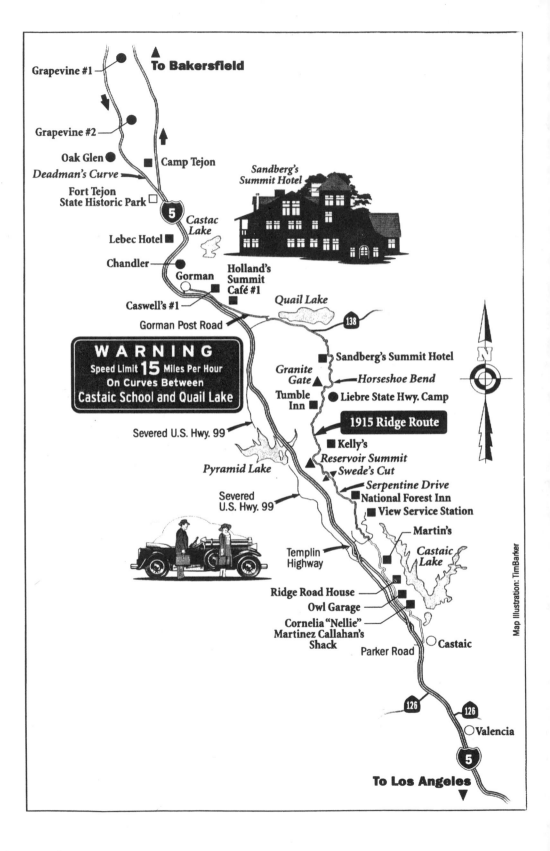

Ridge Route

The Road That
United California

By
Harrison Irving Scott

Published By:
Harrison Irving Scott
Torrance, California
www.RidgeRoute.com

First Printing, 2002
Second Printing, 2003
Third Printing, revised edition, 2003
Fourth Printing, revised edition, 2006

PREFACE

It's strange how your direction in life changes when you least expect it. My youngest son, Jim, and I were traveling north to visit my parents in Visalia. When we started climbing Five-Mile Grade north out of Castaic, Jimmy commented that it was a pretty steep climb and must have been a real challenge for the early automobiles. I told him that the first road over the mountains was east of us and, that I wasn't even sure it still existed. His interest tweaked my curiosity and having some time to spare I found myself heading east at Templin Highway exit. As outlined in the summation at the end of this book, we did indeed locate the 1915 road and, being of an adventurous nature, drove it all the way north to State Highway 138 near Gorman before resuming our trip north on I-5. Our detour on the old road was about to change my life. After spending 32 years with Pacific Bell and 10 years with the Los Angeles Chapter of the American Red Cross, I was looking forward to retirement. Little did I realize how the old, forgotten Ridge Route would replace the proverbial rocking chair we envision when retired. Here I am, not even a member of a historical society, and I've decided to save the old Ridge Route. I look back now and realize how naive I was.

For those not completely familiar with the area, The Ridge Route highway is that section of road that winds over the San Gabriel and Tehachapi Mountains between Castaic Junction on the south (where I-5 junctions with State Highway 126 to Ventura) and extends to the north (where I-5 enters the great San Joaquin Valley). The "Grapevine" is the 6.5-mile segment of the Ridge Route that extends from Fort Tejon to the bottom of Grapevine Grade. Many people erroneously believe that the "Grapevine" got its name because the original 1915 highway had a series of "switchbacks" which allowed early vehicles to gain elevation as they climbed the grade heading from Bakersfield toward Los Angeles. The serpentine path resembled a giant grapevine. Although this observation was true, the name actually came from the fact that early wagoneers had to hack their way through thick patches of Cimarron grapevines that inhabited "La Canada de Las Uvas," (Canyon of the Grapes). Traveling the grade today, look for patches of what appear to be ivy on both sides of the canyon near the truck run-a-way escape ramps. What you see are descendant vines that date back to the 1800s.

What I offer here is the culmination of approximately eight years of research. Most of the research was necessary to qualify the old road for National Register status. Having an engineering background from Pacific Bell, research was right up my alley. Unfortunately engineering "types" tend to be very pragmatic. You will see that I do better research than writing. Nonetheless, I have attempted to document my findings and to present facts and dispel myths as information relates to the original 1915 Ridge Route and the establishments that lined its path. In this book I represent directions in the following manner. Heading north on the old Ridge Route, anything on the right hand side of the road is considered to be "east" of the highway or to the east and anything on the left side of the old road is considered as being "west" of the highway or to the west. Photographs without a reference of credit are from my personal collection. I have made every attempt to be as accurate as possible.

In 1914 The California Department of Highways accepted the challenge of forging a road through the formidable mountain barrier that separated northern and southern California. When completed, the project was hailed as an engineering marvel, the "Magnus Opus" of mountain highway engineering and construction.

Completing the Ridge Route squelched efforts of various groups to divide California into two separate states. Economically, the Ridge Route provided Los Angeles and southern California with a direct link to the agriculture and oil resources of the great San Joaquin Valley. Oil drilling equipment and machinery was transported to Bakersfield and Taft from Los Angeles while produce from the San Joaquin Valley found better access to Los Angeles markets. Today, keeping the current Ridge Route open is a continuing endeavor and major expense. It is said to be one of the most expensive highways in the system to maintain. Slanted and shifting layers of water-laden clay beneath the roadbed keep maintenance crews busy building retaining walls and leach systems to drain thousands of gallons of water from the soil in their attempt to stabilize the road.

While this book focuses on the 1915 Scenic Ridge Route, it also addresses the 1933 Ridge Alternate, (U. S. Highway 99) and the current I-5 Ridge Route highway.

My wonderful wife, Marie, has been most tolerant in my tenacious time-consuming pursuit of information. We have three wonderful children, James John Scott, John Harrison Scott and Kathleen Marie Shaw. We are also blessed with three beautiful grandchildren, Noah and Hannah Shaw and Sophia Scott. When my grandson Noah was four-years old I took him up to Reservoir Summit on the old Ridge Route. I took his hand and walked to a vantage point where you could peer down into the deep canyon to the east. His eyes widened and he exclaimed, "Oh Wow!" That pretty much sums up the majestic views you encounter up on the ridge. Remember it was once referred to as "The Scenic Ridge Route." Although the road shows its age, it still provides a path to the enduring beauty of the San Gabriel and Tehachapi Mountains. This book is dedicated to my grandchildren. Through the eyes of a child: Oh Wow!

Harrison Irving Scott

The author on the east side of the old Ridge Route at Sandberg's Car and Photo courtesy of Daniel Holthaus

TABLE OF CONTENTS

CHAPTER 1

The First Road

El Camino Viejo, "The Old Road", was California's first road of any distance. Beginning at San Pedro Harbor it proceeded north to historic Dominguez Ranch on Alameda Street where water was available. The road continued north through Compton eventually aligning with Main Street to enter the small pueblo of Los Angeles. Teamsters took advantage of a watering hole at Aliso Street and Main where the road split. The eastern portion of the road provided the path to Rancho Verdugo and northeast Los Angeles. The west leg followed Temple Street through the Hollywood area to Cahuenga Pass. The next water was near Universal City at the remains of an old branch of the San Fernando Mission. This old site was constructed before the San Fernando Mission structures were built. John Carpenter and his wife, Chata Moreno, the stepdaughter of Governor Pio Pico, ran this station. Here the road separated again with the western fork leading to Ventura and the coast. The inland route continued 18 miles to San Fernando Mission. Three miles west of the mission water was available at Lopez Station (now at the bottom of Van Norman Reservoir, part of the Los Angeles Aqueduct). The Reservoir is named for Harvey A. Van Norman, former Assistant Chief Engineer of the Los Angeles Water Bureau.[1] The road continued northeast to the eastern end of the Santa Susana Mountains and on to Newhall. At Saugus the road split once more. One leg continued up Soledad Canyon along the Santa Clara River to Acton and Palmdale. The San Joaquin branch continued north to the mouth of San Francisquito Canyon, to access passage to Elizabeth Lake. In earlier days Elizabeth

---

[1] Los Angeles Times, March 25, 1928.

1

Lake was known as "La Laguna de Chico Lopez."[2] About five miles north of the lake was Muddy Springs. Entering Antelope Valley the road went along the edge of the foothills west of Fairmont, Neenach and Crane Lake to Gorman. The only water along this relative level section was at Cow Springs where good water was available.

From Gorman the road led north over a small divide at Tejon Summit on I-5 where shortly, thereafter, another divide appeared. The western branch went through Frazier Park and Cuddy Valley to the entrance of San Emigdio Canyon where it continued to the valley below following the west side of the foothills in a northerly direction to Altamont Pass and San Francisco. This leg followed the general path of today's State Highway 33.

The northern trail went down to Lebec and Canada de Las Uvas to the San Joaquin Valley, on the present path of I-5 toward Bakersfield.[3]

For many years, the San Gabriel and Tehachapi Mountains formed a barrier that separated Los Angeles and Southern California from our neighbors in the upper half of the Golden State. The Butterfield Stage and later, the Southern Pacific Railroad, both wanted to bypass Los Angeles and both companies had to be enticed to route their passage through Los Angeles. There was a strong outcry to divide California into two separate states. The Ridge Route's ribbon of concrete over the barrier effectively joined northern and southern California and in doing so squelched the drive to divide the state. Prior to the Ridge Route, and before California adopted a formal plan to build highways, early motorists utilized wagon trails if they wanted to motor any distance. Cars like the popular Model - T Ford were built with a high clearance that enabled them to utilize a badly rutted dirt road.

[2] Latta, Frank F. Saga Of Rancho El Tejon, Bear State Books, 1976, p. 29.

[3] Ibid. p. 55-59.

CHAPTER 2

Early Exploration by Europeans

The first white man through this area was a Spanish Army officer and acting governor of Alta California, Don Pedro Fages, in 1772.[4] He was also the first white man to penetrate the Tejon Pass, the highest summit on the Ridge Route. Fages called the Tejon Pass, the Pass of Buena Vista (good view).[5] The name may refer to the view that met the gaze of Fages as he emerged from Grapevine Canyon and looked out across the broad expanse of the San Joaquin Valley. A prominent part of the view was the "labyrinth of lakes and tulares." Obviously Buena Vista Lake got its name because it was a part of the "fine view."[6] Before damming the Kern River it emptied out onto the valley floor to form the various estuaries and Buena Vista Lake. Today there is only a small portion of the lake that remains. It is located approximately 10 miles northeast of Taft at the Buena Vista Aquatic Recreational area.

Fages was bent on capturing a group of runaway mission Indians who had stolen some of his cattle, and he was also trailing deserters from the Spanish Army. Fages noticed an abundance of Cimarron Grapes growing wild in the area north of what is now Gorman.[7] Grapevines were so prevalent the wagoneers and soldiers had to hack their way through.[8] To be

---

[4] Hoover, Mildred Brook et al; revised by William N. Abeloe, Historic Spots in California, 3rd Ed., Stanford Univ. Press, p. 123.

[5] Hill, Harlan H. History of the Ridge Route, Unpublished Thesis, Occidental College, p. 8 & 9.

[6] Bolton, Herbert Eugene In The South San Joaquin Ahead Of Garces, Kern County Historical Society, May 1935, p. 7.

[7] Malnic, Eric, "Old Ridge Route: Long, Long Trail A – Winding," L. A. Times, 2-1-1987 Part I p. 30.

[8] Anderson, Gordon "Mountain Pass Winds through History," The Bakersfield Californian, 12-26-1983, p. B2.

historically correct it was really the deserter that Fages found in the valley who was the first white man in the area.[9]

In a letter dated October 18, 1937, Mr. M. C. Kress, president of the New Lebec Hotel Corporation granted permission allowing a monument to be placed on hotel property honoring Don Pedro Fages. Monument number 283, a California Registered Historical Landmark, can be found on Lebec Road approximately 1.6 miles north of the I-5 Frazier Park exit. Wording on the plaque states: "In 1772 Don Pedro Fages, leaving the first written record of explorations in the south San Joaquin Valley, passed this site traveling from San Diego to San Luis Obispo via Cajon Pass, Mojave Desert, Hughes Lake, Antelope Valley, Tejon Pass, Canada De Las Uvas (Grapevine Canyon), and Buena Vista Lake."

For many years it was thought that Father Francisco Garces was the first white man to enter the San Joaquin Valley. Professor Herbert Eugene Bolton of the University of California at Berkeley discovered a diary of Fages and confirmed that Fages entered the valley in 1772, four years ahead of Garces.[10]

The name Tejon originated during an expedition in 1806 from the Santa Barbara Mission into the San Joaquin Valley led by Lieutenant Francis Ruiz. Father Jose Maria Zalvidea accompanied Ruiz and kept a diary of the trip. In his diary the word Tejon was first recorded to designate the area. A dead badger (tejon in Spanish) had been found in the canyon.[11] Due to the large amount of Cimarron Grapes in Tejon Pass the Ruiz expedition referred to the canyon as (Canada de Las Uvas) or Grapevine Canyon.[12]

The name Tejon formerly belonged to another pass 15 miles farther east. This is believed to be the location Father Garces took in 1776 when he entered the San Joaquin Valley

[9] Hill, op. cit., p. 10.

[10] Bolton, op. cit., p. 11.

[11] Hill, op. cit., p. 16.

[12] Hanna, Phil Townsend Dictionary of California Land Names, The Auto Club of Southern California, p. 125.

by way of Cottonwood Creek and the Tejon Canyon.[13] Lieutenant Robert Stockton Williamson of the Pacific Railroad, surveyed this area in 1853. Hearing of a better road further west, he scouted it and found it would be far more practicable for wagons if the bulk of traffic henceforth went that way. The name Tejon was transferred west to today's "Tejon Pass."[14] In memory of Father Garces a twenty-five foot statue stands in the center of the traffic circle at North Chester Avenue and State Highway 204 in Bakersfield.

[13] Bolton, op. cit., p. 11.

[14] Cooper, Frederic Taber California: A Guide Book for Travelers, Rider's Guides, 1925, p. 564.

Random View of Road

CHAPTER 3

Edward Fitzgerald Beale and his Tejon Ranch

Beale was commissioned as a lieutenant in the United States Navy October 3, 1850.[15] In 1852 Beale gained the appointment to serve as California's first Superintendent of Indian Affairs and helped charter a new humanitarian policy toward Native Americans.[16] Fort Tejon was established August 11, 1854, as part of Beale's recommendation to provide protection for the Indians in the area. Fort Tejon, the farthest west of all military outposts, was the only fort built for thc purpose of Indian assistance. On the appeal of the governor of California, the fort was also constructed to discourage bandits and marauding Indians from robbing the ore shipments from the Kern River gold fields.[17] During its active years (1854 to 1864) the fort was a center of social activity.

Fort Tejon, circa 1920
Courtesy Jan McLarty

---

[15] Thompson, Gerald <u>Edward F. Beale & The American West</u>, University of New Mexico Press Albuquerque, 1983, p. 41.

[16] Ibid. p. xi.

[17] Hill, op. cit., p. 25.

Fort Tejon, Inside View, circa 1920
Courtesy Jan McLarty

Fort Tejon looking west, circa 1920
Courtesy Jan McLarty

Fort Tejon looking south, circa 1920
Courtesy Jan McLarty

Fort Tejon, circa 1920
Courtesy Jan McLarty

Whenever Fort Tejon is mentioned, the camel story comes to mind. Jefferson Davis was Secretary of War. At that time, there were expectations of opening the American Southwest with a trail across the desert to California or even building a transcontinental railroad. Camels had been considered as early as 1836 for use in our desert areas, but Washington never took the matter seriously. Davis discussed the idea with various men that were knowledgeable on western travel. Beale was approached and supported the experiment Davis proposed. It was thought that camels would lend themselves better for army use in the desert than the mule, which required larger quantities of water. The government imported 78 camels to San Antonio, Texas. Davis wanted to test the fitness of the animals for military use. In the spring of 1857 John B. Floyd replaced Jefferson Davis. Floyd ordered a survey and wagon road be established from Fort Defiance, New Mexico, to the Colorado River. He directed that some of the camels be assigned to the party so they could be evaluated. Beale was appointed to command the undertaking. Beale was extremely impressed with the camels and sent glowing reports to Washington while he and his men were surveying and building the wagon road west. His terminus was Fort Tejon. The road Beale constructed is pretty much the southern route of the Burlington Northern-Santa Fe Railroad today. On Beale's return trip east, upon reaching the Colorado River he sent the camels back to Fort Tejon believing that they might be needed there in the spring. The camel idea never caught on. The army never had a Camel Corp and the animals were never used in an official capacity other than to transport supplies.[18] After the Civil War, the camels were relocated to Second and Spring Streets where they were corralled with some being auctioned off and others let loose. Some of the animals were spotted wandering about for a number of years.[19]

In 1857 a tremendous earthquake occurred (estimated to have been 8.5 on the Richter Scale) destroying "a good part of

[18] Briggs, Carl & Trudell, Clyde Francis, Quarterdeck & Saddlehorn, Chapter 13.

[19] Rasmussen, Cecilia, "L. A. Then and Now," Los Angeles Times, Metro Section, June 11, 2000.

the fort."[20] The January 10, 1857, edition of the <u>Los Angeles Star</u> newspaper reported: "Yesterday morning, about half-past eight o'clock, a very severe shock of an earthquake was felt here, the vibrations continuing for fully two minutes." A later issue of the <u>Los Angeles Star</u> dated January 24, 1857, outlines the extensive damage wrought upon the buildings of Fort Tejon. The magnitude of the quake is reflected in yet another account of the event. A miner, spending the night camping out near Fort Tejon, leaped to his feet when the ground began to shake just in time to see the ground open and swallow his camping gear. There were reports of cows being thrown down steep hillsides by the shock, and one poor beast was reportedly entombed in a large fissure.[21] This quake, and the 1906 San Francisco 8.3 earthquake,[22] two of the "great" quakes to have occurred in California's history, were a direct result of movement on the San Andreas Fault line.[23] The San Andreas Fault is a giant shear zone that extends some 650 miles through Southern California and cuts directly across Interstate 5 at the 4,144 foot Tejon Summit. During highway construction, the deep cuts for the freeway carved a slice right out of the heart of the fault zone exposing subsurface characteristics of the rift. The line of most recent activity shows up as a band of black "gouge" clearly visible to the passing motorists at the summit.[24]

[20] Anderson, op. cit.

[21] Iacopi, Robert <u>Earthquake Country</u>, 1976, p. 53.

[22] Ibid., p. 30.

[23] Ibid., p. 16.

[24] Ibid., p. 80.

The following letter (sic) believed to be circa 1920 was graciously provided by Jan McLarty.

OLD FORT TEJON—RESTORED
by Clarence Cullimore—Architect

In Central California there is no more historic relic of early days and no more picturesque pile of adobe to attract the research student or the enthusiastic art lover than the ruins of Old Fort Tejon. In sight from the main paved highway between Los Angeles and Bakersfield, near the summit of the narrow pass through the Coast Range, Old Fort Tejon once served its purpose to keep the Indians in check. Set in a vista that recalls the work of Corot, along a formal approach of towering Lombardy Poplars and among a grove of giant oaks the Old Fort buildings, having served their day at military duty now stand guard over the mouth of an exceptionally peaceful canyon, passed unnoticed daily by hords of pleasure-bent auto tourists.

The War Department at Washington gave General Beale a free hand in the design and construction of this interesting fort. This largely accounts for its charm and romantic flavor of Early California Spanish culture, which has left its influence on the original buildings. Although military structures usually bespeak Architecture harsh and severe, Old Fort Tejon adds persuasive notes of appeal and romance, coming from the employment of such accessories as an arched loggia, a balconied window or an outside stairway.

Let us not for a moment confuse the Spanish spirit of Old Fort Tejon with the Mission movement. Its Spanish feeling is gained rather incidentally through the employment of simple natural local material in an honest expression that fell naturally into those similar forms of expression used by the early Spanish Californians.

The Old Fort fell almost by accident and certainly quite naturally into the so-called Spanish style, and the interesting thing is that it is going to be restored quite as naturally by local earth mixed with dried meadow grass and tramped in troughs by the feet of Mexican Laborers, and finally tamped into forms to make adobes.

The real thrill in the restoration of Old Fort Tejon comes from the satisfaction of building truthfully with an honest homely local material and in an Early Californian style. In form and texture and color the restored Fort will truly express its practical constructional and social aspects. Here the adobe bricks in the original buildings will be restored by more adobe mud. It is strange to reflect that ordinary mud can be so satisfactory and thrilling. How superior is the feeling that it gives one to build an adobe wall of adobe bricks, rather than to sham the same effect with wood construction or even hollow tile.

Already the beating winter storms have worn away the outer plaster shell and are melting the old adobe bricks. A hundred squawking jays have placed thousands of acorns in as many pecked out crevices in the walls, to await the development in each of a juicy grub worm to devour.

Yet a few short years and the old land mark would have passed away had not private enterprise come to the rescue to restore this priceless heritage of Early California.

***

In 1861 President Lincoln appointed Beale as Surveyor-General of California.[25] When the Surveyor General's Office in Nevada closed, that district was added to California, also under Beale's supervision.[26] This was an important position Beale tended to neglect. Lincoln dismissed him, but prior to his discharge Beale had used his office to gain title to Rancho El Tejon, one of the largest ranches in the west.[27] In conversation with a senator, Lincoln asked: "what sort of fellow is this man Beale of California?" The senator responded that Beale was a pretty good fellow and inquired why Lincoln had asked. Lincoln said: "Well I appointed him Surveyor-General out there, and I understand he is monarch of all he has surveyed."[28]

[25] Thompson, op. cit., p. xi.

[26] Ibid., p. 138.

[27] Ibid., p. xi.

[28] Ibid. p. 137.

Purchasing Spanish and Mexican land grants, Beale amassed 173,242 acres. The El Tejon Ranchos included El Tejon at 97,616 acres which he paid 11¢ an acre, Castac and Los Alamos y Agua Caliente at 26,626 acres at 11¢ an acre[29] and La Liebre almost 49,000 acres at 3¢ an acre.[30] As surveyor general, Beale had ordered all of these properties surveyed at government expense.[31] Beale's son, Truxtun, sold the property in 1912 to what is now the Tejon Ranch Company.[32]

Despite his problems as Surveyor-General, his accomplishments can be readily noted. He emerged from the Mexican War as the most prominent American hero of the fighting in California.[33] It was Lieutenant Beale who saved General Kearney's men from annihilation at the Battle of San Pasqual by riding to Commodore Stockton at San Diego for help on the 6th of December 1846.[34] In 1848 Beale carried the first samples of gold from California to the East Coast prompting the greatest mass migrations of the nineteenth century. Beale was regarded as "Mr. California," and numbered among his friends such prominent men as Robert F. Stockton, Kit Carson and Ulysses S. Grant.[35] In 1856 Beale accepted a commission as brigadier general in the California State Militia. He later resigned his commission as brigadier general to run for sheriff of San Francisco County. Although he had given up his commission he liked the sound of the title and for the remainder of his life went by "General" Beale.[36]

[29] Latta, op. cit., p. 191-193.

[30] Thompson, op. cit., p. 90.

[31] Ibid. p. 142.

[32] Anderson, op. cit.

[33] Thompson, op. cit., p. xi.

[34] Ibid. p. 15.

[35] Ibid. p. xi.

[36] Ibid. p. 96.

CHAPTER 4

The Butterfield Overland Stage

In 1857 John Butterfield, founder of the American Express Company, received the lucrative contract to organize a regular overland mail service to California. Butterfield and his associate W. G. Fargo, of Wells Fargo, had faced intense competition for the contract. [37] For $600,000 a year, he was to establish a twice-a-week service, both east and west with the running time not to exceed twenty-five days in either direction.[38] He was given only one year to get his 2,757.5-mile[39] line in operation.[40] The Overland Mail Company was a joint stock association formed by men who were substantially connected with one or another of the four major express companies, American, National, Adams, and Wells Fargo. John Butterfield was president of this newly formed company.[41] Butterfield was an administrative genius.[42] He amazingly gathered enough livestock, equipment and workers to meet the deadline. [43] Much of the route went through uninhabited or hostile Indian territory. Way stations were located at approximately ten-mile intervals. He used the best Concord coaches and pulled them with horses of endurance. Stages operated day and night, winter and summer, despite storm, floods or hostile Indians. The trip usually took twenty-three

---

[37] Beck, Warren A. & Williams, David A. California A History of The Golden State, 1972, p. 211.

[38] Lavender, David Sievert The Southwest, 1980, p. 158.

[39] Winther, Oscar Osburn Via Western Express & Stagecoach, 1968, p. 110 & p. 113.

[40] Lavender, op. cit., p. 158.

[41] The Overland Stage, Wells Fargo Bank, p. 2.

[42] Cleland, Robert Glass, From Wilderness to Empire, 1944, p. 308.

[43] Lavender, op. cit., p. 158.

days or less. [44] The first through passenger on the first west-bound trip was Waterman L. Ormsby, a 21 year-old special correspondent for the <u>New York Herald</u>. He made the trip representing the newspaper and was said to have written six very good articles about his experience. The coach in which Ormsby rode had three seats and the backs could be let down to form a bed for four to ten people according to their size and how they lie. [45] The miseries travelers endured were such that most dropped out en route to rest a day or two before continuing on the next stage. Men could alleviate the discomforts of stagecoach travel with whiskey, but women, forbidden to drink in public, had to suffer through the rigors of the trip as best they could. [46] Often passengers that remained aboard arrived substantially ahead of schedule. [47]

The stage line was established to carry mail to the west coast faster than the Pacific Mail Steamship Company. [48] Butterfield carried the mail as well as passengers by a route that connected St. Louis, Missouri, and Memphis, Tennessee, with San Francisco. [49] The starting point in Missouri was really Tipton, being the farthest extension of the railroad west of St. Louis. [50] The two starting points in the east converged at Little Rock, Arkansas, continued to Fort Yuma and on to California. [51]

From Los Angeles the route led through Cahuenga Pass, San Fernando Valley, San Fernando Pass, San Francisquito Canyon, Elizabeth Lake, Fort Tejon into the San Joaquin Valley then over Pacheco Pass to Gilroy to reach San Francisco. [52]

---

[44] Cleland, op. cit., p. 308-310.

[45] Winther, op. cit., p. 114-115.

[46] <u>The Overland Stage</u>, op. cit., p. 15.

[47] Lavender, op. cit., p. 158.

[48] Hill, op. cit., p. 28.

[49] Beck/Williams, op. cit., p. 211.

[50] Winther, op. cit., p. 113.

[51] Lavender, op. cit., p. 158.

[52] Outland, Charles <u>Stagecoaching on El Camino Real Los Angeles to San Francisco 1861-1901</u>, 1973, The Arthur H. Clark Co., Glendale, CA., p. 40.

Mr. Fred Delano, a member of a pioneer family in southern California, gives us the following description of stage stations from Los Angeles north: The Butterfield Stage line had relay stations for changing horses about every 12 miles. The first station north of Los Angeles was at Cahuenga Pass. Coming in order after Cahuenga Pass are Rice Station in the San Fernando Valley, Lyons Station just north of the pass, (refers to San Fernando Pass near the confluence of I-5 and State Highway 14 to Palmdale). Lyons Station was located near the present intersection of Sierra Highway and San Fernando Road inside Eternal Valley Memorial Park. A plaque marking the location reads: "This site was the location of a combination store, post office, telegraph office, tavern and stage depot accommodating travelers during the Kern River gold rush in the early 1850's. A regular stop for Butterfield and other early California stage lines, it was purchased by Sanford and Cyrus Lyons in 1855, and became known as Lyons Station. By 1868 at least 20 families lived here." (California Historical Land Mark # 688). Moore Station was next at the mouth of San Francisquito Canyon. It was established and kept by Charley Moore's father. (This station was later called Hollandsville when Moore took off to pan for gold further up the arroyo.)[53] Chiminez Station followed and then Delano Station, which was an overnight stop. Thomas Abisha Delano Senior, Fred's father, built the Delano Station in 1859. Above Delano's, the relay stations were Mud Springs, Liebre and Gorman.

Mr. Delano declares that freight wagons were not taken over the mountain by winches, but that there was a wagon road over the ridge a short distance east of the Beale cut.[54] Before the cut was made, all travel, including the stages, went around the hill near where the cut is now, and over a grade much steeper than the one in the cut.[55] Teams were massed

---

[53] Reynolds, Jerry, Santa Clarita Valley of the Golden Dream, 1992, p. 29.

[54] " Delano, T. A. Recalls Operation Of The Butterfield Stage Line Through This Area." The Newhall Signal and Saugus Enterprise, Oct. 25, 1940.

[55] Latta, op. cit., p. 197.

on a single wagon and it was dragged to the crest. Then a tree was cut down and fastened to the wagon for a drag, and it was brought down the north side. A ravine at the foot of the road was full of these discarded drag trees, Mr. Delano says. Delano Station was located near Powerhouse No. 1. It originally consisted of a big rambling house, barn, shed and corrals. A room in the house housed the telegraph relay station on the first telegraph line, which ran between Los Angeles and San Francisco.[56] A Western Union telegraph line was completed in 1860 connecting Los Angeles and San Francisco.[57] On October 24, 1861, The Western Union Telegraph Company and its subsidiary, The Pacific Telegraph Company, completed their transcontinental line between Omaha, Salt Lake and San Francisco.[58] This accomplishment brought an end to the famous Pony Express which was established in an attempt to eclipse the mail service of the Butterfield Overland Stage. The Pony Express existed only 18 months, traversing hostile Indian Territory. In all that time, only one mail pouch was lost. The brave riders carried the California mail from Sacramento to Saint Joseph Missouri in the remarkable time of nine days.[59]

The one-way stage fare between Los Angeles and Fort Tejon near the top of the Grapevine was $12.[60] The stage trip from Los Angeles to Fort Tejon took an average of 32.5 hours.[61] When a way station along the route changed ownership it was common practice to change the name of the station. A good example of this is Lyons station. Over the years it was also known as: Hart's, Hosmer's, Fountain's, Andrew's and eventually Newhall.[62]

---

[56] Delano, op. cit.

[57] Latta, op. cit., p. 83 & 84.

[58] Cleland, op. cit., p. 168.

[59] Winther, op. cit., p. 120-136.

[60] Hill, op. cit., p. 30.

[61] Jones, Bob "Winding way over to L. A.," The Bakersfield Californian magazine, Oct. 6, 1990, p. F4.

[62] Outland, op. cit., p. 156 & 157.

The first mail stage from St. Louis stopped at Fort Tejon on October 8, 1858, en route to San Francisco.[63] On April 19, 1861, the Overland Mail via Fort Tejon had been discontinued and all future mails were by the Coast Route.[64]

---

[63] Fluter, A. G. "Grapevine, Historic Canyon Section of U. S. 99 Will Be Eight-Laned," California Highways & Public Works, Jul. - Aug. 1958, p. 10.

[64] Outland, op. cit., p. 4.

CHAPTER 5

Bandidos

By 1850 the gold rush was reaching its peak. Of three possible routes to the gold fields from the south, the Tehachapis offered the shortest. The display of nuggets and dust traveling steadily over the pass attracted bandits by the score. The Ridge was becoming populated, but not with desirable settlers.[65] El Tejon, refugio de los bandidos translated, meant that El Tejon was the refuge of the bandits. Gold from the Kern River was also shipped to Los Angeles via the Tejon Route. "The road was ripe with bandits. A number of the old Joaquin Murrieta gang hung out in the vicinity. Also a few were known to be with Vasquez. The gangs came to the Rancho El Tejon vaquero camps (cowboy camps) and bummed groceries and ammunition."[66]

A party of rangers led by Captain Harry Love killed Joaquin Murietta, the most famous of all California outlaws near Tejon Pass. There was a reward of $5,000 for Murietta's head, and Love, fearing the authorities might doubt that he had actually killed the notorious bandit unless he offered proof, ordered Murietta's head cut off and preserved.[67] Murrieta's career lasted only three and a half years. Tiburcio Vasquez and his band lasted twenty-three years.[68] One of his hideouts was Vasquez Rocks. Another was Robbers Roost.[69] Vasquez, a.k.a. Don Ricardo Cantua, was a man without principle. When not busy robbing someone, he was busy taking advan-

---

[65] Hill, op. cit., p. 19.

[66] Latta, op. cit., p. 225.

[67] Hill, op. cit., p. 20.

[68] Historical Society of Southern California Quarterly, p. 81, 6-1948.

[69] Ibid., p. 83-84.

tage of someone's wife or a young girl. It has been reported that Vasquez hated the los Americanos and preyed on them for vengeance. The fact of the matter was that he treated his own people in a similar fashion. Vasquez was a good-looking man. He wore fine attire and his boots were always polished. He had a fine saddle, a beautiful watch and carried a pair of colt revolvers of excellent quality. He wore a black cape.[70] He was finally captured on March 19, 1875. He was tried, convicted and hanged at San Jose.[71]

[70] Latta, op. cit., p. 236.

[71] Historical Society of Southern California Quarterly, p. 96, 6-1948.

CHAPTER 6

Beale's Cut

In December 1854, twenty-four year old Phineas Banning took a Concord Stage north over the crest of the mountains proving that it could be done. His nine passengers had gotten out and labored up the grade. They could not comprehend how the stage could descend declaring any attempt would be an act of madness. "Banning was said to have laughed and stated that a man who couldn't drive a stage safely down hill was no driver at all and should confine himself to ox team-ing in the valley."[72] Down he went with the horses ahead of the stage and sometimes the stage ahead of the horses. The crude trail over the summit was known as Cuesta Viejo, "Old Slope or Hill" in Spanish and a hill it was. Cuesta Viejo was less than a half-mile from San Fernando Pass. "Banning's treacherous descent landed him where the Southern Pacific (Union Pacific now) Railroad tunnel is today". Banning ex-claimed, "a beautiful descent, far less difficult than I antici-pated. I intended that staging to Fort Tejon and Kern River should be a success".[73] Banning had gone in with David W. Alexander to establish freight routes.[74] The February 1, 1855, issue of the Southern Californian reported that the enterprising house of Alexanders & Banning established a line of stages between Los Angeles and Kern River. Passen-gers seeking their fortune in gold along the Kern River found Banning's advertising misleading. The Alta Californian paper of February 25, 1855, said that miners would be better off to buy a horse in Los Angeles and ride to the mountain sites

---

[72] Historical Society of Southern California Quarterly, "The San Fernando Pass & The Pioneer Traffic That Went Over It," Part III, p. 50, 1947 - 1948.

[73] Historical Society of Southern California Quarterly, p. 113, 6-1948, p. 43, p. 46, p. 47, 3-1947.

[74] Ibid. p. 42, 3-1947.

because Banning's stage line dropped you off a long way from the diggings. In 1852 Don David Alexander had joined with Banning in operating a stage line between San Pedro and Los Angeles. Alexander for a time was owner of what later became Gorman's Station on the Butterfield Overland Stage Line.[75] On February 10, 1855, the <u>Southern Californian</u> reported that a Mr. Hall of the California Stage Company purchased the entire stage property heretofore belonging to Messrs. Alexanders & Banning and the various lines in operation by the two concerns will henceforth be under the sole control of the California Company. The article went on to say that Messrs. Alexanders & Banning retire from the "stage" full of honors, and possessing the esteem of our citizens, for the many kind attentions received at their hands, during the last two or three years. "May their shadow never be less."

The first attempt to lower the elevation at Beale's Cut occurred in the summer of 1854 when the Los Angeles County Board of Supervisors, chaired by David W. Alexander, Banning's partner, voted to spend $1,000 to improve the crude wagon road over the mountain.[76] Contractor William T. B. Sanford, (Banning's brother-in-law) and Sanford's partner, George Carson, hired Gabe Allen to work on the road. Allen, with twenty men, completed the improvement.[77] On December 28, 1854, the Tejon Road was ready for travelers. Allen had cut down the hill a distance of nine hundred and fifty yards, one hundred and thirty of which had been through solid rock at an average depth of thirty feet.[78]

Four years later on June 12, 1858, the Board of Supervisors approved $3,000 to be appropriated from the county treasury to repair the road.[79] The proposed Butterfield Stage route was to by-pass Los Angeles in favor of San Bernardi-

[75] Latta, op. cit., p. 74.

[76] Historical Society of Southern California Quarterly, p. 38, 3-1947.

[77] Ibid. p. 39, 3-1947, p. 117, 6-1948.

[78] The Southern Californian, Dec. 28, 1854.

[79] The Los Angeles Star, June 12, 1858.

no.[80] To entice the stage route through Los Angeles, the road over San Fernando Pass had to be lowered yet again.[81] On July 12, 1858, Gabe Allen once again was chosen to accomplish the task.[82] The $3,000 allotment proved insufficient to accomplish all the necessary improvements required for the Butterfield Stage. With time running out, and fearful the stage would be routed through San Bernardino if repairs were not complete, the Los Angeles County Board of Supervisors appropriated an additional $5,000 to complete the work. On August 28, 1858, with the improvements having been accomplished, the road was ready for service.[83] Film buffs that watch "Stagecoach," the 1939 western that launched John Wayne's career, will see a brief glimpse of Beale's Cut. Although the movie was filmed at Monument Valley Utah, there is one scene as the stage, being chased by the Indians, passes through the Cut.

With the increased use of the Tejon Route, the state legislature in 1861, at the urging of Governor John Downey, empowered Charles Brinley, Andres Pico, and James Vineyard to build a turnpike at San Fernando Hill. The contract gave them one year to complete the turnpike.[84] Construction was to be completed no later than May 7, 1862.[85] A torrential downpour of rain in the winter of 1861 and 1862 prevented the start of any construction. Because of the inclement weather an extension was asked for and granted advancing the completion date to March 7, 1863. The original holders found the project too expensive to complete after the heavy winter rains of 1861-1862 washed out the road.[86] Beale assumed the franchise of Brinley, Pico and Vineyard sometime in 1862. Beale was a man of wealth and apparently saw the

---

[80] Outland, op. cit., p. 68.

[81] Ibid., p. 70.

[82] The Los Angeles Daily Evening Bulletin, July 12, 1858.

[83] Outland, op. cit., p. 73.

[84] Hill, op. cit., p. 32.

[85] Historical Society of Southern California Quarterly, p. 63, 3-1948.

[86] Thompson, op. cit., p. 143.

toll road to be a good investment feeling it might be too costly a venture for the original holders of the franchise.[87] Beale dispatched a crew of Chinese Laborers to deepen an earlier 1858 cut made for the Butterfield Stage. Beale's laborers cut a 12-foot wide passage through 60 feet of sandstone to reduce the climb by 50 feet in 1862.[88] Although toll rates were set by the Los Angeles County Board of Supervisors, Beale received a handsome return on his investment.[89]

Beale's Cut
Newman Post Card Co., Los Angeles, Cal.

[87] Historical Society of Southern California Quarterly, op. cit., p. 113, 115, 116, 6-1948.

[88] Jones, Bob, op. cit., p. F4.

[89] Hill, op. cit., p. 34.

During the time Beale was improving the cut and establishing his turnpike, he had trouble with the Los Angeles County Board of Supervisors. They wanted a much lower gradient over the mountain barrier.[90] In March of 1864 the Los Angeles Board of Supervisors finally approved Beale's work on San Fernando Hill. At the base of the south grade stood the small adobe Toll House of Beale's collector, O. P. Robbins, who was always ready to lift the wooden pole which blocked the road. With his twenty-year contract, Beale averaged several hundred dollars per month. When the contract finally expired, the road had paid for itself several times over.[91] The grade was lowered once again in 1904; see (The challenge of early crossing by automobile).

[90] Ibid. p. 33.

[91] Thompson, op. cit., p. 165.

CHAPTER 7

Saint Francis Dam Disaster

It is worthy to note that the Butterfield Stage traveled through the narrowest section of San Francisquito Canyon where seventy years later at midnight March 12, 1928, the Saint Francis Dam, (part of the 250 mile Owens Valley water aqueduct) collapsed. Billions of gallons of water severed the Ridge Route at Castaic sweeping a path of death and destruction clear to the Pacific Ocean at Ventura.[92] Four hundred lives were lost and twelve hundred homes destroyed.[93] William Mulholland, Chief Engineer and Manager of the Los Angeles Bureau of Water at the time, and Los Angeles' greatest water Czar never recovered emotionally from the effects of this terrible disaster. Next to the San Francisco earthquake of 1906, this was the greatest catastrophe in California's history. To his credit, Mulholland assumed full blame: "If there is an error in human judgment, I was that human." It was an agony he carried with him the rest of his life.[94] It was Mulholland that built the Los Angeles Aqueduct that first brought water from Owens Valley to Los Angeles on November 5, 1913.[95] In the late 1940s the author lived at 415 South Saint Andrews Place at the edge of Hancock Park. The Mulholland residence was at 426 right across the street. Apartment complexes have replaced the stately homes that once lined Saint Andrews Place.

---

[92] Los Angeles Times, "Grand Jury Investigation of St. Francis Dam Break Depends on Verdict of Coroner's Jury," Los Angeles Times, Part 1, March 25, 1928.

[93] Los Angeles Times, Jan. 10, 1999, Magazine section, p. 17.

[94] Watkins, T. H. California An Illustrated History, 1973, p. 315.

[95] Los Angeles Times, Nov. 6, 1913.

Author's Childhood Home
415 South Saint Andrews Place

CHAPTER 8

Petroleum Lines

Gas, petroleum and electric companies were pretty active in the Ridge Route area prior to 1914 when road construction began.

General Pipe Line Company, predecessor of General Petroleum Corporation better known as Exxon Mobil Oil, had spent six months in 1911 traipsing the same mountain ridges surveying for a pipeline they planned to build between the new Midway-Sunset Oil Field in the San Joaquin Valley and Los Angeles.[96] "Nothing like this had ever been attempted and the best engineers of the day said it was impossible. Rea Maynard was engineer in charge of pipeline construction. He was a capable engineer and is remembered as having laid the pipeline by instinct rather than by slide rule. Maynard would ride up on horseback and holler, "Put her there!"[97] Later he became president of the company.[98]

In the early nineteen hundreds there were few automobiles. Captain John Barneson and a group of his friends in the oil business formed the General Pipeline Company. They speculated that if they could get the oil to San Pedro harbor it could be used to fuel ships.[99] This 150 - mile[100] 8-inch "screwed together" pipeline identified as G. P. Line M1 originated in the San Joaquin Valley at Kettleman North Dome. They pumped south to Kettleman, Lost Hills #1, Belridge, Midway, Continen-

[96] Jones, Charles S., From The Rio Grande To The Arctic, The Story of the Richfield Oil Corporation, 1972, p. 85.

[97] Crouse, Harriet "They Built The First Pipeline," Westways, August, 1951.

[98] Barnes, Marvin & Bill, 6-15-1995, 5-17-1998, 5-24-1998, 6-11-1998 & March 2000 Interviews.

[99] Crouse, op. cit.

[100] Ibid.

tal, Pentland, Emidio, Rose and Grapevine. Grapevine Station pumped the oil onto the Lebec refinery.[101]

Mules hauled in all the heavy pipe sections, boilers, steam engines and steel for buildings. A company telephone line was constructed along with the pipeline and connected the various pumping stations. Not only was their route over the mountains a success, they accused the State Highway surveyors of having used their telephone line to site the location for the new highway.[102]

In actuality, their pipeline did not follow the old Ridge Route south of Gorman. From the Lebec refinery their pipeline indeed went south but the alignment was via Piru Canyon, the route that would eventually become the Ridge Alternate, U. S. Highway 99 in 1933. At the location that is now Pyramid Lake was General Pipeline's "La Liebre" Pumping Station. La Liebre lifted the oil upward to the Old Ridge Route at a point just south of Reservoir Summit on the Old Ridge Route. From Reservoir Summit south, the pipeline pretty much followed the old highway. La Liebre pump station was ultimately eliminated. It was all downhill from Tejon Summit and gravity pushed the lighter oil in this line without the aid of that station.[103] The former pump station was located on the 1933 Ridge Alternate highway approximately even with the face of Pyramid Dam and is now under Pyramid Lake. La Liebre pumped to Newhall Station, located at the southeast corner of Highway 126 and the I-5 freeway. Continuing south the pipeline followed San Fernando Road to Fernando Station located near the intersection of San Fernando Road and Lankershim Boulevard. Angeles Station, near Los Angeles, was the last pumping station. From Angeles Station the pipeline followed Alameda Street south to their refinery at 37th Street and Santa Fe Avenue in the city of Vernon. The total cost to build this line was $3,300,000.[104] The first oil through this line reached

---

[101] Cooper, Emmett, Retired Mobil; Pipeline Safety Engineer State of California Fire Marshall's Office.

[102] Crouse, op. cit.

[103] Barnes, op. cit.

[104] Brooks, Ray W., "Many a Man no Longer Alive Failed on Ridge Route Drive," Daily Breeze, Redondo Beach, December 3, 1950.

the refinery in March of 1913,[105] and the first ship to fuel from this line sailed from San Pedro in June of 1913.[106]

General Petroleum also built a branch pipeline from their Lebec refinery to the rail terminal at Mojave. From the refinery the Mojave line headed to Quail Lake Pumping Station that was located on the southeast corner of State Highway 138 and the Old Ridge Route. Antelope Valley Station was next, then Willow Springs Station pumped the oil to the Mojave rail terminal. The stations were approximately 15 miles apart. Each station used superheated steam to warm the crude oil 200 to 300 degrees. The crude was then pumped onto the next station. The pumps were also operated by steam with piston rods similar to those found on steam locomotives. At Mojave the residuum oil, (a residual product from the distillation of petroleum) was loaded into tank cars at the rail terminal and used throughout the country to power steam engines of that era. The branch line was referred to as "The Bank Line" because the oil was like money running through it. In 1948 or 1949 diesel locomotives replaced steam engines and the entire pipeline was removed.[107]

In 1935 Mobil replaced the 1911 M1 line with a 10-inch welded line that connected their Lebec refinery to their new Torrance refinery located at 190th Street and Crenshaw Boulevard. This line was also replaced by 16-inch line (M-70) completed in April of 1993 also terminating at the Torrance refinery.[108] In addition to the Lebec Pumping Station and former refinery, another pumping facility is located on the west side of the southbound lanes of the I-5 freeway a short distance up the Grapevine. This Grapevine Station originally had two bunkhouses and two cottages for the workers. Standard Oil Company never built a pipeline over the Ridge, however SCONY Vacuum (Standard Oil Company of New York) was once the parent company of Mobil.

[105] Finley, Farrell, Mobil Oil, retired, telephone interview, Mar. 8, 2000.

[106] Brooks, op. cit.

[107] Barnes, op. cit.

[108] Sisk, John, Mobil Engineer.

In 1925 Edward L. Doheny's Pan American Petroleum and Transport Company (later Atlantic Richfield Company or ARCO) constructed a 10-inch diameter line covering a distance of 130 miles. Originating in the San Joaquin Valley, Line # 1 terminated at Carson. This line was abandoned due to damage suffered from the 1994 Northridge earthquake. Fortunately they had another line in service that was built in 1950. This line is a combination of 14 and 16-inch pipe sections known as line # 63. It avoided serious damage from the quake due to its eastern alignment away from the San Fernando Valley area.[109] The pumping station for line # 1, although inactive, is still located at the bottom of the Grapevine between the north and southbound lanes of the I-5 freeway where the town of Grapevine once stood. Originally this station had three cottages for the workers. Their active pumping station that formerly pumped oil through line # 1 is located just north of Fort Tejon in a grove of oak trees. This location also had 4 or 5 houses for the workers in addition to a large area where both Richfield and General Petroleum, (Mobil) families gathered for picnics.[110] British Petroleum Amoco recently purchased Atlantic Richfield (ARCO) and will retain the ARCO name. Pacific Pipeline purchased ARCO's crude oil pipeline division.

Beginning in August of 1997, Pacific Pipeline (owned by Philip Anschutz) [111] completed a 20-inch diameter line originating at the Emidio Pumping Station in the San Joaquin Valley. A second pumping station was constructed at the bottom of the Grapevine between the north and southbound lanes of the I-5 freeway located a short distance north of the now inactive Richfield pumping plant. South of Templin Highway and east of the I-5 freeway, they have a pressure reduction station. From this point south it is entirely gravity flow. This 132-mile pipeline generally follows the Golden State Freeway

[109] Cooper, Emmett, op. cit.

[110] Kaufman, Frank, of Bakersfield, interview of 1-7-1997, 6-9-1998, & March 2000.

[111] Los Angeles Times Business Section, February 4, 2001.

from Kern County to the San Fernando Valley, and then runs along the Union Pacific Railroad right of way[112] until it ends on Ultramar Diamond Shamrock refinery property located in Wilmington on the southeast corner of Anaheim Street and Henry Ford Avenue.[113] Strangely, Ultramar does not draw product from this line. The line simply ends on their property. At the time of this writing, Ultramar Diamond Shamrock was being purchased by Valero Energy Corporation of San Antonio Texas in a $4 billion deal that will create the nation's second largest oil refinery.[114] This line does have branches extending to the Chevron refinery at El Segundo, the Tosco and Equilon refineries in Carson and to the Edison Pipeline & Terminal Co. storage facility at Dominguez Hills.[115] The pipeline's owner is Anschutz Corporation.[116]

[112] Hafer, Mark & Stassel, Stephanie, "Building a Pipeline," Aug. 3, 1997, Los Angeles Times.

[113] Finley, op. cit.

[114] "Valero buying rival Ultramar," May 8, 2001, the Daily Breeze.

[115] Meadows, Ted, Ultramar Diamond Schamrock.

[116] Hafer & Stassel, op. cit.

CHAPTER 9

Natural Gas Lines

In 1912 the Midway Gas Company, predecessor of Southern California Gas Company, started construction on the first natural gas line over the Ridge to Glendale. The line was placed in service in 1913.[117] Line # 100, a 12-inch diameter line began at Station 40, approximately five miles east of Taft. Gas was collected from the Taft Midway oil fields Westside District encompassing Taft, McKittrick, Fellows and Maricopa. Station 40, a compressor plant received the gas at 20 to 60 pounds and utilized eight large Fairbanks-Morse engines to increase line pressure to 410 pounds. These engines were 70 feet long and had flywheels 20 feet in diameter. Station 40 was removed around 1960.

The Gas Company had a facility at the bottom of the Grapevine where they had a cottage, garage and pipe yard. Their Lebec station had three cottages. Below Sandberg's, in La Liebre Canyon, was another cottage and garage for the pipeline inspector. This location was vacated in 1939 and was replaced by a two-cottage facility approximately 3 miles north of Pyramid Lake in Hungry Valley. Inspectors patrolled the line from Kettleman Hills to Los Angeles. Going south, the pipeline went up Grapevine Canyon, through Gorman on the west side of the road following what today is Gorman Post Road to the intersection of State Highway 138 and the Old Ridge Route. This is the same corner where General Petroleum had their Mojave Pumping Station. The pipeline was approximately 50 feet west of the intersection. It proceeded up the hill remaining on the west side of the Ridge Route. At Pine Canyon intersection it crossed the road leading up to the Bald Mountain weather station then descended down La

---

[117] King, Denise, Public Affairs, Southern California Gas Company.

Liebre Canyon to a point below the Tumble Inn. Here the line climbed up to the Old Ridge Route highway. From Tumble Inn, the pipeline continued south following the alignment of the road. This is the pipe that used to cross above the old road south of Swedes Cut. If you look close you can see where it was cut away. Other lines cross above the road at the same location today. By the time the gas arrived at Glendale it was down to 10 pounds of pressure. Dressler Couplings had been used to join each section of pipe. Unfortunately this rubber gasket type fitting secured with eight bolts leaked from the very beginning. In 1919 all of the defective gaskets were replaced between Grapevine and Glendale. In 1932 a crew from Chicago trained the men in the operation of the new electric welding machines just coming into use. Using this technology the remaining Dressler Couplings between Grapevine and Station 40 were removed and the pipe sections were re-joined by welding them together.

In 1928 line # 119, a 20-inch diameter line was installed from Grapevine south. This line followed approximately the same path that General Petroleum used in 1911 through Piru Canyon and Hungry Valley to Pyramid Lake. From this point the line climbed east up the hill to Reservoir Summit then followed the alignment of the old Ridge Route south.

In 1930 line # 85 was put through to the Southern California Edison Long Beach generating station, now NRG Energy Incorporated, located on the northwest side of the Gerald Desmond Bridge at Long Beach Harbor. This 26-inch diameter line originated at Kettleman and followed the same route as line # 119 above.

In 1951 a 34-inch diameter line was installed over the ridge. This line is located approximately one-half mile east of the Grapevine and stays near the top of the mountains. It runs east of Castac Lake (Opposite Lebec) and crosses State Highway 138 near Gorman Post road. Following a path west of the Bald Mountain weather station, the line continues south.[118]

---

[118] Kaufman, op. cit.

Installing the gas line on the 1915 Ridge Route

Ridge Route Kern River Line Construction 1906
Courtesy Richard Atmore

CHAPTER 10

Electric lines

About the same time that General Petroleum was building their pipeline, linemen of Henry Huntington's Pacific Light and Power Company were stringing cable between the metal towers they had constructed over the Ridge. This was the longest and highest voltage line yet attempted in the world extending some 241 miles from "Big Creek," a branch of the San Joaquin River and Huntington Lake in the north to the Eagle Rock Substation near Los Angeles in the south. It was the largest hydroelectric project in the United States and was financed entirely by private capital. It used the biggest and best that technology could produce. The project consisted of two three-wire 150,000 volt circuits that converted to 66,000 volts at Eagle Rock. Power began at powerhouse # 1 below Huntington Lake and near the little village of Big Creek. In 1923[119] these lines converted to 220,000 volt operation. The lines were supported on separate but parallel steel towers. The project was completed the first week of November 1913, but the line had not been tested. Ironically, the line was tested by "fire" so to speak. At 7:30 a.m. the electric generating steam plant at Redondo Beach (today owned by Global Power Corp., part of AES) was experiencing a serious problem. A broken water pipe had flooded the boiler room. Unfortunately this plant supplied most of the power that was used by the Pacific Electric and Los Angeles Railways commute trolleys in Los Angeles, better known as the Red Cars and the Yellow Cars. As the steam pressure began to drop, the trolleys came to a halt. Try as they did, the repairs at the Redondo steam plant were taking longer than anticipated. A crisis was at hand. General Manager Davis of the Pacific Light and Power Company decided

---

[119] Redinger, David H., The Story of Big Creek, 1949, p. 66.

to gamble and energize the untested "Big Creek" lines. The newspaper reported that at approximately 8:38 a.m. power from the "Big Creek" lines reached the stalled trolleys and the cars began to move. A little over an hour had elapsed since the failure. On May 26, 1917, Huntington's Pacific Light and Power Corporation was merged into the Southern California Edison Company.[120]

Like General Petroleum, Huntington's Pacific Light and Power company had built a make-shift road over the mountains in 1913 on what would become the Ridge Route alignment. The separate but parallel towers are still visible if you travel the old Ridge Route today.

The first electric line linking the San Joaquin Valley to Los Angeles was placed in service in 1902. Power for this line came from the Borel Power House on the Kern River at Democrate Springs. The 55,000-volt line utilized wooden poles and had three sub stations. Oak sub station was the first, followed by Elizabeth Lake sub station and Castaic sub station. This Pacific Light and Power line was east of the old Ridge Route.

Between 1906 and 1908 a 75,000-volt line was constructed from Kern River # 1 powerhouse up the Grapevine following an alignment, which would become the Ridge Alternate U. S. Highway 99 in 1933. Although designated a 75,000 volt line, by the time the power reached Los Angeles it was closer to 60,000 to 66,000 volts and really became identified as a 66,000 volt operation. This line was the first line ever built on metal towers. The towers were built by a windmill company and are still in use today. If you look close you can spot these old 1906 towers when you travel I-5 between Gorman and Pyramid Lake. Look on the west side of the highway. They are rusty and look like the letter "A".[121] As of 2006 the towers are slowly being replaced.

[120] Myers, Dr. William A., Historian, retired, Southern California Edison, Iron Men and Copper Wires, 1986, p. 109 – 111 and telephone interview, March 1999.

[121] Ibid.

CHAPTER 11

Reservoirs

There were three reservoirs along the old road. Reservoir Summit, (the largest), National Forest Inn, and the third one was located seven tenths of a mile south of Templin Highway on a small knoll on the east side of the road. The property owner destroyed it while I was working to get the old highway placed on the National Register. In 1997 I wrote an article for the California Historian. In that article I believed the Forest Service built the reservoirs for fire control. Additional information now leads me to believe that the reservoirs were constructed by the State Department of Highways as a water source for paving the cement highway. I have attempted to unravel this mystery by interviewing old timers and forest service personnel. Marvin Barnes, a long time resident of Lebec, told me that the reservoir at Reservoir Summit was built by the people that operated the Reservoir Summit Café, Garage and Camp Site. He said they generated their own electricity and used electric pumps to pull water from Liebre Gulch, filling the reservoir for their operations. This may have been true, but how could such a small establishment with only a few cabins afford to build such a massive structure. The reservoirs at Reservoir Summit and the National Forest Inn sites were probably utilized by the leaseholders when the State had finished paving the road. He said Tumble Inn pumped water to their establishment via the same method. The Tumble Inn site did not have a reservoir although the Forest Service has an underground tank located there for use in fighting forest fires. Some believe as I that the reservoirs were built by the State Department of Highways. Others claim the reservoirs were used by the facilities at each location and were filled by pumping water from the canyons below. Another belief is that water to fill Reservoir Summit came from the springs on Liebre Mountain.

I do know this. Reservoir Summit has a 10,000-gallon underground forest service water tank in addition to the reservoir. Jack Rimmer, a forest fire captain, was stationed at Reservoir Summit around 1932. He told me the tank, not the reservoir was their water source. Jack did not recall the reservoir ever having water in it during his tenure there. He said the 10,000-gallon water tanks were installed by the forest service. They are located at various points along the road and, at one time, were filled by tanker trucks to aid in fighting forest fires. The reservoir south of Templin Highway did not have any commercial or other type of facility near it. If the forest service built these reservoirs, then logically I would expect to find similar ones elsewhere on forestland, which is not the case. Also, I have a copy of the January 18, 1915, deed signed by Harald Sandberg and his wife Marian granting the California Highway Commission 40 percent flow from a spring located on land they occupied. The Sandberg's had full claim to the spring on Liebre Mountain that supplied water to their hotel. The document recorded in <u>Book 6020,</u> page 155 of deeds reads as follows: "In consideration of the benefits to accrue to them from the development of their spring hereinafter described, so as to secure the apparent and approximate maximum flow at time of installation, the undersigned, H. Sandberg and Marian G. Sandberg, residing near Neenach, in Los Angeles County, California, do hereby grant to the State of California for its use by the California Highway Commission, for the purposes of construction and maintenance of the State highway and for the use of the traveling public, the perpetual use of forty (40%) per cent of the flow of water now flowing, or as may hereafter be developed from that certain spring located in Los Angeles County etc. etc....... and that the Sandberg's do hereby grant to said State of California and to its employees of the California Highway Commission free access to said spring which they are to develop, together with the right of way to lay or repair the two (2") inch galvanized iron pipe, which pipe shall be fitted with unions at least every 600 feet, and be placed underground from said spring to a point on the State highway etc."

I have seen remains of this pipe the state installed along the highway. It extends from Liebre Mountain south to the reservoir at Reservoir Summit. A section of this original pipe is uncovered and exposed about thirty-five feet north east of the reservoir. Liebre Mountain is higher than Reservoir Summit, therefore, water could have filled the reservoir and the one at National Forest Inn as well. Mr. Frank Kaufman, an old timer and long time resident of Bakersfield, told me that water to fill the reservoir was piped from a spring on the mountain near Sandberg's and that the pipe supplied water to other sites along the highway as well. He also said the forest service may have built the reservoirs. The road was built in 1914, opened in October of 1915 and paved in 1919. An account of 1920 addressing the paving operation indicates water was hauled to the work sites. To quote that portion of the article it states: "Piercing a district almost entirely uninhabited, the commission found themselves faced with a lack of water due to the unusually dry season which had prevailed. Water and materials both had to be hauled to the place where work was being carried on, much of the material being transported in trucks from Lancaster, forty miles away across the desert."[122] The article states that much of the material was hauled from Lancaster. It does not specifically state that water was hauled from Lancaster. Keep in mind the state obtained water rights from the Sandberg's on January 18, 1915. The Ridge Route is in a very remote area and to pave it with cement would have required a convenient source of water. I believe the reservoirs were used for that purpose and the primary water source was the Sandberg spring on Liebre Mountain or one of the other springs close by. It is doubtful we will ever know for sure. I do know that the two-inch diameter pipeline did extend from Liebre Mountain spring to the reservoir. The spring is still active to this day supplying water to former Los Angeles County fire patrol station # 77 at the Pine Canyon-Ridge Route intersection.

---

[122] Henry, William M., "California's New Road," <u>Motor Magazine</u>, June 1920, p. 94.

CHAPTER 12

Beginnings of the State Highway System

At this point it is necessary to review early events that led to the Ridge Route's birth. In 1895, the State Bureau of Highways was created. Governor James H. Budd appointed three highway commissioners, R. C. Irvine of Sacramento, Marsden Manson of San Francisco and L. Maude of Riverside.

These three officials purchased a team of horses and a buckboard wagon and proceeded, during the next year and a half, to cover the state, logging some 7,000 miles. Upon their return they submitted a report to the governor recommending a system of state highways that would connect all large centers of population. Specifically was suggested a direct route from Los Angeles to the San Joaquin Valley to replace the round about Midway Route.[123] Every county seat would be reached. Their recommendation included the utilization of existing county roads to the fullest possible extent. The California Legislature of 1897 dissolved the Bureau of Highways and created a Department of Highways. The members of the new department made exhaustive studies of road construction practices and economics. Members of the department toured Europe to observe methods used in England, France and other countries. (Even then, politicians justified extended trips on tax dollars!)

Their findings on such factors as drainage, roadbed and pavement construction were based on fundamental engineering policies. At the outset, modern highway development in California was on a firm foundation. On November 4, 1902, an amendment to the California State Constitution was adopted giving the legislature the power to establish a state highway system and to pass all laws necessary for highway construction

---

[123] Robinson, John, "The Old Ridge Route: L. A. to Bakersfield the Hard Way," Los Angeles Westerners Corral, No. 163, Spring 1986, p. 3.

and maintenance. This amendment also allowed the state to give aid to counties for their road systems.

In 1907, the Department of Engineering was organized, but due to lack of funds, no road construction began. Before the Tehachapi barrier succumbed to the Ridge Route, there was a strong political movement afoot to carve California into two states.[124]

In 1909 the state legislature passed an act, to issue $18,000,000 in bonds for the acquisition and construction of a state highway system. The voters approved the bond issue and it became effective December 31, 1910. This initial bond provided funds for building the original Ridge Route highway.[125] Fortunately, Los Angeles purchased the bonds when the Commission was unable to market the securities in the east.[126] A resolution in 1911 designated three men as an executive committee to the Department of Engineering to be known as the California Highway Commission. These three gained immediate control over all state road and highway activities, with the Tehachapi region receiving special priority.[127] In 1916 another bond issue provided an additional $15 million, and in 1919 a third gave the commission another $40 million for construction purposes within the state. In 1919 a state gasoline tax was approved which eliminated the need for additional bonds for road construction. In 1921 Congress passed the Federal Highway Act that provided the states with dollar-matching federal grants for the building of the interstate highway system.[128]

On January 25, 1912,[129] an intensive survey was ordered,[130] with 18 months taken in laying out the Ridge

---

[124] Jones, Bob "Mountainous Task" The Bakersfield Californian magazine, Oct. 13, 1990, p. E4.

[125] Hill, op. cit., p. 48 & 49.

[126] "$500,000 Ridge Road Engineering masterpiece," Touring Topics, Dec. 1915, p. 7.

[127] Hill, op. cit., p. 40 & 41.

[128] Watkins, op. cit., p. 338.

[129] "The Great Short Cut Over Tehachapi Mountains," Calif. Highway Bulletin, July 1, 1916, p.2.

[130] Hill, op. cit., p. 43.

Route.[131]   Heavy cement survey monuments were set at various intervals along each side of the proposed highway right-of-way to separate the highway from adjacent private property. The concrete survey monuments were commonly referred to as "C" Blocks, with the "C" indicating a California State route. Monuments were placed at each curve point and at intervals on long straight lines. Ref. CA Hwy. Bulletin, Vol.2, July 1, 1914 Number 1. All four sides of the three-feet, six-inch tall columns were six inches wide. A three-sixteenth inch copper wire is centered in the top of the monument and marked the exact point of the angle. The letter "C" is recessed on one side, one-quarter of an inch into the post. Placement of the three-inch letter is two inches down from the top of the monument.[132]

"C" Block

[131] "Completed Ridge Route Now Open to Traffic," Southwest Builder and Contractor, Nov. 28, 1919, p. 10, & "The Contractor, Building Construction, Bridges and Road Work," Architect & Engineer, vol. LX, No. 1, Jan. 1920, p. 120.

[132] "Standard Structures," Division of Highways map, Kern County, District 6, Section A, Route 4, June 8, 1942.

Survey Party #4. Assistant Resident Engineers, March 1915. This picture was taken somewhere in Section 4C which was between National Forest Inn & Sandberg's.

Courtesy Caltrans

The preliminary study, made by W. Lewis Clark, Division Engineer at Los Angeles, dissipated all doubt as to the feasibility of a direct route over the mountains.[133] To Highway Commissioner N. D. Darlington of Los Angeles belongs the chief credit for the selection of the route.[134]

Since travel to the south first began there had been only two routes followed. The Tehachapi, ("Midway Route," today's State Highway 58) went due east from Bakersfield to Mojave, then south through Lancaster to access Mint or Boquet Canyons. The other being the "Tejon Pass Route," which used an old wagon road to climb up the Grapevine Grade from Bakersfield to Quail Lake (today State Highway 138), then east roughly following the San Andreas rift to the head of either San Francisquito (Turner Pass) or Bouquet Canyon. The Tejon Route was considerably shorter than the Tehachapi Route but neither pass could be called direct, for both curved widely to

[133] "The Great Shortcut ....," op. cit., p. 3.

[134] Hill, op. cit., p. 42.

the east to reach the heads of the canyons while the objective point was almost due south.[135] The Automobile Club of Southern California promoted the "most direct and practicable route" between Los Angeles and the San Joaquin Valley. The Club's engineering department first brought attention to the fact that a mountain road could be built over the Ridge and in so doing the State would benefit the greatest number of people.[136] Before Commissioner Darlington selected the route there had been a bitter feud between Harrison Gray Otis, publisher of the <u>Los Angeles Times</u>, and E. T. Earl of the old <u>Los Angeles Express</u>. In editorials, the <u>Los Angeles Examiner</u> and the <u>Los Angeles Times</u> promoted the direct route that Darlington ultimately selected, while the <u>Los Angeles Express</u> favored the Midway Route.[137] [138]

[135] "Bakersfield is Now Linked to L. A. by Paved Highway: Ridge Route Will Open Saturday," <u>The Bakersfield Californian</u>, Nov. 11, 1919, p. 1.

[136] "All Aboard For Ridge Route-But Watch Your Step!" <u>Touring Topics</u> November 1919, p. 11.

[137] Hill, op. cit., p. 43.

[138] Brooks, op. cit.

Road Construction
Courtesy Caltrans

CHAPTER 13

The challenge of early crossing by automobile

From the southern end of the Tejon Route the early motorist heading north from Los Angeles would lose pavement shortly after crossing the Los Angeles River. The dirt road continued following the alignment of the Southern Pacific railroad tracks, (now Union Pacific) through to the far end of the San Fernando Valley. At this point the road veered away from the tracks and headed toward the mountains. Here you had to deal with the Newhall Pass/Grade, also known as Fremont Pass.[139] General Fremont gave it prominence when he took this route in 1847 to confront the Mexican forces in the San Fernando Valley.[140] Some referred to the area as San Fernando Hill,[141] or San Fernando Pass.[142]

View of the Ridge Route at San Fernando Pass

[139] Dektar, Cliff "Ghost Highway in the Mountains," <u>Westways</u>, March 1955, p. 9.

[140] Cronk, Duane L. "Building the Newest Ridge Route," <u>Westways</u>, Aug. 1970, p. 53.

[141] Thompson, op. cit., p. 143.

[142] "Tejon Pass, Gateways to California," <u>PG&E Progress</u>, Feb. 1967.

Approach to Newhall Grade

Newhall Grade
Mission Art Company, L. A., Cal.

Sunshine Inn, Newhall Grade, Mission Art Company, L.A. Cal.

Courtesy Barbara Hagle

This is the southern approach to Beale's Cut, the divide that separates the Santa Susana Mountains on the west from the San Gabriel Mountains on the east.[143] The early motorist would venture up the grade to the top of the pass that was described in a club tour book as a 30 percent grade![144] It was here at the top of the pass that General Beale, federal Surveyor-General of California and Nevada and a capable engineer, in 1862 had lowered the grade 50 feet for his toll road. Beale's Cut was also referred to as "The Narrows."[145]

A 1911 motoring magazine listed items you should have when attempting travel on the dirt roads of the time. Some of the suggested items were: basic tools, a towing cable, assorted rubber cement patches, a small package of raw rubber for vulcanizing, an assortment of cotter pins, nuts, lock washers etc., as well as emergency food and a two-gallon canvas water bag.[146] Before any pavement, the first car to navigate Beale's Cut was a 1902 Autocar. A McKittrick man had traveled to Los Angeles by train to purchase a car from dealer Ralph Hamlin. Mr. Hamlin accompanied the new owner in driving the car back to the San Joaquin Valley. The grade was so steep at The Narrows that gasoline would not flow to the carburetor. They had to climb the grade in reverse, both men leaping out and chocking the wheels with rocks each time the engine stalled.[147]

In April 1903 T. E. Baker and F. Hughes set out by auto from Los Angeles to Kern City. Records do not indicate which canyon route they took but they drove the 150-mile distance in thirty-one hours, considered to be a remarkable feat for that time. They proudly reported not having one single breakdown and only used ten gallons of gasoline on the entire trip.[148] In

[143] McDonald, P. A. "Elimination of Newhall Tunnel Bottleneck Soon to be Realized," California Highways & Public Works, Jan 1938, p. 10.

[144] "So We Threw Her in Low," Westways, Dec. 1950 p. 23.

[145] Pease, Robert "The Ridge Route and Antelope Valley," Los Angeles Geographical Society, Publication Number one, 1964 p. 94.

[146] Watkins, op. cit., p. 334.

[147] "Evolution of a Pass," California Highways & Public Works, March-April 1964.

[148] Miller,Thelma B., History of Kern County, Chapter VI, 1929, p. 441.

1904 to further lessen the grade at Beale's Cut, men with picks and shovels once more laboriously deepened the cut and the roadbed was graded and oiled. Even with this effort the grade was still challenging, and San Joaquin automobile customers who purchased their cars from dealers in Los Angeles refused to complete the sale unless the car could climb the grade.[149]

In 1907 Mr. Kamprath crossed the Tehachapis with a friend that had a two-cylinder touring car and was anxious to demonstrate its capabilities. The trip was accomplished in sixteen hours. What a time they had climbing up the Grapevine! Kamprath had to follow the car blocking the wheels with boulders when the motor stalled. Travelling down Bouquet Canyon they crossed the creek several times, each time holding their breath for fear of killing the motor in the middle of the stream. The owner was not quite so proud of his machine after the trip.[150]

All of these early intrepid motorists had common challenges when choosing the Tejon Route. They had to contend with the severe grades of San Fernando Pass on the south and the Grapevine Grade on the north. There was no pavement or Ridge Route at that time. The cars made their way over rutted roads heretofore having existed for stagecoaches and freight wagons. Venturing through San Francisquito Canyon or one of the other canyons was an additional worrisome concern depending on the level of water in the canyons creeks. Beale's Cut was the only way over Fremont Pass until the Los Angeles County Road Department constructed the 435-foot Newhall Tunnel just west of Beale's Cut on Sierra Highway, formerly San Fernando Road.[151] The old route through the tunnel to Newhall and Saugus became part of the State highway system in 1917.[152] The tunnel opened October 1910. It was very narrow and had only two lanes. With increasing traffic the narrow tunnel soon became a serious

[149] "Evolution of a Pass," op. cit.

[150] Hill, op. cit., p. 39.

[151] Cole, David L. "Map Historian" Santa Maria California.

[152] "Evolution of a Pass," op. cit.

bottleneck[153]. Loaded trucks often scraped the sloping walls inside unless directly in the center of the tunnel.

Newhall Tunnel south portal with sign advertising "Bowerbank Copper Radiators, They Cool"

Newhall Tunnel, south portal
Mission Art Company, L. A., Cal.

[153] McDonald, op. cit.

Newhall Tunnel, north portal
Courtesy Caltrans

The developing oil industry saw refinery equipment being hauled from Taft south utilizing the Newhall Tunnel. The October 3, 1919, issue of the Newhall Signal & Saugus Enterprise reported an unsuccessful attempt to truck a thirteen-foot diameter "agitator tank" through the tunnel. "The tank becoming stuck had to be dragged out backward with the help of another truck. The tank was taken back as far north as Newhall and unloaded. The truck body was replaced with two wooden sills that lowered the load allowing passage with a clearance of only three inches between the top of the tunnel and the top of the tank."

On January 2, 1920, the same newspaper reported another incident. "A Mr. H. G. Beckley was driving a motor stage through the tunnel when a hay truck crowded him to the wall. He hugged the side of the tunnel so closely that all of the baggage was torn from the top of the stage, (bus) he was unable to avoid the collision." The tunnel was dark as well as low and narrow, 17.5 feet wide and 17 feet high at the center.[154] This obviously created a serious hazard as traffic increased on this singular access north to the San Joaquin and Sacramento Valleys and northwest to the Mojave Desert, Antelope Valley and Owens Valley.

In an article from the Newhall Signal and Saugus Enterprise of November 1, 1928, it is implied that the state assumed the congestion in the tunnel was the results of through travel on the Ridge Route and that the way to solve the matter was to straighten that road using an alignment through Weldon Canyon that would avoid the tunnel. An article from the same newspaper dated December 13, 1928, indicates that the contract for the Weldon Canyon road was let "last week" to LeTourneau & Lindberg of Stockton for $391,391. The work was to be completed in 300 working days. The article went on to say the contract only called for grading and that the paving contract would be let after the grading was complete and well settled.

The May 29, 1930, issue of the newspaper stated, "the new cut-off road south of town (Newhall) was completed Wednes-

[154] "Evolution of a Pass," op. cit.

60

day and thrown open to travel. The paving is of concrete and makes a very fine road though the width is only twenty feet wide." The article states that the connection with the old road was at the tunnel. This comment refers to the southern end of the Newhall railroad tunnel, not the Newhall automobile tunnel. The point where the new Weldon Canyon cut-off road intersected with the old road was also called tunnel station and today is located beneath the Weldon Canyon viaduct where State Highway 14 separates from I-5. As a side note, Weldon Canyon is named after Arthur Weldon, a pioneer railman. He came to California with the builders of the Santa Fe Railroad, fighting Indians as the railroad advanced. After reaching California he identified himself with the Southern Pacific and was a foreman with the crews that drove the tunnel under the Santa Susana Mountains in 1875. He built his home near the southern portal of that tunnel. He passed away in January 1942 at age 89.[155]

Auto congestion through the Newhall Tunnel was reduced when the new route to the west in Weldon Canyon opened for traffic to and from the San Joaquin and Sacramento valleys. Over the next ten years increasing volumes of traffic again began to plague the tunnel especially on Sundays during the wildflower season. The situation became intolerable. On May 5, 1938 the State awarded a contract to "daylight" the tunnel and improve the highway.[156] This famous tunnel, which had served nearly three decades of traffic finally, succumbed to progress.[157]

[155] "Arthur Weldon, pioneer railman, dies in sleep," The Newhall Signal and Saugus Enterprise, Jan. 23, 1942.

[156] Gallagher, John D. "Newhall Tunnel Replaced by Cut," California Highways and Public Works, January, 1940.

[157] Myers, R. C. "Eliminating a Tunnel Bottleneck," California Highways and Public Works, November, 1938, p. 4.

Fresno Scraper
Courtesy Caltrans

CHAPTER 14

Breaking ground on a new pass road

The Tehachapi and San Gabriel mountain ranges present a formidable barrier to any passage in or out of southern California. Mentioned earlier was the fact that in 1858 the Butterfield Overland Stage would have by-passed Los Angeles in favor of San Bernardino had the Los Angeles County Board of Supervisors not subsidized the grade reduction at Beale's Cut in addition to improving the San Francisquito Canyon road. The same problem arose in the early 1870's.

The Southern Pacific Railroad ran into the same mountain barrier. Originally they had intended to by pass Los Angeles while building their line south from San Francisco. Enjoying a monopoly in California, they were suddenly faced with a transcontinental competitor in the form of the Texas Pacific Railway Company. Tom Scott, proprietor of the Texas & Pacific (later Texas Pacific), had acquired some state and federal land grants and his objective was to build his railroad from Dallas all the way to San Diego via Yuma, Arizona.[158] "While the Texas Pacific was building their line toward San Diego from the east, the Southern Pacific made haste building a line down the San Joaquin Valley toward the Colorado River. Southern Pacific was attempting to claim the best southern California route before the Texas Pacific reached the state line. Extremely pressed for cash the Southern Pacific saw an opportunity to squeeze a subsidy out of Los Angeles. Fearing that the main line would by-pass Los Angeles, the city negotiated an agreement with the Southern Pacific that required voter approval. The good people of Los Angeles approved the measure in November of 1872 that guaranteed a large sum of money to Southern Pacific in exchange for placing

---

[158] Yenne, Bill, The History of the Southern Pacific, 1985, p. 52.

Los Angeles on the main line. There was only one problem. The Southern Pacific would have to bore a 6,966- foot tunnel through the mountains near Beale's Cut in order to reach Los Angeles. This tunnel was five times longer than their longest tunnel on the Central Pacific High Sierra transcontinental line. This was one time the Southern Pacific worked hard for its subsidy contending with the extreme difficulty of building the San Fernando Tunnel. At one point after the complexity of the job was revealed, the railroad considered sabotaging the election to free them to by-pass Los Angeles. The line was completed to Los Angeles on September 5, 1876. With some regret the railroad honored its agreement with the city but charged high rates for many years thereafter to re-coup their sacrifice." [159] A gold spike was driven at Lang Station in Soledad Canyon to commemorate the completed rail connection with San Francisco.[160] As a side note, the Southern Pacific had just barely completed its line connecting northern and southern California in 1876 when they turned east. The Southern Pacific took Yuma in May 1877, Tom Scott was defeated and his line was never built west of Texas.[161]

Before Commissioner Darlington of Los Angeles selected an alignment for the new highway, four already existing routes were offered the Commission. Each was successively rejected. Soledad Canyon, the route of the Southern Pacific line, now owned by Union Pacific was subject to frequent washouts. San Francisquito Canyon, the most westerly pass, was too steep and narrow. Bouquet Canyon, a.k.a. Deadman Canyon on some maps offered too many drainage problems. Mint Canyon was judged too long and costly. In their stead, the route chosen was practically a direct line between Newhall and Bakersfield. This proposed route went straight up to the top of the mountains where it would go mile after mile.[162] The road wound around and around the

[159] McAfee, Ward California's Railroad Era 1850-1911, 1973, p. 113-122.

[160] Pease, op. cit., p. 106.

[161] Yenne, op. cit., p. 52.

[162] Cooper, Frederic Taber, op, cit., p. 566.

peaks of the mountain in order to save grading costs at a time when highway expenditures were tightly budgeted.[163] Even then, the engineers knew a better road could be built, but an economical balance had to be struck between the available money and projected traffic volumes. At that time there were less than 126,000 cars in the entire State and 35 miles per hour was "wide open." Had the Ridge Route been engineered "through" the mountain peaks as opposed to twisting around each pinnacle it would have depleted money for highway improvements elsewhere in the state. By building along the ridge, they would minimize drainage problems inherent to mountain highways built on lower elevations. With limited funds, steam shovels were employed only when alternative options were not feasible. The objective back then was to just "get out of the mud."[164] In 1912 the State engineers had also investigated Piru Canyon as a possible route for the new road but because of water rights and a proposal to build a large dam and reservoir in the canyon it was not an option worthy of pursuit.[165] They say history repeats itself. Although it is not the same water project that was envisioned in 1912, Pyramid Dam and Reservoir, part of the state water project, occupy Piru and Violin Canyons today.

When they built the Ridge Route, the average wage for a highway worker was $3.50. The wage scale increased to approximately $6.00 per day if you brought a particular talent or skill to the job.

[163] Buckley, Patricia R. Highway 99: A California Chronicle, Calif. Dept. of Transportation Library, 1987, p. 17.

[164] Gallagher, J. D., "Highways of California," Nov/Dec, 1945, Calif. Highways & Public Works, p. 6.

[165] Myers, R. C. "New Ridge Alternate Highway Opened After 4 Years' Work," Calif. Highways & Public Works, Oct. - Nov. 1933, p. 2.

Swede's Cut
Courtesy Richard Atmore

CHAPTER 15

Road Construction

Construction work on the Ridge Route started in 1914, with the 40 miles of heavy construction between Castaic School and the Los Angeles Kern county boundary divided into three contracts. Section B carried the highway from Castaic School a distance of 12.8 miles to a point halfway up the summit. This section was let to Mahoney Brothers, railroad contractors of San Francisco.

Section C carried the road from the point left off by Mahoney for 14.5 farther, to the summit of Liebre Mountain. Section D was composed of the remaining 12.7 miles to the southerly border of Kern County. Sections C and D were assigned to Lee Moor Contracting Company, railroad and grading contractors of El Paso, Texas.[166] [167] Contractors building the road were concerned there could be a labor shortage if we were pulled into World War I. Fortunately for the contractors, the United States did not enter the war until April of 1917, eighteen months after the Ridge Route was completed.

It is noteworthy to mention that many early maps and documents refer to distance from or to the Castaic School. The late Jerry Reynolds, historian of the area, informed me prior to his passing that Castaic School was located on the southeast corner of the Lake Hughes Road and the old Ridge Route, approximately where a fire station is currently located.

Mule teams hauled equipment from the railroad at Lancaster to the remote northern construction sites.[168] The long, difficult trek was more challenging in wet weather when the

[166] "The Contractor,"<u>Architect and Engineer</u>, Vol. LX, No. 1, Jan. 1920, p. 120.

[167] <u>Southwest Builder and Contractor</u>, "Completed Ridge Route Now Open to Traffic," Nov. 28, 1919, p. 10.

[168] Dektar, op. cit., p. 9.

Culvert Pipe Stuck In Mud
Courtesy Caltrans

Lee Moor contractor company's Jeffery quad truck stuck in
mud between Fairmont and Neenach after a heavy storm
Courtesy Caltrans

roads became a quagmire of mud.

The southern end enjoyed a closer rail access at Saugus. Mules were also used to pull Fresno Scrapers. This primitive device was the primary tool used in grading the road. Teamsters on foot would direct the mules as the scrapers they pulled, gnawed their way through the mountains. In those days, the contractor who bid low on a highway job had to begin by purchasing a lot of horseflesh.[169]

Fresno Scrapers
Courtesy Caltrans

Construction was started in the middle and pushed toward both ends.[170] Grades were not to exceed six percent; however, several seven percent grades existed.[171] One million cubic yards of earth were removed to complete the Ridge Route,[172] with steam shovels brought in for the larger cuts.

[169] Cronk, op. cit., p. 12.

[170] Hill, op. cit., p. 50.

[171] Hill, Ibid.

[172] Hill, Ibid., p. 46.

Bucyrus Steam Shovel 60
Courtesy Caltrans

Marion Steam Shovel Model 3
Courtesy Caltrans

Twelve-hour workdays were not uncommon.[173] One such excavation was "Swede's Cut," also known as the "Big Cut" or Culebra Excavation." Some early postcards also show it as "Castaic Cut." My extensive research shows them all, beyond a doubt, to be the same location. Prior publications have suggested them to be separate sites, but this is not the case.

Swede's Cut

The State referred to the cut as Culebra (Spanish for snake), probably because of the "snaking" of the highway across the top of the mountains. This cut was dug to a depth of 110 feet, the largest on the entire route.[174] Although a Tehachapi-Mojave alignment, the "Midway Route," would have been less expensive to build, it would have been much longer.[175] The Ridge Route shortened the distance between Bakersfield and Los Angeles by 58 miles, as compared with the old path over the Tehachapis. The new road was also 24

[173] Buckley, op. cit., p. 17.

[174] "The Great Short Cut ...., op. ci.t., p. 3.

[175] Myers, op. cit., p. 16.

miles shorter than by way of Bouquet Canyon.[176]At a cost of $450,000, the unpaved road was opened to the public in October, 1915.[177] The opening of the Ridge Route did not mean the elimination of the Bouquet and Mint Canyon roads on the run to Bakersfield. Los Angeles County continued to maintain these roads.[178]

The Ridge Route reached its highest elevation of 4,233 feet on the Los Angeles side[179] just south of Sandberg's Summit Hotel. Due to the elevation and circuitous nature of the new highway, the speed limit was set at 15 miles per hour.[180]

15 Miles Per Hour!
Courtesy Caltrans

[176] "Bakersfield Is Now Linked to L. A....," op. cit.

[177] Henry, op. cit., p. 92.

[178] "All Aboard for Ridge Route....," op. cit., p. 11.

[179] "The Great Short Cut .... op. cit., p. 3.

[180] "All Aboard for Ridge Route.....," op. cit., p. 9.

The speed limit for heavier trucks with solid rubber tires was 12 miles per hour.[181] The Sheriff of Los Angeles County assigned two motorcycle officers to the highway, and they patrolled the ridge at all times. There was no joke about the speed limit edict issued from the Sheriff's office. It was set at 15 miles an hour and vigorously enforced. The Sheriff said: "woe to the man, woman or unlicensed child who tries to speed where there is to be no speeding – none at all, whatsoever and Stages (buses) won't make up their time on the Ridge Route." The words of Sheriff Cline – "I don't want to be killed myself up there and I'm not going to let anyone else take the chance."[182] It took about 12 hours driving time under normal conditions to make the Los Angeles to Bakersfield trip. Before the road was thrown open, the Automobile Club of Southern California was given only 24 hours notice to post signs along the new highway. "Hurling a high-powered Moreland truck through the night hours and up into the higher altitude, the work for which two weeks had been allotted was accomplished between sun up and sunset."[183] From the instant the early motorist set their wheels on the Ridge Route they found themselves in a forest of warning signs. It was the most gigantic feat of road-signing ever achieved anywhere. There were so many signs that they were likened to the "quills on a porcupines back."[184] The Automobile Club erected approximately 150 metal road signs.[185] People complained that there were more signs than trees. Ultimately some of the signs were removed and warning signs were erected at both the northern and southern terminals of the Ridge Route.

[181] Jones, Bob, "Winding Way over to L. A.," The Bakersfield Californian Magazine, Oct. 6, 1990, p. F4.

[182] "All Aboard for Ridge Route...," op. cit., p. 9.

[183] Dektar, op. cit., p. 9.

[184] "All Aboard for Ridge Route...," op. cit., p. 10.

[185] "Paving On Ridge Done; Open November 15," The Newhall Signal, Oct. 31, 1919.

Random view of car on Ridge Route.
Note Automobile Club of Southern California warning sign:
"Slow Grades and Curves Keep to Right."
Courtesy California Historical Society, Los Angeles Area
Chamber of Commerce Collection, Department of Special
Collections, University of Southern California Library

All of those warning signs were a testament to the "never ending" twists and turns of the old road. Unfortunately, the constant merry-go-round caused many motorists to lose the contents of their stomachs. In the 36 miles between Castaic and Gorman the road had 697 curves, which equaled 97 circles.[186] Another source stated that in 35.8 miles you completed 642 curves.[187] A third source said there were 48.36 miles of the original old Ridge Route and in that distance there were 39,441 degrees of turn that equated to driving around 110 complete circles (39,441 divided by 360 degrees).[188] This last reference considers the entire distance of the official Ridge Route, i. e. the distance between Castaic Junction and

---

[186] Bezzerides, A. I., "Trucker On The Old Ridge Route," Touring Topics, Jan. 1941, p. 9.

[187] Dektar, op. cit., p. 9.

[188] Leadabrand, Russ " Let's Explore A Byway Over The Old Ridge Route," Westways, Jan. 1971.

the bottom of the Grapevine. Taking this into consideration, I believe 110 circles is probably correct. My assumption is supported with information J. D. Gallagher, Associate Highway Engineer, published on page six in the Nov/Dec 1945 California Highways and Public Works Bulletin. His information indicates that there were 109.5 complete circles on the 1915 highway that equated to 39,441 degrees of curvature. The same article also supports the fact that the entire length of the road was 48.36 miles. Many writers calculated only the distance along the spine of the mountain, roughly that distance between Gorman and Castaic. Whether there were 697 curves or 642 is a matter of who was keeping tally.

As a side note, younger readers may be surprised to learn that it was the Automobile Club of Southern California that assumed the responsibility of erecting all highway signs in Southern California. Beginning in 1905 their crews extended as far north as San Luis Obispo and Visalia. Their signage reached east to the Nevada line and south to the Mexican border. On the scenic El Camino Real route they posted signs all the way to San Francisco. In 1913 the famous National Old Trails Road was nearing completion between Los Angeles and Kansas City, Missouri. In 1914 the Automobile Club of Southern California elected to erect 4,000 signs covering the entire route, an effort that consumed an entire year. Traveling west the signs would mark the mileage to the next town as well as the distance remaining to reach Los Angeles. You say, "National Old Trails Road," I have never heard of it. Well, it was the forerunner of Route 66! In 1946 the California Division of Highway Services assumed sign posting on state and county roads and the famous Automobile Club of Southern California logo that marked the bottom of each sign slowly faded into history.[189]

My 100-year old late foster mother recalled traversing the Ridge Route in 1918 with her brother and sister on a trip to Yellowstone. They were in an Overland touring car with removable side curtains. Her brother was driving and her

---

[189] Tilford, Kristin, "Signs of the Times," Westways, July/Aug. 1999, p.28 - 30.

older sister sitting in the front passenger seat would lean out, attempting to peer around the blind curves for oncoming traffic. She said signs were posted on curves to "sound your Klaxon" (horn).

The road opened in October of 1915.[190] "The road surface was rock and shale when it first opened, providing an excellent foundation for the temporary surface of oil and gravel giving a roadbed that makes traveling comfortable and permits all the speed that can safely be utilized."[191]

The State of California developed a highway numbering system that was used exclusively for construction and engineering purposes. The numbers were never posted along the highways. Generally speaking, Route 1 was the highway traveling the coast between the Oregon border and San Francisco. It was referred to as the Redwood Highway. Route 2 was the same coast route extending south from San Francisco to San Diego and was known as El Camino Real. Route 3 was the inland route that would become U. S. Highway 99 between the Oregon border and Sacramento and was known as the Pacific Highway. South of Sacramento to Los Angeles it was Route 4[192] and became the Golden State Highway. The Pacific Highway went west from Sacramento over to San Francisco then south on El Camino Real. In other words, Route 2 went by two names. In the early days, town councils, chambers of commerce and groups of people living along a road would promote a name for the route, e.g. "The Lincoln Highway," "The Roosevelt Highway," etc. If the names "caught on" with the motoring public, local communities that lined the route would be more apt to compete effectively for the limited maintenance funds available in that era.

"Road experts claimed the Ridge Route to be one of the most scientifically constructed mountain roads in the world."[193] "This highway is an achievement for the California state highway commission in which it may rightfully take

[190] "Completed Ridge Route Now Open To Traffic," op. cit., p. 11.

[191] "$500,000....., op. cit., p. 9.

[192] California Highways and Public Works, October 1929, courtesy David L. Cole.

[193] "$500,000....., op. cit., p. 7

76

pride. It was a daring conception both from engineering and political standpoints, winding as it does for some thirty miles through the most rugged of isolated mountainous territory. It abandoned the old-traveled route through a somewhat settled territory (refers to the Midway Route) arousing bitter opposition from politically powerful interests who sought to have this trunk line follow the old but longer route."[194] A comment of 1916 reads, "The Ridge Route has already become a great and powerful influence in promoting the unity and integrity of heretofore divided sections of the state, and in discouraging state division agitation."[195] "The road is a gift without price to every commercial vehicle that plies between the Canadian border and the Mexican line."[196] "The Tejon Route is a roadway of first commercial importance. The <u>San Francisco Chronicle</u> reported: "One of the most remarkable engineering feats accomplished by the State Highway Commission. It is Southern California's Magnus Opus in mountain highway construction."[197]

[194] "Completed Ridge Route Now Open To Traffic," op. cit., p. 10.

[195] Fluter, op. cit., p. 10.

[196] "All Aboard For Ridge Route...," op. cit., p. 11.

[197] "The Great Short Cut....," op. cit., p. 4.

Paving Operation 1919
Courtesy Richard Atmore

CHAPTER 16

Paving

The September 23rd 1917 edition of the San Francisco Chronicle reported that the Ridge Route was to be paved! Highway Commissioners had made a tour of the Ridge Route and announced that it would be paved between Los Angeles and Bakersfield. They reported that work had already started on the south end of the route near the Castaic Wash. While work is being done on the first eight miles a detour will be used but once work starts on the Ridge itself it will be necessary to close the road over the mountain.

By Pass South of Chandler's
Courtesy Caltrans

The article goes on to state that with the completion of the paving of the Ridge Route, we can have hopes of seeing the day when a paved highway stretches from Los Angeles to San Francisco. Two years after the road opened, the Highway Commission solicited bids to have the Ridge Route paved. It had been necessary to allow the great fills to settle thoroughly. There were various bids received but on December 31, 1917, the Highway Commission received only one bid in response to its advertisement for paving all three sections. Fred Hoffman of Long Beach offered to do the job for $575,130. The engineers felt that the bid was too high. They calculated the paving job should cost no more than $378,879. They did not enter into a contract, especially as it was doubtful of being completed under the war conditions of 1918.[198] [199]

An article in the December 1918 issue of Touring Topics stated: "The war is over. The embargo is off, highway construction. Fine. Now, let's get some roads built. Let's Go." "The big resumption of road building has not yet begun and will not begin until labor is more plentiful and the wherewithal to pay for the roads is secured in greater volume through sale of the highway bonds."

A poem in the local newspaper stated:

"He's back from war –
he's back from hell –
Back to the land he loves so well!
Back to the home –
back to the farm,
wearing the gold upon his arm.
Back from the fields of blood and stain –
Back to the civil life again!
It's work he wants – right now – today –
Have you a job – what will it pay?"[200]

[198] "The Contractor," op. cit., op. 122.

[199] Southwest Builder and Contractor, op. cit., p. 11.

[200] Dougherty, H. E., The Newhall Signal & Saugus Enterprise, February 21, 1919.

Again, the December 1918 edition of <u>Touring Topics</u> states, "Of interest to motorists of Southern California is the announcement of Commissioner Darlington of the California State Highway Commission that materials will be assembled this winter to commence final paving of the Ridge Route early in the spring. As to the Ridge Route, the state has already completed a total of about twelve miles of paving on it. Four miles of pavement have been laid on the southern end of the Ridge Route and seven miles on the northern end. Between the two extremes there is about one and one-half miles of pavement completed. Beyond this improvement the Commission is unable to proceed without shutting off traffic for the reason that there are no available by-paths or detours that will allow use of the Ridge while the remaining portions are being paved. If labor is available in ample volume the work will be pushed through next summer. During the period of construction traffic will use Bouquet Canyon and this is going to mean temporary construction and maintenance work on this roadway if it is to stand up under the travel to which it will be subjected."

Portions of the twelve miles of pavement mentioned above were actually laid in 1917. During this same time period various points along the road were being improved. It was the intent to have the entire Ridge Route paved by the summer of 1918,[201] unfortunately World War I interrupted the project.

Division Engineer, W. W. Patch, of the State Highway Commission stated in the March 14th 1919, issue of the <u>Newhall Signal</u> that The Ridge Road will be closed on March 17, and will not be opened before fall, in order to pave a 17-mile gap in the highway. In the meantime traffic will be diverted through the Mint and Bouquet Canyon roads. The section to be paved extends from a point four miles north of the Castaic schoolhouse to a point two miles south of the rippers camp. This strip, which is all in Los Angeles County is on the summit of the ridge and it is impossible to by-pass it while the paving is in progress. The commission will do the work by day labor

---

[201] "Paving of Ridge Route From Bakersfield to L. A. Started," <u>The San Francisco Chronicle</u>, September 23, 1917.

and preference will be given to any returned soldiers and seamen who apply for work. Traffic will be diverted from the Ridge Road at the forks at Saugus and at Quail Lake. Mr. Patch said: "Mint Canyon and Bouquet Canyon routes are in excellent shape." It is interesting to note that other references stated the the road closed for paving in February 1919 [202] in addition to April 1919.[203]

Pouring cement over the re-bar
Courtesy Caltrans

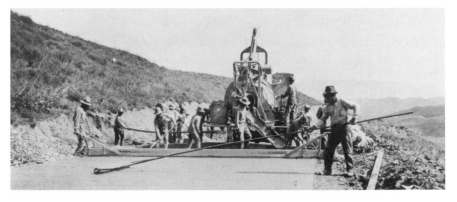

Smoothing the pavement August 7, 1919.
Courtesy Caltrans

[202] Henry, op. cit., p. 92.

[203] "Ridge Route Closed For Paving," Touring Topics, April, 1919, p. 13.

The commission decided to go ahead with the paving it-self in 1919. They completed the job at a cost slightly in excess of $700,000 and claimed a savings of $100,000 had it been done by contract even though they had asked for and received no bids since the $575,130 Hoffman bid of December 31, 1917, mentioned earlier.[204] Judging from the numbers alone, it would appear that Mr. Hoffman's bid was obviously below the Commissioner's cost, but then again, the Commission had delayed the paving for yet another year.

The road was paved with 4.5 inches of concrete with re-inforced twisted iron bars laid transversely 18 inches apart and bound together at each end with longitudinal bars.[205] Substantial concrete curbs were constructed at all dangerous points, six inches wide and ten high to protect reckless drivers and also to assist with drainage problems.[206] The high curbs were installed in locations where it was impossible to anchor wooden guardrails.[207] The high curbing acted as a deflector to the narrow, tired vehicles should they get too close to the edge of the cliff. It has been written that teamsters controlled their decent on the steep grades of the Ridge Route by shifting into a lower gear or by braking or a combination of both. Another practice common in this era was to rub the right front tire along the curbing. This practice did little harm to the solid hard rubber truck tire but inflicted considerable damage to the curbing.

The paving completed, the road reopened November 15, 1919. Commissioner Darlington said: "that for the present the concrete will be left unsurfaced. No surfacing material has yet been developed which would give complete satisfac-tion on the ridge. It is vitally necessary that the surface shall be non-skidding in all weathers and shall not "ripple" under the traffic thrust of thousands of climbing wheels. Virtually all the travel over the ridge is rubber shod and the concrete

[204] "The Contractor," op. cit., p. 122.

[205] Ibid.

[206] Hill, op. cit., p. 54.

[207] "The Contractor," op. cit., p. 122.

surface will stand up under it until such time as a satisfactory surface is developed."

The entire job was finished except for a ten-mile stretch between Lebec and Rose Station on the Kern County side. This section was oiled. A lack of funds prevented this section from being paved until a July bond issue was passed. The following spring would see this section completed.[208] The Kern County portion of the Ridge Route from Lebec to the bottom of Grapevine Grade was graded and paved during the period from September 1919, to May 1921.[209] During the paving of this strip, a detour of one and one-sixth miles was necessary in the vicinity of the famous Grapevine. The detour was a 20 percent climb and the road was adobe, a dangerous soil when wet. Three accidents happened on the detour in the first week, and motorists were warned by guards at both ends not to attempt the steep detour unless using low gear and having good brakes. Early cars without vacuum-feed fuel systems would be advised not to attempt going up the detour as the engine would ultimately be in a higher position than the gas tank.[210]

During the November rain of 1919 a newspaper article stated: "Highways to L. A. Made Difficult By Rain. Detour Around Grapevine Grade Is Now Very Dangerous. Telephonic advices received today by Manager P. J. Powell of the local Automobile Club of Southern California office state that motor routes from Bakersfield south offer many difficulties to travelers as a result of the county-wide rain. The state highway from Bakersfield to Los Angeles is reported all right the entire distance, with the exception of the short detour on the Grapevine Grade near the south Kern County line, where paving is being done and this detour seriously cripples the usefulness of the remaining boulevard. Of adobe soil, its 20 percent incline has become unnegotiable to touring cars without the assistance of two trucks, which are stationed at the detour

---

[208] "Bakersfield is Now Linked to L. A....," op. cit.

[209] Wallace, E. E., District Engineer, "Relocating Grapevine Grade Unit of Ridge Route Cuts Out 95 Curves," California Highways And Public Works, February 13, 1932, p. 24.

[210] Miller, op. cit., p. 443.

and towing motorists up the grade at $5 each. The detour is about a mile long and extremely dangerous, being narrow and slippery. Constructed on the side of a high hill it is almost certain death to topple off the road in a car. The Tehachapi-Mint Canyon route to Los Angeles from Bakersfield is in fair condition, with the exception of the Rosamond-Lancaster 10-mile stretch which has become extremely muddy. This road is marked by deep ruts and heavy soil, which makes it a veritable bog when wet. Mr. Powell stated today that if the rain continues in that section of the county the road will be impassable by tomorrow."[211]

After the Grapevine was paved and the detour eliminated, motorists still faced a healthy seven percent grade.[212] Many truck drivers would wait until evening before tackling the climb to reduce the possibility of overheating.

Another interesting note regarding Grapevine Grade and the Ridge Route Highway is the following clipping from the archives of The Bakersfield Californian newspaper. "BREACH OF MOTOR COURTESY TO LEAVE ROCKS IN ROAD, July 17, 1922. The Automobile club is receiving complaints about big stones that are left along the side of the road on the Ridge Route. It seems to be the habit, said J. B. Best, assistant manager of the club, for motorists to stop along the side of the road, going up the grade, and block the left rear wheels with big rocks. Upon continuing the journey, the stones are left in the road and the next motor passing along 'stubs its toes.' The leaving of the 'props' in the road is considered a breach of road courtesy, and should never be done, said Best."

[211] "Highways to L. A. Made Difficult By Rain," The Bakersfield Californian, November 27, 1919.

[212] Mohawk-Hobbs Grade and Surface Guide, 1926.

Pouring Asphalt, June 1920
Courtesy Caltrans

In 1922 a twenty-mile section of the concrete highway from Swede's Cut south was paved with asphalt.[213] In May of 1924 the California Highway Commission in an attempt to eliminate the dangerous blind curves assigned a twenty-man crew to widen and straighten the highway. The improvement began at the Castaic School House on the south end and had extended northward a mile beyond Big Swede's Cut, a distance of 17.5 miles. The men were operating a three-quarter-yard P. and H. Power Shovel and a small fleet of dump trucks. These improvements were accomplished using gasoline tax funds.[214] Prior to the upgrade, any attempt at passing became a game of Russian roulette. The curves simply blocked your view of oncoming traffic. Remember, once you pulled out to pass you did not have the option of a passing gear as we do today. More often than not the judgment call lead to disaster. Now it was possible to safely pass a slow moving truck because you could clearly see the road ahead.

[213] "State Highway Work," The Newhall Signal & Saugus Enterprise, August 11, 1922.

[214] "Eliminating Curves On The Ridge Route," California Highways, November 1925.

CHAPTER 17

Newhall / Saugus

Oak Glen, (Newhall area)

People would motor north from Los Angeles on San Fernando Road to Newhall. Oak Glen was located north of the Newhall Tunnel and south of Eternal Valley Memorial Park on the east side of the highway according to an undated Southern California Automobile Club map. The1926 <u>Mohawk-Hobbs Grade and Surface Guide</u> gives the following description: Oak Glen Camp, 25 cents, water, comfort station, lights, gas, good shade. A newspaper article of April 1930 states, "Extensive changes are going on at the Needham Ranch at the location known as Oak Glen. The change in grade has furnished a vast amount of dirt that has been used in leveling off a large area on which Mr. Needham has built a new service station and several camp cottages. When the work is completed, it will certainly be a beautiful spot."[215] Do not confuse this site with the small settlement of Oak Glen that was established on the Grapevine after the three lane Ridge Route Alternate was cut through Violin Canyon in 1933. A mile and one half north of the Oak Glen auto camp was Newhall Camp, a newer facility that had cabins under construction. Those not interested in staying at an auto camp could stay at Hotel Swall, a two-story brick hotel in Newhall that was constructed by Albert Swall in 1914.[216] By 1926 the community had a population of 600. Also listed in 1926 were Lowden's Garage and Traveler's Hotel. Rooms at the hotel were purported to be modern but they did not list any pricing information.

---

[215] "Changes at Oak Glen," <u>The Newhall Signal & Saugus Enterprise</u>, April 17, 1930.

[216] "Santa Clarita Historical Society."

Shady Camp

Shady Camp was another auto camp located in the vicinity of Newhall. The camp was most likely located at the south end of town where groves of Eucalyptus trees once provided shade. Do not confuse this location with the Shady Inn located at Lebec. The 1928 Mohawk-Hobbs Grade and Surface Guide notes: Shady Camp in Newhall has best tent space, 25 – 50 cents. An article in the June 14, 1940, edition of the Newhall Signal & Saugus Enterprise outlined, "Fire Damages Cabin At The Shady Auto Court." Two hundred dollars of damage occurred to one of the cabins caused by a leaking gas jet in the kitchen stove. G. L. Webb of Imperial California owned the property.

Saugus Café and Wood's Garage

Up ahead in Saugus the old road veered west after crossing the railroad tracks toward Ventura. The tracks have been removed but were located just south of State Highway 126. On the west side of the highway directly south of the tracks (and State Highway 126) was Wood's Garage and Richfield gasoline. The 1926 Mohawk-Hobbs Grade and Surface Guide touted them to be the largest and best, and they never closed. Their neighbor on the south was the Saugus Café, a local landmark that purportedly opened in 1886. It was originally called Tolefree's Saugus Eating House and was located in the north end of the Saugus Train Station. The restaurant was purchased by the Woods in 1898 and renamed the Saugus Café. In 1905 the café was relocated to the west side of the tracks (and highway) across from where the old train depot used to be. In 1916 Martin Wood expanded his Saugus Café while brother Richard switched from operating a blacksmith shop to running an auto repair shop known as Wood's Garage.[217] By 1926 the Saugus Café had competition in the form of Woodard's Café, a larger restaurant. The small community of Saugus with only 250 people also boasted of having

[217] Reynolds, Jerry, Santa Clarita Valley of the Golden Dream, 1992, p. 69 & p. 88.

the Saugus Hotel, a hostelry having 20 rooms. Eight of them had running water! A double occupancy room could be had for $1.50 per night.[218] Although Wood's Garage, The Saugus Hotel and Woodard's Café are long gone, the Saugus Café remains in business to this day.

By 1915 the Saugus Café had relocated across from the depot just beyond the man in the buggy. A year later Wood's Garage would open behind the telephone pole on the right.
Courtesy Caltrans

After leaving Saugus the road followed what today is State Highway 126. It extended west beyond the I-5 freeway then turned north crossing the Santa Clara River on a metal truss bridge near the northwest parking lot for Magic Mountain.

[218] Mohawk-Hobbs, 1926, op. cit.

Santa Clara Bridge, Mislabeled Castaic Creek Bridge
Western Publishing & Novelty Co., Los Angeles Cal.

Santa Clara Bridge today, looking north

The cement foundations for this bridge still remain, supporting a pipeline. To find this site take Feedmill Road on the north side of the park. Before entering the parking area, the bridge foundations are off to your right in the Santa Clara River bed. This bridge was reduced to rubble when the Saint Francis Dam ruptured in 1928. The road continued north after crossing the bridge to Castaic Junction where State Highway 126 heads west to Ventura and the Ridge Route continued north toward Castaic.

Random View Grapevine Canyon
Courtesy Terry Ommen

CHAPTER 18

Castaic Junction

In the early years of the road, various establishments quickly appeared along the highway. The information on these sites is extremely limited. Pictures are scarcer. Castaic Junction hosted a large Richfield, (ARCO company today) gas station with three gas pumps on the west side of the Ridge Route. The one story Beacon Inn restaurant and small one story frame home sat across Telegraph Road (State Highway 126) just south of the service station. Like most Richfield stations of that era it had a 120-foot high tower with large letters spelling R-I-C-H-F-I-E-L-D vertically from top to bottom.[219] Each letter was eight feet tall. When the towers were first put up in 1929 the letters were red. In later years they were changed to blue neon. The station opened for business in August of 1929. The tall tower and the directional beacon all flashed on illuminating the whole section like a flash of lightning. A Newhall car got the first gas, followed by a San Bernardino car and one from Culver City. The concealed air and water hose were noted as an innovation here. The hose is pulled from beneath the pumps and after use is automatically drawn back to place. Mr. Field, of the Richfield Company was present to see that everything passed off smoothly.[220] In the early 1920s there was a growing interest in aviation. The Richfield Oil Company of California erected these towers at their gas stations on the main highway between California and Washington as an aid to early aviators. The top of each tower supported an 8,000,000-candle power beacon. The Richfield stations were soon referred to as "Beacon" stations. [221] In

[219] L. A. County District 7 Route 4 Section "A" State map of old rights of way # 35, undated.

[220] "Richfield Opens Fine Station," The Newhall & Saugus Enterprise, August 22, 1929.

[221] Cole, David L., "The Richfield Beacon Service Stations," Check The Oil magazine, Jan. 1995.

later years on the Ridge Alternate, Castaic Junction was the site of Tip's restaurant.

Officially the Ridge Route is that portion of highway between Castaic Junction on the south where State Highway 126, (Telegraph Road) to Ventura intersects I-5 and the small settlement of Grapevine on the north that gives entrance into the San Joaquin Valley and Bakersfield. The "Grapevine" section of the Ridge Route is the 6.5-mile stretch of highway between Fort Tejon and the bottom of the grade at Grapevine.[222] I will address this segment of the old road in a later chapter. North of Castaic Junction, the road crossed over another bridge at Castaic Creek. The northern foundation for this bridge was still in place at the time of this writing just west of the freeway. From this point on the freeway has covered over the original alignment between Castaic Creek and Castaic.

North foundation of Castaic Creek Bridge today,
looking east, I-5 in background

[222] Anderson, Gordon, "Steep, tortuous curves marked early travel," The Bakersfield Californian, Dec. 27, 1983.

CHAPTER 19

Castaic

Heading north on I-5 we will take the Parker Road exit to enter Castaic. The United States Forest Service once had a facility on the west side of the original highway two miles south of Parker Road. At the top of the off ramp, turn right. At this point Parker Road becomes the old Ridge Route. From the very beginning, Castaic has been a truck stop and remains so today. In the early days, Parker Road and the Ridge Route actually came together with a "T" type intersection one block east of the off ramp at Castaic Road. The south end of Castaic Road was the alignment of the original Ridge Route. The old road continued south to a point where the freeway covered it up. Locals credit Samuel B. Parsons as possibly having built the first structure in Castaic fronting the Ridge Route. Sometime in 1914 he built a filling station and store. The post office was located in Sam's store.

Sam's

Tommy Adkins of Castaic said the "Days Inn Travel Lodge" at 31410 Castaic Road marks the location of Sam's old filling station and store. The Days Inn Travel Lodge is on the east side of Castaic Road just south of the Ridge Route intersection. A newspaper of 1920 states "Mr. S. B. Parsons of Castaic has a stock of groceries in connection with his filling station at the foot of the Ridge Route."[223] He sold his store and property to Pierre Daries on August 16, 1921.[224] In 1923 the newspaper states "The place belonging to Pierre Daries and known

---

[223] The Newhall Signal and Saugus Enterprise, Nov. 19, 1920.

[224] "Notice, I Pierre Daries, having purchased the station..." The Newhall Signal & Saugus Enterprise, 8-26, 1921.

as Sam's Place has recently changed hands."[225] The late A. B. Perkins, Castaic historian, indicates that Sam sold his property to Anthony Schuyler. This may have been, however I cannot find any information to support this statement.[226] As mentioned earlier, Sam sold his station to Mr. Daries on August 16, 1921. Mr. Schuyler acquired his station on March 11, 1921. Sam also owned 80 acres at the foot of the Ridge Route near Castaic Brick right on the highway.[227]

This poor picture is all that is available showing Sam's Service Station. The caption in the lower left hand corner reads Castaic Cal. to Los Angeles 40 miles
Courtesy the late Jerry Reynolds

[225] "The place belonging to Pierre Daries...," The Newhall Signal & Saugus Enterprise, Nov. 30, 1923.

[226] Perkins, A. B., "The Castaic Story," The Newhall Signal & Saugus Enterprise, June 14, 1962.

[227] L. A. County Division 7, Section B, sheet 4, Highway Engineering map, July 18, 1914.

96

The following locations in Castaic were determined from an early-undated Los Angeles County District Seven State Highway Engineering map.

Castaic Garage

In the road's hey day you would have found Castaic Garage on the northeast corner of the Ridge Route and Castaic Road intersection.

Jack Wilson's Service Station

Directly across the Ridge Route on the northwest corner of the intersection was Jack Wilson's Service Station.

Post Office

The Castaic Post Office sat directly north of Castaic Garage on the east side of the Ridge Route. It had a large front porch. The post office sat between Castaic Garage and Shilling's Service Station and Café.

Shilling's Service Station & Café

Shilling's was located on the east side of the Ridge Route directly north of the post office. There was a small stonewall between the post office and Shilling's Service Station and Café.

Schuyler's Filling Station

North of Shillings Anthony H. Schuyler built a filling station.[228] Another article dated October 1922 states, "A. H. Schuyler is just completing a large garage in connection with his grocery and filling station."[229] In December of the same year he built some small houses for the accommodation of

[228] "Mr. Schuyler's new filling station...," The Newhall Signal & Saugus Enterprise, March 11, 1921.

[229] "A. H. Schuyler," The Newhall Signal & Saugus Enterprise, October 27, 1922.

97

travelers who wanted to stop for the night.[230] Mr. Schuyler's small houses perhaps could have qualified him as having built the first motel. Unfortunately for Mr. Schuyler, three years later San Luis Obispo claimed that distinction.[231] A Newspaper article of November 1923 said "A. H. Schuyler's new restaurant is now open and is one of the most inviting places along the Ridge Route. There are tables for ladies, besides the large lunch counter. Mr. Schuyler has his own electrical plant and has the whole place lighted by electricity. Those who know, say he has a wonderful cook."[232] Mr. Schuyler must have been doing very well. An article listing local court cases states "Mr. Schuyler was arrested November 15, 1923." The charge was for having slot machines. His bail was set at $500. The newspaper stated that this would be a test case on slot machines.[233]

Miller's Service Station

Directly across the highway from Schuyler on the west side of the Ridge Route was Miller's Service Station.

Shadowland Auto Camp

Miller's neighbor to the north was the old Parker home. In 1923 it was converted into the Shadowland Auto Camp.[234]

Ever Green Cafe

Continuing north we cross over Palomas Creek on the small concrete bridge as the water below continues east to Castaic Creek. North of the bridge on the east side of the Ridge Route

---

[230] The Newhall Signal, Dec. 22, 1922.

[231] Roth, Matthew W., "Roadside Dreamin," Westways, May/June 2000. & Daily Breeze newspaper, Dec. 13, 1999.

[232] "A. H. Schuyler's new restaurant," The Newhall Signal & Saugus Enterprise, November 30, 1923.

[233] "A. H. Schuyler, Castaic," The Newhall Signal & Saugus Enterprise, November 16, 1923.

[234] "The old Parker home...," The Newhall Signal & Saugus Enterprise, June 15, 1923.

was Bert Reynold's Ever Green Café, Garage and Gas Station complex that included 5 auto cabins. The café building was directly to the right after crossing the bridge (heading north). There was another café with gas pumps directly across the street on the west side of the Ridge Route. The Ever Green Cafe had gas pumps out front. The auto cabins were north of the café and north of the cabins was the Ever Green Garage building that also had gas pumps in the front.

Castaic School, (An Early Mileage Marker)
Start your self-guided tour here

Directly north of the Ever Green garage, still on the east side of the road was Castaic School. The school was one of the first structures in Castaic and because of this held a place of importance on early maps. Distances to and from Castaic were measured using the schoolhouse as a reference point. The schoolhouse was located just south of the Ridge Route and Lake Hughes Road intersection and sat behind the Los Angeles County fire station that occupies the site today. Like the maps from an earlier time we will also measure distances from the Lake Hughes Road, Ridge Route intersection forward to each venue as we continue our journey back through time. (Please note your odometer.)

White Star Auto Camp

Crossing over Lake Hughes Road we continue north on the Ridge Route. The White Star Auto Camp was once located on the Northwest corner of this intersection.

Clark's Service Station

North of the White star Auto Camp was Clark's Service Station.

Jones' Service Station & Garage

Diagonally north of Clark's on the east side of the road was Jones' Service Station and Garage. Today on our right is Castaic Lake State Recreation Area. North Lake development has constructed hundreds of homes in this area. Unfortunately their housing project destroyed a portion of the original highway and alignment. The road originally (now Castaic Lake Drive) wound up the hill west of the Castaic Lagoon parking area and continued up a small canyon passing in front of Castaic Brick Yard and joined the original alignment north of West Pine Crest Place. The new alignment takes us through the housing development.

Corneila Martinez Callahan's home, store and
Union 76 gas station.
Courtesy Eva Rogers

CHAPTER 20

Service Stops & Landmarks on the Ridge

Queen Nell's

Beginning our climb we will travel 2.2 miles to the former location of "Queen Nell's Castle," Cornelia Martinez Callahan's home. A large water tank on the east side of the road marks Nell's old homestead. Prior to the water tank a grove of Pepper Trees identified the site. She and her late husband home-steaded here in 1909.[235] In the future, with the expansion of the North Lake housing development, it is proposed the road be relocated and placed on the east side of the water tank. If this occurs, the water tank will be on the west side of the highway at this location.

Cornelia Martinez Callahan's home

---

[235] "Wastes Reclaim Trail that Taxed Early Driver,"L. A. Times, May 29, 1947.

On October 30, 1914, Nell deeded some of her property to the State for the new road. She had a small green[236] wooden shack and sold gasoline and cold "pop" to motorists. [237] [238] The old road veered west here and was in the direct path of the new southbound lanes of the I-5 freeway. From Nell's, north to the Owl Garage the road was realigned and now parallels a portion of the freeway. Back in 1924, a 1500-foot curve in the same area replaced seven shorter curves. This re-routing of the old road was referred to as the "Callahan line change."[239] In 1929 she deeded more property to the state so they could build the Ridge Alternate Highway.[240]

Callahan Line Change
Courtesy Caltrans

[236] Hillinger, Charles, "Old Ridge Route Trip Turns Back to 20's," L. A. Times, Mar. 14, 1960.

[237] Dektar, op. cit., p. 9.

[238] Los Angeles County Book of Deeds, 5893, p. 250.

[239] "Eliminating Curves On The Ridge Route," op. cit.

[240] Los Angeles County Book of Deeds, 8140, p. 116.

Some locals referred to Nell as the "witch of the Ridge Route," possibly because of her remote location and the shack she lived in but more likely because she was a self-determined soul.[241] Back on March 15, 1891, Thomas Marple from Lea Wood England, married Leovigilda Del Campo Martinez of Ventura. Leovigilda Del Campo Martinez had a sister Cornelia Martinez, "Nellie" or "Nell" Callahan of Ridge Route fame. Nellie had a brother Carlos, "Charlie" Martinez. It is believed that Nellie had many brothers and sisters; however, nothing is known about them or her husband Mr. Callahan. Family members recall Mr. Callahan leaving before 1935. A Los Angeles Times article written about the Ridge Route and published on September 8, 1952, states: "shortly after her husband's death, Mrs. Callahan deeded to the State a portion of the right of way needed for the new venture." The Los Angeles Times had interviewed her prior to publishing their article and the interview intimates her husband passed away in 1914. The family remembers Nellie as having lived alone. It was Nellie's sister Leovigilda Del Campo Martinez, that chased General Petroleum off of her land with a shotgun when their pipeline caused damage to her vineyard. Thomas Marple, named after his grandfather, related another story regarding his grandmother. A couple of men wanted to hunt on her property. She refused their request, and they said they were going to hunt whether she liked it or not! She fired a shotgun at them. Her property was in the canyon at the bottom of 5-mile grade and today is that land between the north and southbound I-5 freeway. Leovigilda's husband, Thomas Marple, passed away in 1910 and was buried in Marple Canyon where the old homestead was. When the new I-5 freeway was constructed the state relocated his grave to Chatsworth. Nell's property was farther up the Old Ridge Route where a large water tank is currently located. It appears that Nell, like her sister stood ground to any confrontation. A newspaper account of January 1925 reads, "Mrs. Callahan who resides on a ranch west of the Ridge Route was arrested by the local police Wednesday. She is charged with assault and battery on Mrs. C. Pierce,

[241] Azhderian, Sam, Author's interview.

mother of Mrs. Pierre Daries of Castaic. The accused furnished bonds and her trial is set for January 16."[242] Although Nell lived alone in a remote area, the forest service entrusted her to be a "fire spotter" and provided her with a forest service telephone so as to report any forest fires[243] in the area.

Sun freeze Ice Cream Sign

Northwest of Nell's shack, across the highway on a small knoll, was the large "Sunfreze" ice cream sign. It was constructed of cement with river-rock pillars on each side of the display surface. When the new 3-lane Ridge Alternate bypassed the old route in 1933, anyone climbing Five-Mile Grade north of Castaic could spot the famous old sign across the canyon standing sentinel to a road left to the elements. In 1932 Nell won a reprieve for the old sign when workman arrived to tear it down. She ultimately acquired ownership of the sign and produced the deed to prove it.[244] The sign was destroyed during the construction of the southbound I-5 freeway.

"Sunfreze" Ice Cream sign
Courtesy Ridge Route Communities
Museum & Historical Society

[242] "Mrs. Callahan," The Newhall Signal & Saugus Enterprise, Jan. 8, 1925.

[243] "Memories Haunt Old Ridge Route," Los Angeles Times, Sept. 8, 1952.

[244] Ibid.

Owl Garage

One mile north from Nell's at odometer 3.2 miles was the Owl Garage. Ed Adkins built the small garage once located on the east side of the highway. He sold Standard (Chevron company today) gasoline. A large metal high-tension electric tower next to the road marks the location.

This is the only known picture of the Owl Garage. Ed R. Adkins (standing), Mildred is behind the wheel and Georgia Hutchings, Mildred's niece is seated on the running board.
Courtesy of James E. and May Jean Graves

South of the tower is a piece of the original alignment. Extensive building in the area will most likely destroy this remnant. Mr. Adkins, in addition to his garage, was the founder and owner of Castaic Brick. The original brickyard was not far from the present site. Down at Castaic Lake State Recreational Area if you were to turn from the Ridge Route onto Castaic Lake Drive (the original Ridge Route alignment) heading north past the parking area the road curves left and dead ends at Castaic Brick. If you were able to continue straight ahead a short distance without curving left toward Castaic Brick, you would locate the original location of Mr. Adkins brick works. Ed Adkins sold Castaic Brick around 1952 or 1953 and continued with the new owner as acting superintendent until 1957 or 1958. In the early 1960s Ed opened Castaic Clay Products on Castaic Road at the north end of town. The construction of Interstate 5 destroyed Ed's Castaic Clay Products Company.[245]

Ridge Road House

The next establishment, 5.2 miles from the Castaic School House was the Ridge Road House. On some maps it is shown as the Ridge Road Garage. The earliest record I have found for the Ridge Road Garage is on page 454 of the 1918 Auto Blue Book, volume 8. In 1926 it was mentioned in a touring guide thusly: "Reputed very fair, lunch."[246]

This poor photograph is the only known picture of the Ridge Road House. This view shows the gas station and café on the west side of the highway

[245] Adkins, Tommy, of Castaic, interview September 2000.

[246] Mohawk-Hobbs, 1926, op. cit.

View of road between the Owl Garage
and the Ridge Road House

Sam and Gloria Azhderian, former owners of the property, built a beautiful home directly above the old site. Sam told me that the garage and restaurant were on the west side of the highway and the foundations are still visible. The Ridge Road House sold Richfield gasoline and advertised with a high pole and a sign sporting a race car perched on top of it. Across the road on the east side there was a grouping of green and white sleeping cabins among a grove of Pepper Trees. Mr. Azhderian, founder of the Castaic Water District, said that after purchasing the property he removed chunks of foundations where the cabins once stood. They did not have in-door plumbing. There is a large wooden water tank located on a small hill behind the home they built that supplied water to the gas station and store. Travelers relied on out-houses for toilet facilities. Sam, a real estate developer and former Castaic town councilman, said Porter B. Markell and his sister Ruth owned the station. Porter was a crippled man The <u>Newhall Signal and Saugus Enterprise</u> of September 3rd 1920, reported the Ridge Road Garage was now owned and operated by Jimeson & Wiesmann. A year later the November 18th edition of the same paper reported that H. S. Birdsell recently sold the

Ridge Road Garage. Whoever purchased the property must have defaulted because Mr. Azhderian said the Markells sold to Clarence A. and Bertha M. Swanson on August 10th 1948, recorded on instrument # 1130. This is most likely correct as the L. A. County Assessor's records show Nelly B. Markel transferring ownership to Ruth Markell in 1938.[247] Irving A. Swanson, father of Clarence A. Swanson, homesteaded 320 acres in 1897 mostly in Violin Canyon but some acreage in Marple Canyon. In 1962 Sam entered into an option to purchase the property from the Swanson's. Sam put his horses onto the property and in later years after Bertha Swanson passed away, Clarence and Sam came to an agreement on a price and title was transferred to the Azhderian's in 1980. Sam Azhderian and Art Lewis founded the Castaic Water District in 1964. Sam was the first chairman to serve the district. Sam remembers traveling the road when he was a small child. His parents had a farm in Fresno and would take their Dodge Brothers truck down to Los Angeles quite often. Some of the other trucks on the highway were the old Mack trucks, the Sterlings, the Fageol and the Reos. He recalls the chain-driven rigs giving a sharp snap when they pulled out, and the constant string of lights along the road at night.

Random View. Sign above the truck cab reads: "Geo. J. Saul Livestock Trucking, Phone Lafayette 1519 Los Angeles."

During the Great Depression, according to Azhderian, the Lebec Hotel would allow motorists to camp on the lawn in front

[247] L. A. County Assessor's Records, book 170.

of the hotel if they could not afford to pay for a room. The road tested the endurance of the early vehicles, with many breakdowns and people begging for help and extra water along the route.

It was between the Ridge Road Garage/House and Martins a mile north that J. D. "Dave" Brodine was involved in an accident. Fortunately no one was hurt. For Brodine, the Ridge Route and the Grapevine hold special significance. He drove the treacherous road in 1925, before the days of good asphalt, guardrails or six-lane interstates. Born in Spokane Washington in 1904, he eventually came to Los Angeles. He worked as a truck driver, hauling freight for several different companies. In 1924 he was hired by the San Joaquin Valley Transportation Company to haul freight from Los Angeles to Tulare. The process of moving goods across long distances was a far cry from today's transportation system. The round trip took 48 hours in one of the company's 1922 Packard four-cylinder trucks. The trucks didn't have stop, clearance or directional lights. The top speed was 28 miles per hour and hand signals were used. A hand brake was used for the rear wheels. There were two drivers assigned to each truck. Above the cab was a wooden box for the relief driver to sleep in. The trip would begin with the truck leaving Los Angeles at 6 p.m. via Alameda Street and San Fernando road. They would travel over a hill, through two tunnels and down the hill to Newhall and Saugus. Turning left at Wood's Garage in Saugus, the road angled northwest to Castaic at the foot of the old Ridge Route. Brodine remembered several stops along the ridge, including Caswell's at the head of the Antelope Valley. They had a sign across their garage that read, "No, the wind never blew this way before." The seven-mile stretch going down the Grapevine had to be driven in second gear all the way, using a small hand brake as well. From there it was about an hour's drive into Bakersfield. "We ate breakfast at Karnes & Klotfellers Restaurant on Roberts Lane. Diamond Tooth Annie frequently waited on us. She had a diamond between her two front teeth". Even in the days before high-speed travel, accidents were frequent. Crews were constantly working to widen and straighten the highway. One rainy night, a stretch of dirt left by the maintenance crew turned into mud. It was so slick travel was hazardous. A Mack truck and trailer loaded with oil-well casings slowed nearly to a stop as the driver saw the dirt ahead. Brodine's San Joaquin Valley Transportation truck was coming down a steep grade on a curve. The Packard, loaded with eight tons of olives, skidded sideways and hit the Mack, pushing it backwards. The Packard nearly went off the grade. Brodine eventually formed J. D. Brodine and Son, a crane company that he ran for many years.[248]

Brodine's San Joaquin Valley Transportation
Packard over the side
Courtesy Mrs. J. D. Brodine

[248] Brodine, Edna and son David, graciously granting permission to use information given Jon Hammond of the <u>Tehacapi News</u> and subsequent article appearing Feb. 8, 1989.

View showing both trucks. The accident location was
on a curve between Martin's and the Ridge Road Garage
Courtesy Mrs. J. D. Brodine

Martin's

Up the road one mile, (6.2 miles on your odometer) was
Martin's, a small gas station that sold Standard gasoline operated by Mildred & Martin Deceta.[249] Ed Adkins' sister, Mildred,
married Martin Deceta, and Martin's sister Ignacia Deceta
married Ed Adkins. May Jean Deceta, Mildred's daughter,
married James E. Graves of Castaic. Until recently, Mildred
lived alone; occupying the original building which at one
time was the gas station and store.   A two-story unpainted
house was once located directly south of the gas station.[250]
Martin's was sometimes pronounced "Marteen's" because he
was a Frenchman.[251] The 1926 touring guide simply states:
"Garage, gas and water."

[249] Hillinger, op. cit.

[250] Adkins, Tommy, opt cit.

[251] Author's Interview with Mildred Deceta, Apr. 25, 1992.

Martin Deceta in front of his garage on the Ridge Route
Courtesy James E. and May Jean Graves

When the Ridge Alternate opened in 1933, Martin Deceta and Ed Adkins opened a garage on the east side of the highway at the Paradise Ranch turn off, that today would be Templin Highway. The Decetas eventually went back to ranching.[252]

Heading north we will cross Templin Highway. People mistakenly believe that Templin Highway was established as an access road for the building of Castaic Reservoir and Powerplant, part of the California State Water Project. Mr. Templin, formerly a Los Angeles County highway commissioner proposed connecting a highway from the I-5 freeway east to Spunky Canyon Road above the Bouquet Canyon Reservoir. The proposal became part of the Los Angeles County Highway Plan in 1975. Pavement was laid east as far as the old Ridge Route. Unfortunately, in 1980 they officially deleted the proposal and the completed section of Templin Highway did in fact become a large driveway to the reservoir and power facility.[253]

[252] Adkins, Tommy, op. cit.

[253] Riedel, Hans, Los Angeles County Dept. of Public Works.

View Service Station

The original alignment of the Ridge Route where it crosses Templin Highway was at a higher elevation. Just prior to reaching the intersection, up above to the east, is a remnant of the original pavement. At 10.4 miles, the View Service Station was the next establishment. It was on the right, or east, side of the road and did indeed command a sweeping view of the San Gabriel Mountains. Early maps seem to place the gas station near the intersection of Warm Springs Road and the Ridge Route. The dirt-surfaced Warm Springs Road is north of Templin Highway, just before you reach the forest boundary gate. Today it leads westerly to a small grouping of homes down the canyon. At one time, Warm Springs Road continued east down into the canyon to access various campgrounds including a California Conservation Corp camp where the bridge is located. With the construction of Castaic Dam, this section is no longer accessible. In conversation with James E. Graves, mentioned earlier in association with the Martin site, I learned that the true location of the View Service Station is a bit farther north of this intersection. A small clump of bamboo marks the location today. The flat area north of the bamboo was created in recent years. The foundation for the gas station was located directly in front of the bamboo and included a cement service pit that vandals filled with cans and trash. All remains of the site were bull dozed over the hill. Although indicated on a couple of early maps, virtually no information is available regarding this site.[254] A photograph of the site has yet to be found.

Just one half mile south of the View Service Station site is the 7.5 mile Angeles Tunnel. Water from the south end of Pyramid Lake flows through the 30-foot diameter tunnel before it falls 1,000 feet into the turbines of Castaic Power plant. The water then enters Elderberry Forebay, a small reservoir separated from Castaic Lake. During hours of low demand for electricity, water stored in Elderberry Forerbay is pumped back into Pyramid Lake where it stays until it is needed again

---

[254] Adkins, Tommy, op. cit.

to spin turbines that turn generators to produce electricity. This method of operation is called pumped storage. Although it uses more power than it produces, pumped storage ensures a water supply to produce electricity regardless of the natural supply, and it produces electricity during peak demand. Castaic Lake actually has two branches. The lake is shaped somewhat like a V. The eastern arm is called Elizabeth Lake Canyon, while Castaic Canyon extends to the west. Castaic Dam is at the south end of the lake, and Castaic Lagoon lies below the dam.[255]

National Forest Inn

At 12.2 miles we reach the National Forest Inn. Located on government-owned land, all that remains today are cement steps on the west side of the road. It was described in a 1932 highway beautification pamphlet with this unkind caption: "The sort of filling station that gets into a national forest and is no addition thereto." Unlike Sandberg's, which was constructed of logs, the National Forest Inn sported neatly-trimmed, white clapboard buildings. A gentleman named Courtemanche built the Inn. This same article stated Mr. Courtemanche, after having built the National Forest Inn, also built the French Village in Newhall.[256] A newspaper article of 1920 mentioned that a Mr. Nelson Courtemanche from Los Angeles was spending his vacation with his parents on the Ridge Route.[257] Another clipping states that Harry Courtemanche and Charles Courtemanche, with their sister Miss Louise Courtemanche, entertained a number of friends with a theatre party at Cody's.[258] A gossip column in the Newhall Signal and Saugus Enterprise of March 11, 1921 reported: "Miss Gladys Parsons and Mr. Charles Courtemanche were

[255] Department of Water Resources, State of California.

[256] "National Forest Inn Fire Sets Big Blaze," The Newhall Signal & Saugus Enterprise, Oct. 20, 1932.

[257] "Mr. Nelson Courtemanche," The Newhall Signal & Saugus Enterprise, November 19, 1920.

[258] "The Messrs Harry and Charles Courtemanche....," The Newhall Signal & Saugus Enterprise, August 19, 1921.

seen 'flivvering' Sunday afternoon." A newspaper clipping of January 1, 1925, indicates a Joe Palmer as proprietor of the National Forest Inn Garage.[259] Another article of February 12, 1925, states: "1924 was a banner year at the Forest Inn. The popular resort enjoyed a very prosperous season during 1924. Frank Lambert and William Rose, together with the able assistance of their wives, built up an exceptionally worthy patronage. It is with regret that a number of loyal friends learned of their departure from the Ridge on January 25, on which date their lease expired. The Courtemanche's, original owners of the Inn, are now in charge of both the Inn and the Inn's Garage, the latter being maintained throughout the 1924 season by Joe W. Palmer, under a sub-lease from Lambert and Rose. Mr. Palmer built up as substantial a patronage for the garage as Lambert and Rose did for the Inn, and he too, made many friends who regret his departure."[260] In 1926 Mr. Courtmanche was building a new road camp across the road from the Eucalyptus grove south of town. He will have a store, garage and ten cottages.[261] This refers to construction of his French Village in Newhall on San Fernando Rd. near Sierra Hwy. Mr. Courtmanche was French Canadian and had the National Forest Inn ready when the road opened in 1915. At one time it was called the Forest Reserve Garage and Accomodations. The 1926 touring

National Forest Inn

[259] "Joe Palmer, Proprietor of the National Forest Inn Garage," The Newhall Signal & Saugus Enterprise, Jan. 1, 1925.

[260] "1924 A Banner Year At Forest Inn," The Newhall Signal & Saugus Enterprise, February 12, 1925.

[261] "New Road Camp," The Newhall Signal & Saugus Enterprise, February 11, 1926.

guide indicated that there were nine rooms in cottages, most with running water at the National Forest Inn from $1 to $2, lunch 75 cents; garage; camp 50 cents. A sign painted on the south side of the restaurant advertised General Gasoline. A metal sign in front of the establishment also indicated they sold General Gasoline. The large sign in the middle of the picture by the car states: "National Forest Inn (page 115), Heated rooms & Cottages, Home cooked meals & Lunches, Cold Drinks."

A 1926 topography map spots a ranger station at this location. All of the accommodations were on the west side of the road. A large metal building on the east side of the road housed the highway repair facility and a ranger station.[262] Also located on the east side of the highway was a water trough for vehicles that required radiator water. Keep in mind that many of the early automobiles did not have pressure caps for their radiators and that the steep climbs would cause the radiator to boil much like a teakettle loosing water and causing the motor to overheat.

Panoramic View of the National Forest Inn

---

[262] Kaufmann, op. cit.

Close-up View of the National Forest Inn

Water trough for boiling radiators, National Forest Inn
M. Kashower Co., Los Angeles Cal.

On a hill, on the eastside of the highway above the National Forest Inn site are foundation remains of an old airplane beacon. The beacon site is also shown on a 1928 topography map of the area.

National Forest Inn Airplane Beacon

On Friday October 14, 1932, a fire started in the National Forest Inn garage. It quickly spread to the dry brush and other buildings at the site. The fire started around 9:00 a.m. and was still out of control the following afternoon. Hundreds of men battled the 1200-acre blaze that destroyed valuable water shed. Mr. Martin, owner of the resort, was reported to have carried his cash register from the burning garage to a location where he sat it down near, or in another structure. Unfortunately the out of control fire consumed the entire complex and he lost considerable cash. The National Forest Inn was on United States Forest Service property.[263] The Inn was never rebuilt because the traffic would be diverted with the opening

[263] "National Forest Inn Fire...," op cit.

118

of the Ridge Alternate in 1933. The National Forest Inn was one of the more popular places on the ridge.

Immediately north of the National Forest Inn site, if we look to the west, we can see the Ridge Route Alternate and the new I-5 highways.

Serpentine Drive, Swede's Cut, Big Cut, Culebra Excavation and Castaic Cut

Serpentine Drive is located north of National Forest Inn at 14.2 miles. It begins where the old Midway natural gas line crosses above the road.

Serpentine Drive looking south

This 1920 view looking south taken from the top of the hill at 4,000 feet states Sandberg's Hotel is still 13 miles farther north! The Flag Studio, Pasadena, Calif.

Serpentine Drive climb looking north
Western Publishing & Novelty Co., Los Angeles, Cal.

Many post cards "imaged" Serpentine climb that at the top entered the largest cut on the road, Swede's Cut, also referred to as the "Big Cut," "Culebra Excavation" and "Castaic Cut" all referring to the same location. Steam shovels provided the muscle for this lengthy dig.

Swede's Cut
Courtesy Caltrans

Swede's Cut today with Angeles National Forest archaeologist
Michael J. McIntyre and the author, view looking south.
Courtesy Brian Smale

Reservoir Summit

Farther on at 17.4 miles we find Reservoir Summit with
an elevation of 3,883 feet.   Although referred to as a summit it was not the highest point along the road. Liebre was
the actual summit at 4,233 feet, a short distance south of
Sandberg's. Reservoir Summit was a high-class, popular
restaurant with men waiters in solid white uniforms. Truckers were welcome.[264] The front of a two by nine inch souvenir
menu from the Reservoir Summit Café, garage and service
station states, "24-hour service, large sanitary rest rooms,
plenty of parking space, home cooked meals and pastries,
fountain, cigars, candies, tobaccos." The proprietor was I.L.
Avis and he was a member of the Tourist Wayside League.

[264] Kane, Bonnie Ketterl-, Dodge interview, June 8, 1995.

Some of the items listed on the menu were: Hot Cakes and Coffee, 25 cents; Toast and Coffee, 25 cents; Hot Cakes, Ham or Bacon and Coffee, 45 cents; Two eggs in Butter, Spuds, Coffee 45 cents; Beans, Bread and Butter, 35 cents; Sandwiches ranged from 15 to 20 cents; Home Made Pies, per cut 15 and 20 cents; and you could have Coffee, Milk or Tea for 10 cents. On the backside of the souvenir menu was a strip map listing mileage between the various towns and auto camps between Oakland and Los Angeles.

Front view of Reservoir Summit Café souvenir menu

The 1926 <u>Mohawk-Hobbs Grade and Surface Touring Guide</u> lists: garage, lunch, rest rooms and camp. The same guide of 1928 omits the auto camp and the 1930 guide does not show anything at the site. An article in the newspaper of 1933 stated that Ira Avis, proprietor of the Reservoir Summit Service Station on the Ridge Route, died at the Community Hospital Monday night September 11, 1933, of heart failure. His widow and a daughter survive Mr. Avis.[265] The restaurant, gas station and garage were all located on the east side of the road. The restaurant had a fabulous view, literally hanging over the side of the cliff. The garage and restaurant were built on stilts. Remains of the cement foundation supports can be found on the east side of the road. The restau-

<hr/>

[265] "Ridge Route Man Dies," <u>The Newhall Signal & Saugus Enterprise</u>, September 14, 1933.

rant was green with a screened porch, not very deep, having a lunch counter with three or four tables. The garage was very small, approximately 15 feet wide and 20 feet deep. It housed a tow truck, and was directly south of the restaurant. A wider area on the west side of the road had parking and a water trough for overheated radiators. The auto camp and six to eight half wood, half canvas tent cabins were located on top of a small hill above the road. Directly west of the former auto camp is the large cement-lined water reservoir, originally having a wooden top.[266] A short walk to the west end of the old reservoir provides a view looking down upon I-5 and the face of Pyramid Dam. Unfortunately, as of this printing, a picture has yet to surface showing the restaurant and garage.

Reservoir Summit reservoir today

The 1926 topography map shows "Reservoir Hill." The 1931 map shows "Reservoir Summit and "Reservoir Hill" with a Ranger Station. An article dated August 4, 1932, from the <u>Newhall Signal and Saugus Enterprise</u> states: "New Fire Truck for Ridge Route. The new truck will be stationed at

---

[266] Kaufmann, op. cit.

Reservoir Summit." Jack Rimmer, of Pear Blossum California, former Forest Service Guard at Reservoir Summit Guard Station, recalls being assigned to the station around 1932. He told me that they did receive a new fire engine and remembers it being painted red when all of the other Forest Service fire engines were green. He does not recall any trace of the restaurant or auto camp. The only structure was an old, gray ship-lath combination mess hall / bunkhouse ranger station. It was located down near the highway. The Forest Service was in the process of building a new garage for the fire engine and associated fire fighting equipment as well as a new combination home and look out station for the ranger. The new house was dark brown with green trim and was located right on top of Reservoir Hill. They had two magneto crank telephones, one connected to the Forest Service line and another to Pacific Bell. The house had indoor plumbing and a long covered porch to be used as the vantage point to spot fires. The porch floor was painted gray. They would take azimuth readings from the porch and report the degrees to the Newhall Ranger Station.

Jack moved all his personal belongings, his green uniforms, boots, a new .22 rifle and a beautiful 6'x 9' white, red and black Indian rug into the house. Lester Drake, a Forest Service supervisor, had also moved his belongings into the new building. Lester was there to oversee that finishing touches were completed on the new house and garage. In the process of completing the job, flooring in the home had been treated with linseed oil. Unfortunately, they had only occupied the house one week when the oily rags used to treat the floor ignited, burning the house to the ground. It was never rebuilt. It was replaced with a look out tower.

Reservoir Summit Lookout Tower
Courtesy Jack Rimmer

Jack explained that a Guard Station had a fire truck and a crew. A Patrol Station was a one-man operation with no crew or fire truck assigned to the station. Standard procedure for a Patrol Station was to assign a pickup type vehicle that carried approximately two to three hundred gallons of water for fire control. Most forest stations were Guard Stations. At Reservoir Summit, the crew of men, approximately eight including the cook, were older men recruited through some type of government program identified as SERA. They functioned in a manner similar to the California Conservation Corp.

Fire crew with Bunkhouse & Mess Hall in background
Courtesy Jack Rimmer

Jack said that occasionally one of the oil company lines or the natural gas line would rupture causing a brush fire. He would prevent these fires from spreading while the pipeline company worked to shut down the line. His crew also cleared brush and did control burns along the Pacific Telephone Long Distance pole line that ran between Bakersfield and Los Angeles. South of Sandberg's and Liebre Mountain, the telephone lines dropped down into the canyon roughly following the road that extended to Kelly Ranch. From the ranch, the lines continued south down Cienaga Canyon and Castaic Canyon to Castaic. Today, nothing remains at Reservoir Summit except the old reservoir and remnants of the restaurant's foundation. A picture of the once popular roadhouse has yet to be discovered.

Kelly's, a.k.a. "Kelly's Half Way House," "Kelly's Half Way Inn" & "Half Way Inn"

Our journey at 19.7 miles places us at Kelly's, which is how it is indicated on early maps. Others mark it "Half Way Inn." It was 62 miles from Los Angeles and 64 miles from Bakersfield. There was a Kelly Ranch in the canyon to the south, but I have been unable to verify if Kelly's Ranch had any connection with Half Way Inn. Old timers in Castaic told me Kelly's Half Way Inn was not in any way connected with Kelly's Ranch. Richard Atmore of Ventura tends to agree and offered the following information. Richard's Grandparents purchased the old Miller adobe near what today is Paradise Ranch. Paradise Ranch is located near Templin Highway and the present I-5 Ridge Route. His grandfather homesteaded property adjacent to the adobe thereby creating a rather large ranch. Richard's grandparents sold food stores from their ranch to the crews that built the power lines over the ridge in 1913. They also sold supplies to the road gangs buildings the Ridge Route in 1914. Richard's aunt, (his father's sister) Minnie Mable Atmore married Arthur Earl Killingsworth. Mr. Killingsworth's nickname was "Kelly." Minnie and Kelly operated the Half Way Inn sometime between 1916 and 1919. They were only there a short time and Richard believes the buildings were there prior to Minnie and Kelly's tenure.

A newspaper clipping of November 3, 1922, stated: "the popular and well known mechanic at Kelly's Garage, Clarence Swanson, is no longer seen with a smiling face as his Chevrolet was stolen last week."[267] A January 1925 newspaper article states Mrs. Ella Palmer, wife of Joe Palmer, who during the past year had maintained the National Forest Inn Garage, died January 3rd leaving behind her husband, Joe, and a daughter, Evelyn.[268] A May 1925 article states, "Joe Palmer who maintained the National Forest Inn garage has purchased the Kelly's place formerly operated by C. O. Cummings." [269]

Anna Pickner was a waitress for Joe Palmer at the Half Way Inn between 1926 & 1928. Joe must have remarried as Anna recalls his wife's name as being Theresa. Anna worked six days a week. She met her husband, Monick Pickner, who worked at the Richfield gas station there. The Half Way Inn had a restaurant near the road with three or four cabins below and was kept very neat. They had running water in the restaurant and outdoor toilets for the public behind the gas station. There was a tin garage with a tow truck west of the restaurant. The restaurant had about 12 to 14 stools at the counter and several tables. Joe Palmer and his wife lived in the restaurant building, which had two bedrooms and one indoor bathroom. One of the bedrooms was in the front of the restaurant and the other toward the rear.

Kelly's
Courtesy Richard Atmore

[267] "Castaic News," The Newhall Signal, November 3, 1922.

[268] "Mrs. Ella Palmer...," The Newhall Signal & Saugus Enterprise, January 15, 1925.

[269] "Joe Palmer Buys Kelly's Place on Ridge," The Newhall Signal, May 14, 1925.

Ridge Route - Los Angeles 62 Miles, Bakersfield 64 Miles.

(Kelly's Half Way Inn and view from Kelly's looking
toward Reservoir Summit.) Sign above the rear of the car to
the left reads "Kelly Service Station, open day &
night. A "Lunch" sign is positioned on the roof
above the front of the car. The sign on the peak of the garage is advertising "Arrowhead Ginger Ale."
Richard Atmore speculates the picture
above is that of Minnie and Kelly with their daughter Lila.

The Palmers took Anna in like a daughter. They gave her
one of the bedrooms in the restaurant. She said it was always quite busy and a lot of trucks stopped there. The facility was open 24 hours. They generated their own electricity.
Later Anna moved to the Gorman area where her husband
took work driving the school bus for 30 years. Anna's father,
Albert Bernhardt Young, retired from General Petroleum having worked at the Quail Lake Pumping Station for a number
of years. Frank Young, (Anna's brother) said that his dad
purchased the Half Way Inn building and tore it down using
the wood and kitchen equipment to open a new restaurant,
(Young's Café) on the Ridge Alternate four miles south of Gorman on the east side of the road near the I-5, State Highway
138 junction.

Bakersfield & Los Angeles Fast Freight
truck plying the Ridge Route

Frank said that he was around 12 or 13 years old, born in 1921 at Gorman in a midwife's house. His dad had homesteaded 640 acres where the restaurant was, and their home was about one quarter mile north of the restaurant site. His dad had built the restaurant before he retired from General Petroleum after World War II. Anna and her husband worked at the new restaurant. Anna ran the restaurant and "Pic" ran the Mobil gas station and garage. Frank thought the restaurant closed around 1950 or 1951, about the time they made the Ridge Alternate a divided highway. They later sold the property to the Sattlers of Gaffers & Sattler of the appliance firm. They kept the house and about two acres of the original homestead that was located on the west side of the Ridge Alternate. Later they sold that property to the state for an off-road park.[270]

Jack, (Anna's son) told me that one time when he was a teenager he and his friends went down to the Castaic 5-mile grade on the Ridge Alternate. A truck loaded with watermelons was laboring up the hill. The driver had a brick on the throttle and was hanging out of the cab, which was a common practice of the truck drivers, to avoid the engine heat. Jack and his buddies grabbed a couple of watermelons from the truck and

[270] Pickner, Jack, telephone interview, June 12, 2001.

the driver was helpless to do anything about it.

A topography map of 1926 reflects the site as Kelly's. Maps of 1931 and 1933 have it as Half Way Inn. The 1926 touring guide states, "Half Way Inn; rooms, cabins, lunch, small garage." They sold Richfield gasoline.[271] A 1932 newspaper account references a "Mr. & Mrs. Avis of the Half Way Inn."[272] Could these be the same folks formerly associated with Reservoir Summit Restaurant? Most likely they were. Anna reflected how people would work at one establishment for a while then move up or down the road to another. The Highway Department had a repair yard and sand tower dispenser here used to sand the road when it got icy.[273] Located on the right hand side of the road heading north, Kelly's was situated on a small knoll. It is difficult to find today, marked solely by power lines crossing above the road and one remaining tree. Cement remnants of the restaurants foundation can still be found in close proximity to the road. The flat area below the grade of the road is where the cabins were once located. The entire area here was bulldozed into the canyon below years ago. The old tin garage west of the restaurant was also shoved over the side into the canyon. One lonely tree stands sentinel on the knoll to mark this historic location.

Random view of cars on the Ridge Route

[271] I found the original Richfield sign down the canyon at the site.

[272] "National Forest Inn Fire Sets Big Blaze," op. cit.

[273] Kaufmann, op. cit.

Kelly Ranch

Some newspaper clippings misspelled Kelly as Kelley. I had the opportunity to visit the old ranch site accompanied by Angeles Forest archeologists, Mike McIntyre and Doug Milburn. In my investigation I discovered "Kelly Ranch" stenciled on a rafter inside an old storage shed laying rest as to the proper spelling. I have not found any clear information about Kelly, but I do have information regarding Frank Knapp, the last owner of the ranch.

Kelly Ranch House

The Angeles National Forest was once a part of the old Santa Barbara National Forest, created in 1900. In 1925 the Santa Barbara National Forest was divided into the Angeles National Forest and the Los Padres National Forest.[274] The Kelly Ranch was an island of private property within the Angeles National Forest. Kelly apparently homesteaded the

---

[274] Reynolds, op. cit., p. 92.

320-acre parcel prior to 1900 when the National Forest was created.

Frank Knapp purchased the old Kelly Ranch in 1962. Tommy Adkins of Castaic told me he was quite sure a man by the name of Rance Pierman owned the ranch before Frank acquired it. He recalls Mr. Pierman being president of the Community Bank. They had two branches, one in Los Angeles and the other in Burbank on San Fernando Road. Mr. Adkins said that prior to Mr. Pierman, a Mr. Reese might have owned the property. Frank was from San Fernando Valley, (Canoga Park) where, over a period of time he had acquired 106 acres that he called "Dry Gulch Ranch." Frank was a cement contractor by trade and also did plastering and dug cesspools. He had learned his trade from his father. He had a brother, Joe Knapp, who is deceased, another brother, Walter Knapp, who gave me this information and a sister on the east coast. Frank was married to Florindi Olive who was Portigi, but they had divorced years ago. They had one son, Edwin Frank Knapp, a fighter pilot during the Second World War that was shot down and killed in Italy. Franks father was born in Switzerland and came to this country in 1909. Frank donated some of his property to Canoga Park in memory of his son. It is Knapp Ranch Park located roughly at Valley Circle Boulevard and Kittridge Street.

When Frank acquired the Kelly Ranch he built a new house, guesthouse and barn. The property has a natural spring that supplied ample water to the house and for irrigation. An electric line from Castaic brought power up the canyon to the ranch. He also had telephone service from the original old toll lead that used to go between Bakersfield and Los Angeles. When the toll lead was removed Pacific Bell was obligated by their franchise to maintain a line to the ranch.

After Frank passed away the property was vacant for a period of time while in probate. During this time the buildings were vandalized but remain in reasonable shape except for the barn and the original Kelly home. The Kelly home is a "bat & board" California type structure. A large tree had fallen onto the screened front porch. There was an old upright piano on the porch under the rubble of the roof and tree branches. The old Kelly house has an interesting basement built with native stone and timbers. Upon Frank's death, no family member was interested in the ranch. The Bank of America administered Frank's estate, which was purchased by the "Trust for Public Lands," and turned over to the Forest Service. The Forest Service will ultimately demolish the buildings and return the land to its natural state. The discovery of asbestos siding on the Knapp house has delayed the planned demolition.

There are several old gold mines south of the ranch in Bear Canyon. The largest mine being the Gillette Mine. King Gillette of razor fortune was looking for the Los Padres Gold Mine. The legend of the Los Padre Gold Mine is that Spanish priests residing at Fort Tejon found a gold deposit and mined it. In the process they enraged the local Indians because the mine site was on a sacred burial ground. The Indians ran them off and destroyed evidence of the mine. Another rumor held was that when the Civil War broke out the mine was dynamited closed for fear Southern sympathizers would find it. In the late 1920s Gillette brought a bulldozer to Bear Canyon and ploughed up the graveyard looking for the mine. He never found it. Gold was not the only thing being looked for up in the canyons. A newspaper report of March 1922 states that a new oil well is under way on the place owned by Ben Kay. The location is eight miles above Castaic. The oil well was identified as Paduca Number 1. The lessees were private individuals headed by a C. W. Ellsworth, formerly a Texas man.[275]

Frank Knapp's Dry Gulch Ranch at the end of Vanowen in San Fernando Valley was near the Gillette estate. Frank had done cement work for Gillette at his elaborate home in Malibu Canyon. After Frank purchased the old Kelly Ranch, Annie Rose Briggs befriended him. She was a colorful character and was known to have hitchhiked up and down the Ridge Route. She lived somewhere down in Castaic and was married to Adrian Briggs who worked for the Newhall Refinery. Annie dressed in work clothes and would walk up Castaic Canyon to the Ranch. Annie was into gold mines and selling gold

---

[275] "A new oil well...," The Newhall Signal & Saugus Enterprise, March 3, 1922.

mine maps. After Gillette left, Annie filed claim to Gillette's old mine. An article in the <u>Newhall Signal</u> of December 22, 1922, states: "The gold mine of Miss Annie Rose has closed down until after the winter rains are over. Not every one knows that we have a rich gold mine in our midst, but such is the case." She and Frank at one time tried to locate the old Los Padre Mine. They dug around digging up Indian bones but never located the mine. In 1968 Frank uncovered an entire skeleton while hiking in Bear Canyon. An examination of the relic indicated the Indian stood five foot, eight inches tall, and that he was 30 years old when he died 150 years earlier.[276] Annie believed in the spirits and solicited their help without success. For additional information regarding Annie Rose and gold, see "Liebre State Highway Maintenance Camp" in Chapter 20. Frank's brother Walter told me that Gillette or his son had another mine down toward Castaic having a long shaft that Gillette had dug under Castaic Wash hoping to locate gold. Walter said that exploring around, Frank had dug into support timbers for the old tunnel.

It was Annie's brother, Billy, that put an end to a long-standing feud. The Rose family and the William C. Chormicle family had property down in Castaic. William Wirt Jenkins, "Bill Jenkins", a shady character and former lawman, had tried to steal portions of their property. A long-standing feud ensued. Billy Rose, Annie Rose Briggs' brother, was camping with his cattle in the area today that would be the after bay of Castaic Dam. Jenkins approached and they got into a fight. Billy fired his shotgun killing Jenkins' horse. The horse fell on Jenkins injuring his leg. Billy hid out for a while but ultimately gave himself up. Billy had to pay for Jenkins horse but was never prosecuted for the incident. Jenkins, an older man at the time of the incident later died from complications of his injury.[277]

[276] Stalk, Jeff, "Deep In The Forest Lives An Antiquarian Extraordinaire," <u>The Newhall Signal & Saugus Enterprise</u>, June 29, 1980.

[277] Adkins, Tommy, op. cit.

Tumble Inn

Continuing our drive toward the summit, we reach Tumble Inn at 22.1 miles. This site is on the left side of the road; it is listed on topography maps of 1926, 1931, 1933, 1937 and 1988. The <u>Mohawk-Hobbs Grade and Surface Guide</u> of 1926 does not show the Tumble Inn, however, their 1928 guide does and gives the following description: "rooms, dbl. $2, meals, gas, free camp space, water and rest rooms." It was also shown again on their 1930 <u>Mohawk-Hobbs Grade and Surface Guide</u>. The sign on the main building read "Tumble Inn Hotel and Restaurant, elevation 4,144 feet." The restaurant and garage were constructed of round river rocks and were level with the grade of the highway. The garage and Richfield gas station were located on the north end of the building and the restaurant was on the south end. A long retaining wall, also built with river rocks, sectioned off an area for parking. Steps built into the wall accessed a higher area where the sleeping rooms and comfort station were located. One of the steps has "Tumble Inn" etched into it. The rooms were in a building made of river rock and wood. River rock pillars supported a large covered porch and observation area on the north end of the structure. A stone arch was at the top of the steps and beyond the arch was the small building housing the "comfort station," (an older term for public toilets). The rooms being on a higher level afforded a panoramic view of Liebre Gulch. In 1914, before the Tumble Inn was built, this site was one of the largest construction camps for workers building the highway.

According to Michael Cunniff his grandfather Alfred Courtemanche, a carpenter and builder by trade along with his brother Frank, a stone mason, built the Tumbler Inn some time in the early 1920's. They also constructed the National Forest Inn as well as the French Village in Newhall. Michael's aunt Mary Louise Ella Courtemanche managed the Tumble Inn for her uncle Frank.

Tumble Inn Road Construction Camp
Courtesy Caltrans

At some point in time the name was changed from "Tumble Inn" to "Mountain View Lodge."[278] Jack Rimmer, Forest Fire Captain, was stationed at Reservoir Summit in 1932, a year before the Ridge Alternate opened, siphoning all of the traffic from the old highway. The Tumble Inn was closed then, but Jack said a man and his wife lived there. The man did mining in the surrounding canyons and in that pursuit lost a couple of fingers. Shortly after this accident his wife left. With his run of bad luck he quit mining and went to work at the new highway maintenance station down on the Ridge Alternate.

Tumble Inn

[278] "Waste Reclaims Trail ... op. cit.

This May 29, 1947 <u>Los Angeles Times</u> photo shows an un-identified man looking at the abandon Tumble Inn restaurant. The Inn was operating as the "Mountain View Lodge" when it closed. Courtesy <u>Los Angeles Times</u> Photographic Archive Department of Special Collections Charles E. Young Research Library, UCLA

Clayton J. Mill and his brother Howard secured the Tumble Inn lease some time in 1942 during the Second World War. Clayton worked for Douglas Aircraft in the South Bay. He and his brother were afraid our coast could be the target of an enemy attack. They wanted an alternative residence where their families would be safe. Clayton moved his wife, Catherine, and two small children, Paul T. Mill, and his little sister, Jean Anne Barnhill, (both currently living in Oregon) to the Inn where he felt they would be safe. Paul told me that at that time the small lodge/hotel on the upper level had been razed, and they lived in the former restaurant down next to the garage on the highway. The stone arch at the top of the stairway had also survived along with the Comfort Station. Paul remembers having gaslights in the old building. (The Southern California Gas Company has a main line that climbs up from Liebre Canyon to the Inn, then follows the road south). When they occupied the old restaurant building, the faded sign above the establishment read "Mountain View Lodge." After the war in 1946 George Kinsey of Kinsey

137

Ranch, employed Paul's father as a Caterpillar operator and his brother, Howard, as a cowboy. Although they moved over to the ranch, they kept the Tumble Inn lease. In 1947 they relocated to northern California.[279] By 1952 the buildings were gone, however, three fireplaces stood among the rubble of broken glass and torn roofing paper.[280] The retaining wall and steps are all that remain today. All of the rubble has been shoved into the canyon below.

Liebre State Highway Maintenance Camp

At 23.3 miles we reach the Liebre State Highway Maintenance Camp. It is shown on the 1926, 1931 and 1933 topography maps. There were various wooden barracks on both sides of the road as well as two long metal buildings on the west side of the highway. The metal structures were similar to the one located at the National Forest Inn. From this facility crews maintained the highway. Rex Farmer was Forman of the Liebre road maintenance station. Jack Farmer, his son, gave me the following information about the camp and his father. Jack was born in Daly City just south of San Francisco in 1918. His natural mother died when he was three-years old of a blood disease, in Alhambra. Jack said that his father, Rex, was a civil engineer for the city of Alhambra before coming to the Liebre State Highway Maintenance Camp. He said that jobs were hard to get at that time, and that his dad had a difficult time getting the job at Liebre. They needed a qualified engineer in addition to someone that could handle a crew, and his father had those qualifications.

The Liebre maintenance district went from the Kern County line south to about Reservoir Summit. His stepmother taught school in Alhambra so Jack and his sister, Martha, stayed with her after his dad took the Liebre job. On the weekends and during summer vacation, they would go stay with their father at the maintenance station. His stepmother did not drive so they would take the bus to San Fernando Valley at which point his father would meet them and take them on up

[279] Mill, Paul T., Interview, Nov. 2000.

[280] Crouse, Harriet, "Ghost Road To Bakersfield," Jan-Feb Lincoln-Mercury Times, 1952, p. 12.

138

to the maintenance camp.

On the east side of the road at the maintenance camp they were provided with a small three-bedroom house constructed of corrugated tin and wallboard. They had a kitchen with a pantry of sorts and a family-type room off the kitchen. They did not have an icebox or refrigerator. The bathroom had a flush toilet, bathtub and a Cole Oil heater. He said that they had hot water at certain times of the day, but it was limited. There was an old Model - T Ford sedan that had been converted to run a direct current generator in another structure near their house. They got their water from a spring above the camp.

Liebre State Highway Maintenance Camp looking northeast
Courtesy Caltrans

Liebre State Highway Maintenance Camp looking southwest
Courtesy Caltrans

Across the road were the bunkhouse, a large metal storage shed, eating area and kitchen. The shed housed a four-wheel-drive snowplow. On the back of the snowplow there was a Liberty V12 aircraft engine that ran the rotary mechanism that threw the snow off to the right side of the highway. His dad had a crew of eight to 10 men. A man with one leg by the name of George Miles was their cook. The men would go home on the weekends and Jack recalls his dad taking him to eat at the Tumble Inn or Reservoir Summit on the weekends when the kitchen was closed. They delivered ice for the camp kitchen. Jack remembers the cook fixing sandwiches for the men working along the highway. He would put the food in an apple box with a large pot of coffee. He said when they were out along the road the men would build a fire to perk the coffee and eat their sandwiches. Jack said he would drive the maintenance station's Model - A Ford pickup truck while his dad sat on the fender spraying puncher vine with his Hudson Sprayer. Puncher vine produced a five-sided thorn that caused many flat tires. The maintenance station did not have a blacksmith so they took all their work to Tom Frew's shop in Newhall.

When the Ridge Alternate opened up, the road camp was relocated to what is now Pyramid Lake. (The new facility was located approximately two miles north of the face of Pyramid Dam on the new three-lane Ridge Alternate). Their new camp was on two levels. The living quarters were beautiful. It was near the road on the east side of the highway and 20 to 30 feet below were located the cookhouse and bunkhouse. The bunkhouse accommodated two men to a room. They also had a garage and blacksmith's shop to maintain the road equipment. The redwood ship lath home had three bedrooms, a good size living room, dining room, basement and back porch. It had a fireplace as well as butane heat and a Servel gas refrigerator. Near the house was an electric generator that supplied power to the entire facility. He said they had a telephone in dad's office that was located in the garage. The snowplough driver and cook came from the old camp. The new facility was large and had quite an expanse of lawn and shrubbery. They had a gardener named Louie Nye. Jack said that when he was older he started staying here when his sister was attending college. When Pyramid Dam was constructed it flooded the entire facility. He said they didn't tear it down before filling the dam. His mom came up on the weekends. He went into the Navy on November 20, 1935, and was discharged April 7, 1939. He worked for the Standard Oil station at Gorman as well as the stations at Castaic and Newhall. While at the Standard station in Castaic he recalls Carol Lombard and Clark Gable stopping as they were heading north, possibly to the Lebec Hotel. He recalls cleaning their windshield.

He planned on getting into the oil fields with Standard, but that did not happen. He went to work for "Oil Field Trucking" of Bakersfield owned by the Phoenix brothers. One brother was in construction, the other in transportation. It was his first real paying job other than the gas station work. He drove a big open-ended dump truck for them. Jack went to Lancaster School. He said that at that time it was the largest school district taking in five counties. His dad would take him to Gorman to catch the school bus to Lancaster and the ride took one and a half-hours. If bad weather or a snowstorm threatened and they couldn't get home, the school had a dormitory. The school superintendent was a Mr. Roy A. Knapp. His father was on the Gorman School board. Jack remembers Kelly of Kelly's Ranch as being a sick man. He vaguely recalls Kelly ending up in Los Angeles County Hospital having a nurse named Rose or maybe later known as "Ridge Route Annie" caring for him. She wore lace boots that extended to her knees. She took care of him at the hospital before he died and to show his gratitude drew her a map of his property showing where he thought there was gold. Later the entrance was dynamited shut. He said there was also an Indian working there. The ranch had a lot of cattle, and they had riders patrolling to keep people out. He said he was never down there, and he did not know how much of this story was truth or legend. He said that at Reservoir Summit you could look down toward the ranch and see large pumps. He thinks the mine flooded and the pumps were to clear the mine of water. He did not recall Kelly owning the Half Way Inn, but felt that he probably did.

Jack recalls Harry Holland, said he always wore bib over-alls and ran bootleg. He recalled Caswell's and said they were famous for their turkey dinners. He recalls Young's Café down on the Ridge Alternate. He remembers the airplane beacon at National Forest Inn. There was another beacon on Bald Mountain and another at the Richfield station at Castaic Junction.

Jack remembers a truck driver breaking down somewhere down around Serpentine Drive. He had a load of oranges. There was a large tree near the road that looked like an apricot tree but wasn't. While he was waiting for help he had nothing better to do so he used bailing wire to hang oranges on the tree. He said motorists would see this and slow down causing all kinds of trouble so his dad removed the prankster's work.

Jack recalls the Richfield "Beacon" service station at Castaic Junction where State Highway 126 heads west from I-5 to Ventura. A Tip's Restaurant was also located at Castaic Junction. In Castaic he recalls the "Screwball Café" run by Harry Royle's wife. Harry worked for his dad on the maintenance crew. Jack's sister, Martha Forth, was born in Alhambra and attended the University of Redlands and received her teaching credentials from USC. Her stepmother, Mildred Rose Merril, (maiden name) was a schoolteacher in Alhambra. Martha was a schoolteacher at a one-room schoolhouse in Leona Valley near Elizabeth Lake teaching there between 1937 and 1941. She was married to Leo Forth a chemical engineer. The WPA built the Gorman School in 1939. She taught first through eighth grade at Gorman in 1941, '42 and '43. She said she was the second schoolteacher at Gorman. Dewey Ralphs and his wife, Marie, provided Martha with a room at their ranch the first year she taught at Gorman. In her second year she lodged at the Ralphs' Motel Gorman, each unit being a cottage with a small front room, bedroom and a bath. At this time Martha's husband was in the service. Martha's friend was Amie Sattler. Amie's father was Mr. Sattler of Gaffers & Sattler Appliance Company. He let Amie manage the ranch and only visited occasionally. Amie's husband was also in the service and, being a bit lonely, invited Martha to live with

her. Martha stayed in the Sattler mansion with Amie the last
six months before she retired and moved back to Alhambra
to be with her husband who was stationed nearby. Martha
recalls Amie having a radio they would listen to for enter-
tainment. She also had servants that tended the house and
cooked their meals.

Granite Gate

At 24.1 miles we see "Granite Gate," today marked by the
large rock situated to the west. At one time prior to shaving
the cliff to the east, the road veered closer to the monolith
giving the appearance of a passage or "gate."

Granite Gate, looking southwest

Horseshoe Bend

At 24.6 miles we locate "Horseshoe Bend." A close look at
the remaining pavement reveals that at one time the road cut
deeper into the cup of the horseshoe. Horseshoe Bend and
Granite Gate were popular views on early postcards.

Horseshoe Bend
Western Publishing & Novelty Co., Los Angeles, Cal.

Sandberg's Summit Hotel

Later called Sandberg's Lodge, at 26.0 miles, is located just north of Liebre Summit (4233 Feet). The hotel stood at 4,170 feet. Harald Sandberg built his hotel in 1914 beside the brand-new Ridge Route highway and had it ready and waiting to accommodate motorists when the road opened in 1915.

A great deal of mis-information has been written concerning Harald Sandberg and his hotel. Some articles state his name as Hermann, others Harold. Additionally, some writers said he was Swiss-German. What follows is an attempt to clarify matters of the Sandberg family and will probably give you more information than you really care to know. Early in my research I checked the Los Angeles County U. S. Census records and found a Harald Sandberg, native of Norway. There was no Hermann listed. Additionally, David L. Cole provided me a copy of an original personalized Christmas card pre-printed in script that the Sandberg family mailed; it is signed Harald Sandberg. (Dave is editor of <u>The Way of the Zephyr</u>, a magazine of the Lincoln Zephyr owners'club. Dave also has an extensive collection of early maps without which

I would have been unable to identify accommodations available at various sites). Considering the Census record and the personal Sandberg Christmas Card, it is very evident he spelled his first name as Harald. It is still interesting to note that some of his legal documents and deeds had typed his first name as Harold.

Harald (not Harold) Sandberg was born in Kongsberg, Norway on September 4, 1867. His father, Harald Christian Sandberg, owned one or more sail ships and spent several years at sea with his family on board. He immigrated to California in 1880 and became part of a co-op colony in Kaweah, Tulare County. Harald Jr. got his education as a farmer in California from 1890 forward. Harald had a brother, Albert Sandberg, born May 6, 1869, in Cardiff Wales and a sister, Marie Sandberg, born on June 1, 1871, in Odderness, Norway. Marie stayed with her father, Harald Christian Sandberg, at the Kaweah cooperative colony in Tulare County California until his death, speculated to be November 1891. It is recorded in a local newspaper that while in Kaweah Marie performed on stage with song and recitation and was a member of the Drama Club. After her father died, Marie joined her brothers, Albert and Harald, in their farming endeavor. Ultimately Harald took over the entire farming operation, buying out Albert and Marie. (Harald had homesteaded the ranch property on the second day of April 1897).[281] On another parcel south of the ranch he built a hotel, restaurant and several cabins. In 1918 the labor situation deteriorated due to World War I, prompting Harald to accept the position of postmaster. The place was now named Sandberg.

After Harald took over the farming, Albert relocated to San Francisco and taught music and literature. Albert never married and had no children. He died in 1941. Marie moved to Los Angeles, working as a typesetter in a print shop. On October 7, 1901, she married Count Edger Stanislaus V. Piontkowski who was born in Warsaw Poland November 23, 1869. He was educated as a civil engineer in the United States and worked construction projects in Mexico between

[281] Robinson, John W., Copy of Homestead Certificate No. 2788, Application 5333, Vol. 6a page 298.

1901 and 1906. Thereafter he was chief engineer in railroad construction in the Philippines. Later in Mexico he continued railroad building until he settled down in 1930 as a building entrepreneur in Los Angeles. He died August 31, 1949. He was the son of a Polish Count – Piontkowski and wife Anna, born Von Schmidt.

Harald met Marion Grant, the daughter of John Grant and Alice Ross from Ontario, Canada when they relocated to the Antelope Valley from Indiana. Marion, born in 1868, was educated as a nurse. They were married September 4, 1905. Marion Grant died in 1955 in Los Angeles. Harald stayed in the job as postmaster until his death on July 9, 1939. Harald and Marion did not have any children.[282] An obituary in the July 11, 1939, <u>Los Angeles Times</u> states: "Funeral services for Harald Sandberg, 71 year-old Antelope Valley pioneer and founder of the hotel and post office station of Sandberg on the Ridge Route, will be conducted tomorrow at 2:30 p.m. in the Wee Kirk o' the Heather, Forest Lawn Memorial Park, Cremation will follow. Sandberg, a native of Norway, went to Antelope Valley 57 years ago and with his brother, Albert, developed large acreages there. He built the hotel at Sandberg 25 years ago and later became postmaster for the district. He leaves his widow, Mrs. Marion Sandberg, his brother, Albert, and a sister, Mrs. Marie Von Piontkowski."

Marion and
Harald Sandberg
Courtesy
John W. Robinson

[282] Sandberg, Otto A., Interview November 11, 1997.

Sandberg's original structure
The Flag Studio, Pasadena, Calif.

Sandberg's Summit Hotel

When the Sandberg hotel first opened it was a one-story structure. Some time after 1921 Harald enlarged the hotel turning it into a three-story log hostelry set amid a grove of California Live Oaks. Sandberg had his own sawmill and cut down trees on the property to build his hotel. Upon entering the hotel there was a telephone booth, (Toll Station). The number was Sandberg # 1. You would crank it to get the operator. Being a retired Pacific Bell engineer, I will explain what a toll station was. Sandberg's was too remote to have local telephone service. The closest local exchange service would have been Bakersfield or Newhall. Fortunately the telephone poles near Sandberg's supported the main long distance circuits that connected Los Angeles with Bakersfield. To provide service in remote locations like Sandberg's, phone companies would often swipe one of their toll circuits and turn it into a great big party line wherever they installed a phone along the highway. The only catch was that public utility tariffs mandated that only payphones could be connected to lines specifically built for long distance (toll) service. It did not make any difference if you lived in a house or ran a business, if you wanted a phone it had to be a payphone. Long distance circuits generate lots of revenue, therefore, the phone companies did not like to dedicate more than one of their toll circuits for this type of service. This being the case, all of the payphones up and down the route were on one great big party line and you would hear your ring along with everyone else's. Toll Stations were installed in remote locations where local service was unavailable.

Beyond the telephone booth directly to your left in the tower structure were the stairs leading to the upper floors. Left of the staircase and parallel with the front wall of the hotel was the post office. Opposite the post office was the large lobby having couches and chairs. On the back west wall was a large stone fireplace.

Sandberg Fireplace

A myth written about Sandberg was that he would charge his hotel guest five cents to warm themselves by the fireplace, a ridiculous story conjured up to help sell newspapers. The entrance to the lady's room was on one side of the fireplace and the men's room on the other side. Located to the right upon entering were the counter and dining room.

Sandberg's Dining Room

The second floor of the hotel was used exclusively as living quarters for the Sandberg's. The third floor contained guest rooms. There were several cabins behind the hotel. North of the hotel was a large garage having a second floor with rooms upstairs.

Sandberg's was the high-class place. This is where you would see the Cadillacs, Packards and Studebakers parked. It was said they had a sign, "Truck Drivers and Dogs Not Allowed."[283]

---

[283] Jones, Bob, op. cit., p. F4.

Sandberg's Summit Hotel

An early touring guide reflects: "Sandberg's Summit Hotel, 25 good rooms in hotel and cottages; most with running water and toilet; sgl, $1.50-$2.50; dbl $2-$4; lunch 85 cents, dinner $1.00." It was a small tourist community, post office, telephone and all-night restaurant. It had a garage that gave almost complete service. "Labor $2, after 6 p.m. $3; never closed."[284] They sold Richfield gasoline. The Sandberg's had an apple orchard a short distance away at their ranch. Travelers stopping at the hotel would look forward to having a piece of Mrs. Sandberg's apple pie. Motor Stages would stop at Sandberg's for meals. Other locations along the road needing the bus to stop would place a sign to flag a stop.[285]

The Sandberg Hotel was on a separate homestead from the Sandberg Ranch property. The late Walter "Lucky" Stevens, the last leaseholder of the hotel, related the following information: Because Harald had used his homestead option to acquire the ranch property, he could not make another filing for the hotel site. Lucky said Grant, Mrs. Sandberg's brother, filed a homestead for the hotel property. It is not clear if Grant was going to become a partner with

---

[284] Mohawk-Hobbs, 1928, op. cit.

[285] Kaufman, op. cit.

Harald on the hotel venture, or if he simply filed on the property to acquire it for Harald. To gain clear title under the Homestead Act you had to make improvements to the land over a five-year period. The hotel was constructed during this time but Harald and his brother-in-law, Grant, had a falling out and Grant left. With Grant's departure the five-year improvement requirement was broken and the property reverted back to the government. Harald had to lease the property thereafter and never gained ownership to the site. Because the hotel was on federal land it is impossible to do a title search to determine who the various leaseholders were. The Angeles National Forest administered the Sandberg Hotel lease. Unfortunately, older lease records have been discarded. Even with this obstacle there are bits and pieces of information regarding various leaseholders of the hotel. Harald's obituary indicates he remained postmaster until his death in July of 1939. Keep in mind that the post office was located within the hotel. An article in the <u>Ridge Route Rambler</u> newspaper of 1939 states: "Grand Opening and Free Barbecue Sunday, May 28, 1939. Sandberg Lodge and Dude Ranch, Larry Brock Proprietor, Harry Moss Manager."[286] From this advertisement it is apparent that the Sandberg's sold their lease on the hotel some time prior to his death in July. The Sandberg Ranch, north of the hotel, was on land they had homesteaded. Records indicate they sold the ranch to Mr. Bruno Brodersen on the 28th of January 1938. Brodersen sold to the Federal Land Bank of Berkley on the 25th of October 1938. They sold the ranch to James H. Cox on the 10th of October 1940.[287]

To summarize, Mr. Sandberg died on the 9th of July 1939. Mr. Brock had the hotel lease on the 28th of May 1939, and the Sandberg's sold their ranch to Mr. Brodersen on the 28th of January 1938.

Lucky told me that Mr. J. H. Cox purchased the hotel and ranch long after the Ridge Alternate had opened bypassing the old hotel. According to Lucky it was Mr. Cox that

[286] Kane, Bonnie Ketterl-, courtesy of. From <u>The Ridge Route Rambler</u>, 1939.

[287] Los Angeles County Assessors, Book 122, sec. 301, p. 122.

151

tainted the hotels reputation by allegedly bringing in booze, slot machines and "ladies of the night." [288]   Harald Sandberg ran a high-class hotel. He did not have "ladies of the night" or allow gambling. Lucky mentioned that over the years various syndicates attempted to convince Sandberg to allow gambling. Sandberg did not compromise his principles, so they finally gave up and established gambling up the road at the Lebec Hotel in Kern County.

We will probably never know for sure if Mr. Cox profited from any alleged shady activities at the hotel, but we do know that he was doing pretty well selling apples from the old Sandberg orchard. Yes, apples! The Sandberg Ranch had a rather famous apple orchard, and Mr. Cox's apple crates prominently displayed his name as owner of the property."[289]

Mr. Cox sold the hotel lease to Lillian Grojean, a German lady. She turned the old hotel garage into a ceramics factory and manufactured beautiful platters and tableware under the brand name of "California Originals." The larger department stores in Los Angeles carried her merchandise. Lillian had been in the Tehachapi Women's Prison for writing bad checks. She helped out other women that had been released from prison. She would bring them to Sandbergs to help them get on their feet but they stole her blind. "Boots" Solaguard was one of the women from prison helping Lillian. Boots was a rough sort and dressed like a man. The gas line went by Sandberg's when Grojean was there. In the 1950s Leonard Baker was in the propane business and indirectly represented the Southern California Gas Company. A gasman would contact Leonard when a prospective customer wanted to convert from propane to gas appliances. In those days you could buy gas appliances on time from the gas company. Lillian had not paid her gas bill and Leonard, on behalf of Southern California Gas, removed her Wedgewood range and Servel gas refrigerator. Boots threatened him with a pipe, but Leonard repossessed the appliances anyway. Even though the gas had been shut off for non-payment, they had built a

---

[288] Stevens, Walter "Lucky," Interview January 6, 1997 & Bonnie Ketterl-Kane interview of "Lucky" May 7, 1995.

[289] Robinson, John W., courtesy of.

wood fire in the oven that ruined it. He said they had also broken the door on the refrigerator.

A former historian in the Newhall area wrote a clip in the local newspaper on the history of Sandberg's claiming the FBI arrested a German family during World War II for transmitting military secrets to the Germans. This snippet has been perpetuated because other newspapers have repeated the story. I have not found anything in newspaper archives to validate the article. Lucky Stevens, last leaseholder of Sandberg's Hotel told me there was no proof this ever occurred. In 1947 Jack Rimmer had given up his forest guard position at Reservoir Summit to work for Los Angeles County at Quail Lake Patrol Station # 77. This former fire station, located at the corner of Pine Canyon Road and the Ridge Route was not far from the Sandberg Hotel where Lillian was manufacturing her pottery. Mr. Rimmer corroborates Lucky's statement regarding Lillian. He told me that although Lillian had her share of trouble she never transmitted messages to the Germans. Marvin Barnes got out of the service in January of 1946, and Lillian asked him to repair the electric generator that supplied power to the hotel. Marvin had worked on generators while in the service. She paid for his services by giving him some of her beautiful ceramic tableware. Marvin said that while there were a lot of strange people helping Lillian she never transmitted messages to the Germans during the war. Marvin told me that his dad Roy Barnes knew Sandberg and had helped him dynamite some large Oak Trees to clear the land for his apple orchard. He also mentioned that Sandberg was president of the stamp collectors club and had spoken before his high school class. Lucky was loosely connected with the Hollywood crowd having been a stunt man and bit actor. He also ran a ceramics business in Burbank. Lillian Grojean apparently stopped at Lucky's business in Burbank and with their mutual interest in ceramics became acquainted. Lillian was manufacturing pottery up at the old Sandberg Hotel. She had leased it and the surrounding 14 acres from the Angeles National Forest for $90 a year. In 1950 or 1951 Lucky offered her $15,000 for the badly dilapidated hotel, out buildings and lease. She accepted his offer. Lucky had designs to turn the site into a "camp-type operation" for under privileged children. He would call it Sandberg, "TOWN FOR LUCKY CHILDREN." In April 1960 he formed a non-profit organization to help bring his dream to fruition. With his connections in Hollywood he successfully acquired money, furniture, and used clothing. By giving a donation you could become an honorary citizen of Sandberg, "TOWN FOR LUCKY CHILDREN."

Sandberg Lodge Guest Ranch

With drive and dedication Lucky set out to completely re-habilitate the old hotel. On the 29th of April in 1961, he was burning trash in the big stone fireplace at the far end of the lobby. Sparks from the chimney ignited the dry wood shingled roof setting the landmark hotel ablaze. Within a matter of minutes the place was reduced to ashes. Lucky moved into one of two cabins that survived the fire. He wanted to rebuild but the forest service dashed all hope when they cancelled his lease in 1963. The only remnants that remain today are portions of foundation and part of the rock wall that was on the south side of the hotel. One of the cabins was moved to a nearby ranch; it is not clear what happened to the other one. Lucky speculated that it was vandalized and later destroyed. Judging from photographs, the original old two-story garage north of the hotel was apparently torn down some years before the fire and replaced with a smaller facility where they had made pottery. This garage survived but was later torn down. Lucky passed away February 18, 1998.[290]

In 1925 Sandberg was planning to open another resort in Libby Canyon. It would primarily be a hunting and fishing lodge. The summer resort was to have a number of log cabins for guests and would be reached by a four-mile pack trail.[291] Sandberg built the lodge in an extremely remote location at the bottom of the canyon on Paso Creek. It was difficult to access and a credit to his determination that you could build anything in a location so inaccessible. The lodge was three stories. The first floor, built partly into the side of the mountain had bathrooms, showers with large sunburst showerheads and a kitchen with a huge wood burning range approximately 10 feet in length. The dining room and large common area were located on the second level and had a huge stone fireplace. The third level was a large dormitory where cots were located. The lodge had a cement-reinforced foundation. Bob and Westley McKenzie did all of the stonework and Harry Priddy did the carpentry. They used a motor from

[290] Stevens, op. cit.

[291] "New Sandberg Outing Resort," The Newhall Signal & Saugus Enterprise, March 5, 1925.

an old Franklin automobile to power an electric generator for lighting. The large door hinges were hand forged and quite unique. North of the lodge, down the canyon are the remains of one of his cabins. The foundation is visible along with a fireplace. A large tree is growing where the center of the structure once stood.[292] The lodge was originally accessed from State Highway 138. Unfortunately, shortly after its construction it was determined that the structure was accidentally built on Tejon Ranch land. Sandberg had to vacate the property and the facility was never really used by anyone. The newspapers blamed the Tejon Ranch, however, it was really an error in judgment by Mr. Sandberg.[293] The remains of the dilapidated lodge are approximately eight to 10 miles southeast of the old Tejon Ranch headquarters off of Sebastian Road.

Sandberg's remote hunting lodge down in the narrow canyon
Courtesy Tejon Ranch Company

[292] Meeks, Jerold Ray, telephone interview, June 11, 2001.

[293] Wiebe, Mildred, Historian, (retired) Tejon Ranch telephone interview, June 13, 2001.

Partial view of structure and entry steps
Courtesy Tejon Ranch Company

View of hand forged hinges
Courtesy Tejon Ranch
Company

157

The old Sandberg ranch house still stands on Pine Canyon Road just east of the Ridge Route and is currently owned by Ed & Dorothy Levitt. It is in a beautiful setting and has an inviting front porch. When the Sandberg's occupied the property the ranch supplied fresh eggs, poultry and vegetables for their hotel.

The hotel's history would not be complete without mentioning the following report in the September 27th 1929, edition of the <u>Los Angeles Times</u>. "Ulysses S. Grant, Jr., son of General Ulysses S. Grant, famous soldier-President, was found dead in bed yesterday morning in a room at Sandberg Lodge, a hotel on the Ridge Route about seventy miles north of Los Angeles. He is believed to have died while asleep as a result of a heart ailment. He was 77 years of age." The article continues to reveal that Mr. Grant and his wife were devotees of outdoor recreation and spent much time in automobiling and extended travel. They were returning to their home in San Diego from a trip to northern California. Ulysses S. Grant Jr. constructed the U. S. Grant Hotel in San Diego, it claimed to have been the first, large reinforced concrete building in San Diego. He maintained his home at the hotel. Ulysses' father, President Grant, was a friend of Edward Fitzgerald Beale, first owner of the Tejon Ranch property.

Sandberg's Final Days

The Sandberg Hotel site is shown on the following Topography maps: 1926, 1931, 1933, 1937 and the 1988 map as a historical site.

Los Angeles County Fire Patrol Station # 77

Back on the old Ridge Route we continue north a short distance to Pine Canyon Road. On early maps, that portion of Pine Canyon Road between the Ridge Route and Three Points to the east was called Oakdale Canyon Road. Off to the right is the former Los Angeles County fire patrol station # 77. This patrol station was established on property across from, and north of Sandberg's Lodge. The Sandbergs deeded the property to the County of Los Angeles on August 19, 1929, for erecting and maintaining suitable housing to be used by the Los Angeles County Fire Warden. A stipulation of the deed stated that should the county abandon the site or use it for an alternative purpose, it would revert back to the grantor. On August the fifteenth 1989, the county, deeded the property to Ray Cobb and his sister, Dolores Berry, current owners of that portion of the old Sandberg Ranch. The fire station had been closed and was no longer needed. I mentioned above that Pine Canyon Road was formerly Oakdale Canyon Road. Another point of interest is that old deeds of the Sandberg property refer to the Ridge Route as the "Elizabeth Lake and Gorman Station Road."

I mentioned earlier that Jack Rimmer was assigned to this station in 1947. It was a one-man operation. He did not have a crew. He had a pick-up truck that carried approximately 300 gallons of water for fire control. Jack said the same gas line that serviced Sandberg's, serviced the fire station. All of the lighting, cooking and heating ran off of natural gas. He did not have any electricity at the fire patrol station.

If you were to turn left at Pine Canyon intersection there is a dirt road that leads up to the Bald Mountain weather station. It had been a manned station from 1933 up until it was automated in 1978.[294] The weather station is still active,

---

[294] Gerrard, Marika, "Town Offers a Lot: Wind and Solitude" <u>Los Angeles Times</u>, May 6, 1981.

reporting weather conditions from "Sandberg" California. Occasionally you will hear a weather report on television from Sandberg and no one knows where Sandberg is. At one time there was an airplane beacon at Bald Mountain. If you have a computer and would like to know the current weather conditions at Sandberg, this is the address: http://weather.noaa. gov/weather/current/KSDB.html

The address is case-sensitive and must be typed exactly as presented above.

General Petroleum's Quail Lake Pumping Station

After crossing through the intersection at Pine Canyon Road we will begin our descent into Antelope Valley. At the bottom of the grade the Ridge Route ends at State Highway 138. To our right on the southeast corner is an abandoned wooden house and oil tank. I described this site earlier in my segment on Pipelines and Electric Lines. This was the Quail Lake pumping station, one of several belonging to General Petroleum that forwarded oil from the Lebec refinery to the rail terminal at Mojave.

Quail Lake Pumping Station
Courtesy Caltrans

Marvin Barnes and his brother, Bill Barnes, long standing denizens of the area, told me that the boilers at each pump station produced superheated steam. Utilizing the steam they would elevate the temperature of the crude oil 200 to 300 degrees. At this temperature the pumps could push the oil through the line. The same boilers that heated the oil at the Quail Lake station also provided steam to power electric generators for lighting the facility and living quarters. A large surge tank also occupied the site. Originally there were three structures, a bunkhouse for the workers and two small family homes. Marvin Barnes and his brother, Bill Barnes, said their dad, Roy Barnes, was engineer for the site in 1923, and they occupied one of the homes. After the plant closed around 1948 or 1949 the other home and bunkhouse were razed. Marvin's bachelor days ended in 1952. His old childhood home at the pump station had been vacant for over a year, and he and his wife Carolyn decided to make it their home. The abandon pump station and the telephone company repeater facility were on leased property belonging to the Kinsey Ranch. Marvin rented the old house for $45 per month. Considering Marvin's childhood years and his married life he spent thirty-five years at the site. How long the abandon house and old tank remain standing at this location is anyone's guess.

Pacific Telephone Voice Repeater Station

The pumping station's neighbor on the east was Pacific Telephone's long distance voice repeater facility. When Pacific Telephone was building their repeater station in December 1929, they had Edison bring electricity down from Gorman. At that time the pumping plant also connected to the power line.

The site was comprised of the main reinforced concrete repeater building, a power and lighting plant, water system, garages and living quarters for the employees. Married men enjoyed the provision of a single family home. Single men were provided with dormitory type accommodations. It cost $85,000 to construct the buildings at this remote location. An additional $150,000 was spent to install the amplifying equipment that would boost telephone conversations on the new telephone cable being laid between Los Angeles, Bakersfield and San Francisco.[295] After the pumping station was closed down, and about 12 years after the Second World War, Marvin worked four hours a day at the repeater station. At that time all the telephone resident workers had left because the repeater station had been automated. In subsequent years

[295] "New Long Distance Telephone Booster Station," The Newhall Signal & Saugus Enterprise, December 26, 1929.

the telephone repeater station became obsolete. All of the equipment was removed and Pacific Bell vacated their lease on the property. Today the old concrete building is occupied as a private resident.

Marvin had three uncles. Tom Barnes poured concrete during the construction of the Ridge Route. Charlie Barnes ran a grading crew during the road's construction and also operated the Fresno Scrapers. Pete Barnes worked at the three rock quarries where rock was obtained during the road's construction. One quarry was located at Grapevine, one south of Gorman on what is now Gorman Post Road. The third was two or three miles south of Sandberg's Lodge.

Crane Lake (now) Quail

We will make a left hand turn onto State Highway 138, the Lancaster road and continue toward Gorman. This section of highway was once the old Ridge Route. A short distance ahead on our right we see Quail Lake.

Quail Lake
Western Publishing & Novelty Co., Los Angeles, Cal.

This 4D Station 200 October 13, 1916 photo
locates this picture as Quail Lake
Courtesy Caltrans

The lake has been modified to serve as a reservoir for the
California water Project. In 1919 maps show Quail Lake as
Crane Lake. The lake was named after Rony Crane, a fellow
of questionable character, that had homesteaded in the area
around 1887. He occupied a small shack at the south end
of the lake, approximately one-half mile east of the Kinsey
Mansion just up ahead. Allegedly Rony, (pronounced like
Sony) acquired some of his income from selling stolen horses.
The original road wound around in this area and was a hair
north of the present alignment. Rony's place along with the
old road is now under water. From Tejon Summit the San
Andreas Fault aligns with Gorman, Quail Lake then follows
a path along Pine Canyon Road, Elizabeth Lake Road all the
way to Palmdale and beyond. Quail Lake is technically a sag
pond created by the fault. Smaller sag ponds are evident
along Gorman Post Road.

Kinsey Mansion

Directly ahead on the left is the Kinsey Mansion, once part
of the Bailey Ranch. General Petroleum (Exxon-Mobil Oil

Company) was looking for a duck-hunting location for their employees. At that time there was a small cottage on the site where the mansion stands today. Being directly across from the lake, it was an ideal location for their purpose. They persuaded Bailey to sell them his ranch that included the small cottage they wanted for their duck hunting headquarters.

In my segment on Pipelines & Electric lines you may recall that Rea E. Maynard, chief engineer for General Pipeline, (later General Petroleum) engineered and directed the construction of the first pipeline over the Ridge. Rea later became president of the company. Captain John Barneson was one of the founders of General Pipeline. When the ranch property transferred from Bailey to General Pipeline, records reflect Rea E. Maynard and Harriett E. Barneson as co-owners of the property.[296]

Mr. Sattler, of Gaffers & Sattler gas ranges, acquired the property at a later date. Mr. Sattler had racehorses and had built a racetrack in Hungry Valley about a mile and one half west of the Ridge Tavern on U. S. Highway 99, the Ridge Alternate. George E. Kinsey obtained the property from Sattler around 1945 and more than doubled the size of the original house. Kinsey was from Kentucky and his southern roots influenced the design in building the large white colonial mansion. Kinsey owned apartment buildings and restaurants in the Los Angeles area. He also owned racehorses.[297] Max Sennet of Hollywood fame owned property directly across the lake from the Kinsey Mansion. He was said to have had wild parties with his Hollywood friends, and they would swim nude in the lake.

Bailey Ranch

At the west end of the lake on your right was the old Bailey Ranch headquarters. There were two Bailey brothers, William and Marcos. They had purchased the Alamos Rancho five miles south in Liebre Canyon near Hungry Valley Road and Pyramid Lake from Cawley and Hayes. The ranch house

[296] Division 7, L. A. County, Route 4, Section D, Sheet 9, map dated April 13, 1914.

[297] Kaufman, op. cit.

164

was originally located here in Liebre Canyon. It was a two-story house having two bedrooms on the ground floor with a kitchen and pantry that appeared to have been added on. An oak staircase in the center of the room led to second floor bedrooms. A severe storm in 1907 gouged deep cuts through their pastures destroying crops, orchards and valuable topsoil forcing them to leave.[298]

Between 1906 and 1908 the power company was busy building their transmission line down through the canyon. Using mules and wagons, they hauled in all their equipment including the large metal transmission towers. The wagon road created by this endeavor was a perfect channel for run off from the storm. The wagon ruts became deep caverns as the water rushed through the canyon. Assessing the damage, the Baileys decided to relocate to the west end of Quail Lake parallel with the new Ridge Route highway. They jacked up the house and placed several beams under it. Wagon wheels were attached to both ends of each beam. A large winch anchored in the ground extended a cable connected to the beams. Two mules, walking in a circle were used to wind the winch thus moving the house. This procedure moved the house about an eighth of a mile at which point the anchor and winch mechanism were relocated and the entire process repeated. After successfully moving the house to the new foundation and basement at Quail Lake, a third floor was added.[299]

Bailey Ranch, view looking north, car heading south.
Courtesy Caltrans

[298] Lata, op. cit., p. 211.

[299] Barnes, op. cit.

Bailey Ranch
Courtesy Caltrans

The Bailey ranch had four corrals and a slaughterhouse at the west end of the lake. A large barn was constructed west of the corrals. The house stood at the far west end of the complex. In between the barn and house, away from the highway, stood the chicken house, blacksmith shop and bunkhouse. There was a beautiful rosewood piano in the house that no one ever played. Cottonwood trees surrounded the house while Poplar trees lined the property along the highway.[300]

Quail Lake is part of the California State Water Project, a system of reservoirs, pumping stations and the 444-mile California Aqueduct. The old Bailey house was destroyed when the water project increased the capacity of the lake by turning it into a reservoir. A 1915 Automobile Club of Southern California map incorrectly shows Bailey's as a hotel and gas station. The property always functioned as a ranch and never offered accommodation to early motorists.

[300] Division 7, op. cit.

Quail Lake

Up ahead, turn right onto Gorman Post Road (formerly the Ridge Route). If it were possible to turn left (south) at Gorman Post Road you would drive right into the original location of Quail Lake. Quail Lake was directly across from the Gorman Post intersection at State Highway 138. What today is Quail Lake was originally Crane Lake.

That portion of State Highway 138 that continues a short distance west to junction with I-5 was constructed when the interstate was built. Bill Barnes told me he and his brother, Marvin, attended the old Quail Lake Grammar School formerly located in the middle of State Highway 138 half way between the Gorman Post turn off and the I-5 freeway. One teacher taught grades one through eight. According to Bill the school averaged about 20 to 25 students. Most of the children were from families employed by the pipeline and oil companies. When the Ridge Route was being built, enrollment increased to 46 students. Children from the road gangs building the highway attended the one-room school. Bill said they were a pretty rough bunch of kids, and the teacher had her hands full. As the highway advanced, the children would be uprooted and have to relocate to another district. After eighth grade you had to attend Antelope Joint Union High School in Lancaster.

Quail Lake Inn

Shortly after turning from State Highway 138, Gorman Post road curves to the left. If you look to your right you will see a dead-end stretch of the old Ridge Route heading toward Quail Lake. After the road turns left toward Gorman, watch for the Southern California Edison sub station directly on your right. This area has been filled and leveled but identifies the location where the Quail Lake Inn once stood. George Barton ran the Inn. Barton had homesteaded 160 acres and built a small restaurant with a counter having four or five stools. He cooked on a wood-burning stove. Barton had a couple of rooms in the back he rented out. He was a huge man and at one time was employed as a bouncer in San Francisco. He was known to play the fiddle at all the local dances. The Quail Lake Inn was a one-story structure having a two-pump service station and a small garage. There was a spring above the Inn on the side of the hill. Barton piped water from the spring to a storage tank then down to the Inn. Abe Fromberg ran his garage. Later Fromberg became the wholesale distributor for Mobil gas in the area. Fromberg is credited for having invented the patch for tubeless tires. The old location is buried under 50 feet of fill.[301]

Holland's Summit Cafe

Back on the highway at the top of the rise with our mileage indicating 32.3 miles, we locate the first Holland's Summit Café site. "It was located on the right side (east side) of the road and was a trucker's joint. Tourists did not frequent Holland's in the early days where trucks jammed the roadside as well as the parking lot." [302] In addition to the café there was a Standard Oil gas station, small garage and a couple of cabins.

Holland's Summit Café number 1
Courtesy Bonnie Ketterl-Kane

[301] Barnes, op. cit.

[302] Bezzerides, op. cit., p. 9.

When the Ridge Alternate opened in 1933, Harry Holland moved his operation over to Tejon Pass on the new three-lane highway. He purchased the old Pershing School house Number One at Lebec and moved it to the summit and converted it into a bar and restaurant.

Holland built a new gas station and several cabins at his new location on the Ridge Alternate, (U. S. Highway 99). In fact, he moved a couple of the cabins from his old location over to the new site. Unfortunately when Interstate 5 was being constructed in the mid 1960s, it devoured his operation along with the old three-lane Ridge Alternate. Today at Tejon Summit (4,144 feet) on Interstate 5 you would never know it was once the location of Holland's popular restaurant. The highway displaced Harry twice, yet at the time of his death he had plans to open again on property west of the Interstate at Frazier Park exit. Harry and Gladys Holland had four daughters, Emily, Harriet, Ruth and Dolly Holland.

Caswell's

At the bottom of the summit on the old road was Caswell's at 33.0 miles. There were 10 rooms with running water in cottages, a double, $2, garage, restaurant and a pay camp.[303] The restaurant, garage and gas station were located on the east side of the road with the auto camp and store on the west.

Caswell's number 1

[303] Mohawk-Hobbs, 1926, op. cit.

Caswell's number 1

Caswell's number 1
Western Publishing & Novelty Co., Los Angeles, Calif.

170

It was a very nice place with a long restaurant that sat perpendicular to the road; they even used tablecloths on the tables. They had two gas pumps and a swimming pool in the marsh. Mrs. Caswell first worked for Chandler and then as a waitress in Gorman before opening Caswell's on the old road. The wind whistled through this place. Caswell relocated to the east side of the Ridge Alternate (U. S. Highway 99) in 1934. Today, the Pyramid Lake Recreational Vehicle Resort at 45100 Copco Avenue located 1.2 miles north of Smokey Bear Road on I-5, marks the site of the second Caswell operation. The former 3-lane alternate pavement at this location has been covered over with the northbound lanes of the I-5 freeway.

German Station

German Station was located two miles south of Gorman, between Gorman and Caswell's. According to Marvin Barnes, it was located on the west side of the road directly across from the property Lorraine Ralphs (Dewey Ralphs' daughter) used to own. German Station dates back to the stagecoach era. Nothing remains today. The house, barn and corrals of a German family that once occupied the site were located near a large Cottonwood tree that has since fallen. Marvin's father told him that he had found wagon parts and an old harness there.[304]

Gorman

At 36 miles we reach Gorman. The story of Gorman is tied to the history of the Ridge Route. Gorman was first called Reed's Ranch then Gorman Station and finally, Ralphs' Ranch. A bachelor named Reed took up land in the early 1850s and built a substantial one and a half story log house that became the Butterfield Station in 1858. In the early 1860s Reed sold the property to Charles Johnson. After Johnson passed away, his widow ran the station for several years. During that time

---

[304] Barnes, op. cit.

it was referred to as Rancho La Viuda, (widow) in Spanish. Mrs. Johnson sold the station to Don David W. Alexander. Alexander, if you recall, was the partner of Phineas Banning in operating a stage line between Los Angeles and San Pedro. Alexander sold the place to Gorman in 1867 or 1868. James Gorman Sr. was a veteran of the Mexican War and had been at Fort Tejon hunting fresh meat for the soldiers and laborers while the Fort was being constructed. He had a son, Jim Gorman, that lived near Bailey's Ranch.[305] [306]

Glen Ralphs told me his father, Oscar, bought the 2,700-acre Gorman Ranch and old log station house from Mr. Gorman in 1898. A second floor had been added and the exterior covered with siding. James A. McKenzie worked at the Tejon Ranch and upon his retirement purchased 26 acres in Gorman. His daughter, Mary McKenzie, married Oscar Newell Ralphs in 1901, thus joining the two ranches.

The Ralphs' family came out from Utah, and they all settled in San Bernardino. Glen's uncle, George Ralphs, his dad's brother, started Ralphs' Grocery Store at Los Angeles in 1872. George was a bricklayer and during a hunting accident lost his right arm and at that time began the grocery business. Oscar and his brother, Walter Ralphs, were equal partners. After George passed away his children and Walter's children took over the stores. Oscar only worked at Ralphs a couple of years and returned to Gorman to pursue ranching. Oscar was the only one to move to Gorman. The Ralphs' family sold the Ralphs' stores in 1968.

Glen's parents had a large two-story house just south of Gorman on the west side of Gorman Post Road (formerly the Ridge Route). It had five bedrooms and a bath upstairs. Downstairs there were two bedrooms, another bath, kitchen, dining room and two large living rooms along with a basement. They had a spring for their water. They used kerosene lamps for lighting. This was the original Gorman Station building and former stagecoach stop in the 1850s.

---

[305] Latta, op. cit., pgs. 74, 79-81.

[306] Conkling, Roscoe, Platt, The "Butterfield Overland Mail," Publisher, H. Clark, 1947, Glendale, California, Vol. 2, pgs 269-270.

Gorman Station, "Ralphs' Ranch House" January 19, 1913
Courtesy Caltrans

Ralphs' Ranch House May 28, 1913
Courtesy Caltrans

The house was torn down in 1933 when the Ridge Alternate came through. It was determined during the demolition that the hand-hewn logs put together with oak pins were as sound as the day they were cut.[307] Caltrans built his mother, Mary, another house about 200 yards from the old one south west of Carls Jr's restaurant. Unfortunately the new house was in the path of the future I-5 freeway. Caltrans moved the house to the west side of the Interstate and south of Gorman School. Mary ultimately built a new home directly north of Gorman School on a small knoll. This was her last residence prior to her death. Mary McKenzie Ralphs passed away at age 96 on September 19, 1978. She had served on the Gorman School Board for 57 years and in 1965 received a special recognition from Vice-President Hubert H. Humphrey for her community service.[308]

Glen Ralphs was born in Lancaster California in 1919 by a midwife. Glen has six brothers and two sisters. They are, James Lloyd, the oldest, (deceased); Clarence, (deceased); Dewey, (deceased); Harry, (deceased); Elmer "Bud" (deceased); Frank Albert, a sister Florence, (deceased) and a sister Marion, (deceased) "Dunny" was her nickname. Frank Albert worked for Ralphs' grocery for 40 years. He lived with his uncle Walter while attending school in Los Angeles. Bud was run over and killed by his own truck when he was 22 years old on the Ridge Route near Bailey's Ranch. He was hauling a horse in the back of his truck when it spooked, jumping partly onto the roof of the cab. Bud was standing on the running board trying to get the horse down when he fell under the wheels.

Gorman Hotel & Café

[307] Conkling, Ibid., p. 270.

[308] "Mary Ralphs Dead at 96," The Mountain Enterprise, Frazier Park, September 22, 1978.

Standard Station now Chevron in same location today

Glen first went to school in 1925 at Manzana School, a one-room building approximately one mile south of Gorman on the east side of Gorman Post Road. The only students were himself and his three brothers, Harry, Albert and Dewey. When the Manzana School building was torn down he continued his classes at Quail Lake School mentioned earlier in my writing. After graduating from Quail Lake School he attended high school in Lancaster. In 1939 the WPA (Works Progress Administration) built the Gorman School. They had grades one through eight but did not have a kindergarten class. The school bus for Lancaster began at the Kern County line. Glen would board in Gorman around 6:45 in the morning and get home about 5:15 in the evening. After having graduated high school he attended Antelope Valley Junior College located next door. He was graduated from the junior college in 1940.

Glen's oldest brother, Lloyd, started building up Gorman in 1925. The Greyhound Bus Company had loaned him money to build the old Gorman Coffee Shop and Hotel that was the bus depot in 1925. The building was constructed of adobe bricks with an exterior finish of plaster. The 1928 touring guide described Gorman as, "a small settlement:

store, garage, café."[309] After 47 years as a fixture in Gorman it was demolished on February 24, 1972, to be replaced by a new structure. Lloyd built Motel Gorman, a grouping of small cabins with attached garages for the motoring public. It did a fair business but never flourished as he felt it would. In later years after the motel closed, the cottages were used as dormitories for the restaurant help. In 1956 he put in the Caravan Restaurant. Lloyd also acted as postmaster for the growing community. About the only thing that did not belong to Lloyd was the Standard Oil gas station that was built in 1923. Glen went into the Army (seacoast artillery and 16 inch-gun battery) in Galveston, Texas, and was deployed along the coast in November 1941. He was discharged in December of 1945. When discharged he moved to Lancaster, California, where he lives today.

The entire town, including a market, gas station, sheriff's substation and cattle ranch were placed on the market for 4.2 million dollars in February 1997. The package comprised seven properties totaling about 2,866 acres.   Ruth Ralphs, the family's 74 year-old matriarch said, "We're getting older and as the family gets larger we need to see to our tax and estate planning.[310]

Chandler

North of Gorman Interstate 5 has covered the old road. Two miles ahead was the small settlement of Chandler once located one-quarter mile south of the Frazier Park exit. To-day it is under the northbound lanes of the freeway. Volume 8 of the <u>Automobile Blue Book</u> of 1918 indicates Chandler's Tejon Hotel & Garage. It was a stone and frame building.[311] A man named Lawrence O. Chandler owned the site. There were several small houses, a motel, Richfield gas station, ga-

[309] Mohawk-Hobbs, 1928, op. cit.

[310] "Shopping for a buyer: Ralphs family cuts price on town," <u>Daily Breeze</u>, February 3, 1997.

[311] State Highway Engineering Map, District 7 L. A. County, Route 4, Section D Sheet 10, May 25, 1931.

rage and restaurant.[312] The touring guide of 1926 indicates: Lodging, meals, small garage, reputed reliable and good, labor $1.75 day or night. Mr. Chandler raised pigeons in the back and served them in his café.[313] It is interesting to note that a State Camp and cabins were under construction at this location in 1928.[314] In the late 1930s a Mobil station occupied the site.[315]

Chandler
Courtesy West Kern Oil Museum Taft

Exit I-5 at Frazier Park and head west to the first intersection. To your left is Peace Valley Road; to your right is Lebec Road. To see a remnant of the old Ridge Route in this area, turn left (south) onto Peace Valley Road and proceed to Falcon Way, the road leading to the high school. Proceed one tenth of a mile west toward the school. Park your vehicle and walk south to the hill in front of you. A piece of the old Ridge Route curves off to the left along the knoll and then turns south paralleling Peace Valley Road at a higher level. Near Tejon Summit, I-5 has destroyed the old alignment. If you are not

[312] Barnes, op.cit.

[313] Kaufman, op. cit.

[314] Mohawk-Hobbs Guide, 1928, op. cit.

[315] Lenke, op. cit.

interested in this side trip, turn right (north) onto Lebec Road. Most of this road is the original Ridge Route alignment.

Lebec Hotel

Mark your odometer and travel 1.6 miles north to the former Lebec Hotel site on the west side of the road. The hotel was the last major structure in place during the highway's glory days. The hotel was the brainchild of entrepreneur Thomas O'Brien, a saloonkeeper from Bakersfield, and Cliff Durant.

The following information was graciously provided courtesy of Sandra O'Brien in memory of her late husband, Michael O'Brien, who at the time of his death was compiling the O'Brien family history.

Thomas O'Brien grew up in Ashland Kentucky. When he was 12 years old his father, Michael, while fishing, fell from his boat and drowned in the Ohio River. With the loss of his father, young Thomas left home seeking work so he could help support the family. He joined up with the Santa Fe railroad as a water boy for the men laying rails to open the west. He made 50 cents a week and promptly sent it to his mother to ease the burden of taking care of his brother and three sisters. As the railroad proceeded west, Thomas distinguished himself by becoming, at 17, the youngest engineer on the Santa Fe Railroad. In the process of this odyssey he also managed to buy two saloons, one in Kingman, Arizona, and another in Needles, California. Ultimately he sold both of them taking the money to invest in oil leases in section 25 between Fellows and Taft near Bakersfield, California. "Black Gold" was discovered in the late 1890s and the return on his investment allowed him to build the "Louvre" Saloon at the corner of 19th and "K" in Bakersfield. He also had an interest in the "Del Monte" Saloon. Additionally, he built the Empire Theater, the first theater in Bakersfield. When his Empire Theater was not booked for vaudeville he would show silent movies.

In 1901 Thomas O'Brien and his friend, Jack Wooley, went to Alaska where O'Brien opened a saloon and gambling joint.

Wooley had worked for O'Brien in Bakersfield and from this early association O'Brien entrusted Wooley to run his saloon in Alaska. Unfortunately, after O'Brien's departure, Wooley lost O'Brien's saloon in a poker game. A situation of this magnitude would normally terminate any friendship, however, O'Brien remained loyal to his friend, and he forgave Wooley for his indiscretion.

In 1905 Al Jolson was one of the more celebrated entertainers that appeared at his Empire Theater in Bakersfield. On the same bill and following Jolson was a pretty young singer from San Francisco, famous in her own right by the name of Cowee A. Erskine. Thomas was enamored by her beauty and voice. After five years of courtship they were married at the Sheraton Palace Hotel in San Francisco on Valentine's Day 1910. He had retired the year before at age forty. His investments were netting between eighteen and twenty thousand dollars per month! At the time of their marriage, Thomas was residing in Los Angeles at 2244 South Western Avenue. Thomas built Cowee a beautiful new home on Crenshaw Boulevard, a short distance from Pico Boulevard.

Cowee A. O'Brien at her Crenshaw home in Los Angeles.

a.k.a. Coie Fancis Bower the lady with two voices because she could sing soprano as well as contralto.

Courtesy Sandra O'Brien

Thomas O'Brien was an eternal optimist and entrepreneur. In 1913 he purchased acreage in Lebec from a man named Taylor. Taylor had a small general store and lived nearby in an old thick-walled adobe home that had been whitewashed on the outside.

Located across from the Lebec Post Office this is thought to be the Taylor home O'Brien occupied after purchasing the property. Building a new home in the canyon where his Lebec Hotel would eventually stand, he added a dining wing to this structure for guests occupying his cabins.
Courtesy Caltrans

Lebec Post Office on left, note Bell System Pay Station Sign. Photo was taken March 10, 1912, before actual construction started on the Ridge Route.
Courtesy Caltrans

In late 1913 or early 1914 Thomas decided to move his family and their maid from the Crenshaw home to their diminished accommodations at Lebec. Mrs. O'Brien was not completely receptive to the move and cried when she left her beautiful home in Los Angeles and was relocated to Taylor's old adobe. Thomas proceeded to build a temporary home for his wife and family at Lebec. He placed it at the rear of a canyon. The house had a large front room with a high ceiling where Cowee located her grand piano. Every room had wallpaper. The temporary roof of tarpaper always leaked. A hard wind would drive the rain down the inside walls. Although the aforementioned description sounds dismal, a photograph of the house indicates it was quite nice for such a remote area.

O'Brien built this home for Cowee at the rear of a canyon.
He would eventually build his hotel in front of the house
Courtesy Sandra O'Brien

In 1919 construction would begin on his grand hotel that would be located between the house and the highway. He promised Cowee that he would build her a proper home in due time but all of his money would ultimately be consumed building the opulent Lebec Hotel. The house never materialized. In the meantime, he set out to develop his property.

He constructed several cabins on the west side of the highway. By attaching a large dining room addition to an existing structure, he created an "L" shaped facility. The dining room had a screened porch and you could eat inside or dine at one of the tables along the porch.

O'Brien's first Dining Room was
an addition to the existing structure
Courtesy Sandra O'Brien

The first sleeping accommodations were the individual cabins that were located behind the new dining room addition that was built parallel with the highway. The one-room cabins were an instant success with early motorists, so much so that additional units were added in back of the original structure that was perpendicular to the highway and formed the short leg of the "L" formation. The cabins and dining room comprised the first Lebec Hotel.

View of Dining Room and Sleeping Cabins
Courtesy Sandra O'Brien

Rear view of Sleeping Cabins
Courtesy Sandra O'Brien

Rear view of complex with Castac Lake in background
Courtesy Sandra O'Brien

In 1915 the Ridge Route highway pushed through to Los Angeles over the Tehachapi and San Gabriel mountains. With an increase in automobile traffic, Thomas tore down an old barn down by the highway and built three new structures. The first building housed his general merchandise store. The second structure hosted a lunchroom, grill and private dining room. The largest building to the north was his Lebec garage. They were all located on the west side of the highway. By this time he had twenty-five cabins, and they were always full. At some point in time, O'Brien accepted the job of postmaster for the area, probably early on when he took over from Taylor.

O'Brien's Store, Lunchroom & Garage. In the lower left you can see O'Brien's house behind a rear portion of the Lebec Hotel
Courtesy Sandra O'Brien

184

He purchased 11,500 additional acres in the surrounding area. At one time he had 4,000 head of cattle on the property. O'Brien was doing quite well. He donated property and a building to the county for Pershing School in Lebec. When the hotel opened in 1921 he ran direct current electric lines from the hotel to the school so the children would have adequate lighting. Prior to this the children were attending class in a small building on the east side of the road across from Taylor's old general store. A large drainage ditch paralleled the east side of the highway so you had to cross a small footbridge to gain access to the building.[316] The small building that was being used as the school was the original grocery store and post office run by J. A. Johnson.[317]

When O'Brien's children graduated from the eighth grade at Lebec Grammar School, they had to commute forty miles to Bakersfield to attend high school. Charlie Bustillos was O'Brien's right hand-man all of his business life and even managed the Lebec Hotel a short time after it had opened. O'Brien assigned Bustillos the duty of shuttling his children forty miles into Bakersfield each day in O'Brien's big black Locomobile. It was one of the few cars of that era having an electric starter. The entire scene gave the appearance that they were rich kids being driven to Kern County High School in a limousine.

Charlie Bustillos
Courtesy Sandra O'Brien

---

[316] McLarty, Jan C., "The Story of Two Grapevines," Unpublished history of Leonard Lawrence McLarty, chapter 8, p. 7.

[317] Early photo showing the small building as the post office and grocery store. Courtesy Sandra O'Brien.

Russell Clifford Durant had stopped at O'Brien's Hotel and noted his success with the cabins and dining room. He encouraged him to build a first class hotel on the property. Cliff Durant was the playboy son of William "Billy" Crapo (pronounced Cray-po) Durant, founder of General Motors. Cliff was a racecar driver and airplane instructor headquartered in Oakland, California. Cliff's father had a hotel in the east and perhaps Cliff wanted to emulate his father's success. O'Brien could see the possibilities due to the popularity of his sleeping cabins. Cliff Durant and Thomas O'Brien became equal partners financially and pushed forward to build the huge first class hotel.

Durant's Simplex
Courtesy Sandra O'Brien

Taylor's old adobe had to be razed in 1919 when construction got underway for the famous hotel. The reinforced concrete hotel was designed to be fire-and quake-proof. Part of the hotel project included 24 mountain bungalows. The architect was Mory I. Diggs of Sacramento, who also was the architect for the clubhouse at Bay Meadows. The grounds encompassed 22 acres, four of which were occupied by the hotel.

Lebec Hotel Construction, view 1
Courtesy Sandra O'Brien

Lebec Hotel Construction, view 2
Courtesy Sandra O'Brien

The dining room could accommodate 400 guests. A finely appointed billiard room was located on the second floor. A modern steam-operated laundry was in the basement of the hotel. The steam plant also powered a direct-current, electric generator that supplied electricity for the hotel. There were two main wings each extending 260 feet from the main entrance. In addition to a standard room, each wing had 30 suites, each having two rooms with a private bath, direct current electric lights, gas and modern furnishings. The hotel switchboard not only served the hotel but also had lines to several nearby homes, a grocery store in Frazier Park, and a line to the Kern County Forestry and fire Department across the road from the hotel. Seaborn "Pete" Jones worked at the fire station in 1942, and said he actually received two separate paychecks; one from the county and one from the forestry service. The hotel was built with an eastern exposure to provide guests with a commanding view of Castac Lake.

Lebec Hotel

The lake takes its name from old Rancho Castac, one of the ranchos that Beale combined to form the Tejon Ranch. Today the Tejon Ranch Company refers to it as Tejon Lake. Do not confuse this lake with Lake Castaic in the community of Castaic.

O'Brien had acquired a large amount of acreage in the

vicinity of the hotel and, together with Durant, had planned to lay out a town site farther down the canyon.[318] [319]

Durant planned to build an airfield in O'Brien's wheat field directly across the highway from the hotel, but that never came to fruition. Nonetheless, Durant and other early aviators used the field as a temporary landing strip. The grand opening celebration for the hotel was Friday, May 21, 1921. Despite stormy and threatening weather approximately 300 registered guests checked into the $225,000 hotel. The hotel opened in a blaze of glory as Hotel Durant.

Durant Hotel Dining Room
Courtesy Jerold Ray Meeks

Durant Hotel Front Desk

[318] "$200,000 Fireproof Hotel Under Way for Thomas O'Brien at Lebec," The Bakersfield Morning Echo, Oct. 9, 1920.

[319] Lenke, op. cit.

Lobby, Lebec Hotel
Courtesy Sandra O'Brien

Lobby, Lebec Hotel
Courtesy Sandra O'Brien

Lobby Fireplace, Lebec Hotel
Courtesy Sandra O'Brien

Because Cliff's father was the founder of General Motors, the Durant name was well-known throughout the country. Both O'Brien and Cliff Durant would hopefully benefit by using the famous name for their hotel.

Charles A. Cooke, manager of the new hostelry, arranged the opening fetes.[320] Cooke had managed the fashionable Hotel Hollywood in Los Angeles, and previous to that was general manager of the Fairmont Hotel and the Palace Hotel in San Francisco. He also managed the El Encanto Hotel at Santa Barbara prior to assuming the managerial duties at Hotel Lebec. [321]Jack Dempsey, the heavy weight champion of the world, was a registered guest when the Lebec Hotel opened. Other celebrities that visited the hotel were silent film stars Rex Bell, Clara Bow and Buster Keaton. Charles Lindbergh and his wife, Anne, were guests at the hotel around 1929. This was after his famous solo transatlantic flight piloting "The Spirit of St. Louis" from New York to Paris in 1927. From 1929 to 1935, the Lindbergh's flew across the United States

[320] "Hotel Durant is Formally Opened," The Bakersfield Californian, May 23, 1921.

[321] "Fine New Hotel for Lake Castaic Soon," The Newhall Signal & Saugus Enterprise, April 8, 1921.

on tours promoting air travel as a safe and convenient method of transportation. Lindbergh was a big, tall, nice-looking fellow. Anne Lindbergh, his wife, was a small woman. She always had her meals sent up to her room. She very seldom showed herself in public and when she did, would not mingle with people possibly because she felt self-conscious being far along in her pregnancy. Gertie, one of the hotel's waitresses, probably spoke to Mrs. Lindbergh more than anyone else. Gertie would take Mrs. Lindbergh's meals to her room. Mrs. Lindbergh liked chocolate malts, and would order five or six of them a day. Lindbergh had a glider trucked up to Lebec and assembled it in the wheat field across from the hotel. Using a car to pull the glider he would catch the wind current and fly around all day. According to Mrs. Lindbergh's obituary, she was "a painfully shy woman." She was thrown into the spotlight of her famous husband immediately after they met in 1927, shortly after he made his famous solo flight across the Atlantic. In 1932 the already-famous Lindberghs drew worldwide attention when their first child, 20-month-old Charles Lindbergh Jr., was kidnapped and murdered. In addition to the kidnapped child, the Lindbergh's had five other children – Jon, Land, Scott, Reeve and Anne, who died in 1993. Charles Lindbergh died in 1974 and Anne, age 94, passed away in February 2001."[322]

Cliff Durant's father had bankrolled part of the hotel's construction. Shortly after the grand opening he ran into financial difficulties and withdrew all support from Cliff in financing the hotel. With this unfortunate event, O'Brien was forced to buy out Cliff's half of the investment. O'Brien had to front a sizeable amount of his wealth to become sole owner of the hotel. At this point he changed the name from Hotel Durant to Hotel Lebec. The hotel never was the "cash cow" they thought it would be. For one thing, cars were constantly being improved and were able to cover greater distances. Why stop at an expensive hotel in Lebec when you could continue another 40 miles and be in Bakersfield. Most of the time the hotel broke even.

[322] "Anne Morrow Lindbergh Obituary," Daily Breeze, Torrance, February 8, 2001.

O'Brien sold the hotel to Foster Curry (son of the concessionaire at Yosemite). Early postcards from this period show the hotel under its brief stint as "Curry's Lebec Lodge." It was during Curry's brief ownership that the general store, restaurant, garage and a number of houses burned to the ground. The $60,000 fire in November of 1923 started early on a Sunday morning. The Lebec Lodge (at this time it was called the Lebec Lodge) miraculously escaped the flames.[323] Curry had not attended to cleaning the grease from the restaurant's flue on a regular basis. The flue ignited and destroyed all three buildings down on the highway.

Curry had the hotel about a year when a dispute developed that ended in court with a judgment favoring O'Brien. O'Brien once again became full owner of the hotel. In 1925 he constructed a large stone building to replace the three structures he had built years earlier and were destroyed in the fire. Constructed of stone, O'Brien vowed it would never burn down again. The new building occupied the same general location as the buildings consumed in the fire. Located on hotel property, the new stone structure housed a coffee shop, bar, grocery store, post office, Richfield gas station and an extensive garage. The garage had a large tow truck and two mechanics.

Lebec Hotel's Stone Coffee Shop down on the Ridge Route. Pershing School #1 is the first structure to the right in the distance.

[323] "$60,000 Fire at Lebec," The Newhall Signal & Saugus Enterprise, Nov. 9, 1923.

A 1926 touring guide describes the Lebec Hotel as: new and high class, 80 rooms, thoroughly modern. Single $2-$3; dbl. $3, with bath $4, coffee shop open 24 hours." Lebec Garage is the largest and best equipped on the Ridge. Labor $1.75, after 6 p.m. $2.40 an hr.[324] The hotel had an enormous kitchen but, people had the mindset that it cost too much to eat there so they closed the kitchen and moved the eating accommodations into the coffee shop down by the highway.

Lebec Hotel Kitchen
Courtesy Sandra O'Brien

With this change, hotel guests desiring to eat had to stroll down to the coffee shop. On the positive side, the facility was open 24 hours. As before, the coffee shop, bar, grocery store, gas station and garage generated $50,000 clear per year, a far better return than the hotel. O'Brien's downfall was that he had a propensity to do everything first class. He used all of his wealth to keep the hotel afloat.

[324] Mohawk-Hobbs, 1926, op. cit.

Thomas O'Brien in front of his hotel
Courtesy Sandra O'Brien

On Monday December 21, 1925, O'Brien's wife, Cowee, and two of her lady friends, Mrs. Alberts, whose husband ran the Lebec Garage and Mrs. Mahoney, wife of the hotel manager at that time, all went to Bakersfield to do some last-minute Christmas shopping. The lady driving this huge all metal Studebaker touring car was Mrs. Alberts. She was a small petit Victorian lady. Hydraulic brakes had not been invented. Stopping a car with mechanical brakes relied on the amount of pressure one could apply to the brake pedal. It is theorized that the women were excited about their shopping trip totally forgetting about the dangerous Santa Fe railroad crossing three miles from Bakersfield. When they heard the engine's blasting whistle, it was already too late. Little Mrs. Alberts who was driving applied the brakes in ample time to stop a modern car but simply did not have enough strength in her leg to push hard enough on the pedal to bring the 2,000-pound car to a halt. All of the women expired in this horrific and tragic accident just before Christmas. Cowee was laid to rest December 23, 1925, at Union Cemetery in Bakersfield.

At 57 years of age, O'Brien remarried a lady by the name of Gemma Martina on Christmas Day 1926. It had only been a year since his first wife was killed in the tragic accident. Gemma was a smart women having been educated by the nuns in Italy. Ray Benjamin was O'Brien's attorney in San Francisco. Gemma was Benjamin's secretary, and that is how she became acquainted with O'Brien. The depression was approaching and O'Brien had to borrow money to keep his operation viable. When O'Brien's money ran low, Gemma wanted to torch the old house behind the hotel and collect the insurance money, but O'Brien would not hear of it. It was after O'Brien had remarried and before there was a serious money problem that O'Brien's son, Thomas Erskine O'Brien, and his sister, Jane O'Brien, were removed from Kern County High School and sent to private Catholic boarding schools in Ojai, a small community near Ventura. His younger daughter, Betty O'Brien, was still in grammar school at Lebec. Just prior to the stock market crash, O'Brien recalled his son and daughter from Ojai in order to save money. He sent both of them to live with their grandmother at 2028 17th Street in Bakersfield. This was the house O'Brien purchased in 1905 for his mother when he brought her out from Kentucky. Thomas and Jane reentered Kern County High School where they completed their education. A short time later when O'Brien lost the hotel, his second wife divorced him and left for Washington D. C. She eventually became a personal secretary for Richard Nixon before he was selected by Eisenhower to run on the Republican ticket as vice-president in the 1952 presidential campaign.

O'Brien had hired Clarence Mark Fuller, an intelligent young man fresh out of college, as his bookkeeper. They became instant friends. Around 1913 Fuller left O'Brien to work for Richfield Oil. With perseverance and purpose he worked his way up and became president of the company.

The year was 1929 and with the stock market crash the roaring twenties came to an abrupt halt. O'Brien still owned two casinos, one in Las Vegas and the other in Reno. The Las Vegas casino was one of his first investments, but it never turned a profit. The patrons had mainly been the men building Hoover Dam. O'Brien trusted Charlie Bustillos and in 1930 sent him to Las Vegas to run the gambling there. This same year O'Brien approached Fuller for a loan. After Fuller had left O'Brien's employment, they had remained friends over the years. Fuller told O'Brien he would loan him any amount he wanted. Fuller had not forgotten O'Brien's kindness in hiring him fresh out of college and advanced a loan so O'Brien could keep his hotel solvent. On December 24, 1930, Richfield was under pressure from the banks to make payments on overdue notes. Fuller, along with his vice president and four directors tendered their resignations. Three weeks later the company went into receivership. [325] In 1932 Fuller and two other Richfield Oil Company executives were convicted of grand-theft in misappropriating company funds.[326] "After a sensational trial, all three were convicted and sent to prison. Fuller and McKee were later pardoned. Talbot died while on parole before his pardon application was acted upon."[327] In 1931 attorneys for Richfield approached O'Brien wanting the money Fuller

[325] Jones, Charles S., opt. cit., p.154.

[326] "Richfield Oil Officials Found Guilty Of Theft," Los Angeles Times, May 17, 1932.

[327] Jones, Charles S., opt. cit., p. 155.

had advanced. Richfield had placed foreclosure signs on the hotel as well as the coffee shop down on the highway. They were not interested in running the hotel and wanted O'Brien to continue managing the property during foreclosure. He agreed to stay on if they removed the signs. Richfield refused to take the signs down claiming that the law required their posting. At this point O'Brien, being too proud and stubborn for his own good, instructed Charlie Bustillos to throw the keys to the hotel and coffee shop across the table to the attorneys. This was an unfortunate error in judgment because on the surface, although the attorneys refused to remove the foreclosure signs, they implied he could do so after their departure. Had good sense prevailed, he most likely could have managed the hotel until the mortgage was satisfied and still maintained ownership.

O'Brien's Palace Casino in Reno was located at 232 North Virginia Street downtown, right on the corner where the now closed Harold's Club stands. In the winter of 1932 one his patrons hit a large jackpot. O'Brien called Bustillos in Las Vegas and told him to sell his place there and bring the money to Reno so he could pay the patron his jackpot. The Las Vegas gambling saloon sold for about the same price he paid for it. O'Brien was relying on recouping his loss the following spring when the gambling business picked up. Regrettably this would not happen. A lingering winter in Reno delayed an early spring, and he lost the casino.

His last business venture was in Bakersfield. He scraped up enough money to open the Saint Francis Café on Chester Avenue. He only lasted about seven months. He was short on cash and got in trouble with the union. He closed up two or three days before Christmas 1936.

There are many stories associated with the Lebec Hotel. One of the more troubling ones is believed to have occurred in 1929. It involved the man that ran the hotel's laundry operation. O'Brien had hired a fellow from Los Angeles experienced in the cleaning business. He was a good worker and ran the laundry quite smoothly. One day he asked if he could bring his daughter up to stay awhile. O'Brien said sure, go ahead. The Kern County Sheriff had heard about this girl. She was allegedly a prostitute and tied up with a gangster ring in Los Angeles. The sheriff sent an officer to Lebec to talk to the man about his daughter. The girl's father was not expecting anyone in the middle of the night. The deputy sheriff went to the bungalow behind the hotel where the cleaner lived and demanded to be let in. The man refused and the deputy broke the door down shooting the girl's father to death in the process. O'Brien tried to get the deputy fired because he was so mad about what had happened. The only disciplinary action that was taken against the deputy was a reduction in pay. O'Brien said that if the over-zealous deputy had gone to him first; there would have been no trouble whatsoever.

Another interesting story is that O'Brien had gambling at his hotel. The late Thomas Erskine O'Brien, (son of Thomas O'Brien), on a tape interview of the O'Brien family history empathically states that his father did not allow gambling at his hotel. This is somewhat an incongruity considering his father did have a gambling operation about this same time in Las Vegas. After O'Brien lost the hotel to foreclosure there were several owners. It is a fact there was gambling at the hotel after 1931.[328]

O'Brien, in his final years prior to his passing, became a little senile and would drive or take the Greyhound bus up to Lebec all dressed in his best suit and hat and try to sell property to travelers who wanted to build a home. Because he once owned 11,500 acres of Lebec he thought in a delusional way it was somehow still his! He passed away March 14, 1942, at age 73 and was laid to rest next to Cowee on March 16, 1942.

Road north of Lebec.
View looking south.
Courtesy Caltrans

[328] Lenke, op. cit.

Road north of Lebec. View looking north.

A Hollywood screenwriter by the name of Frank Butler eventually purchased an interest in the hotel. Butler wrote all of the "Road Show" pictures for Bob Hope and Bing Crosby. Two other screenwriters lived in the Lebec area. [329] The hotel became a hang out for the Hollywood elite. Although illegal, those desiring to gamble could indulge in poker or take their chance at the roulette wheel. Clark Gable and his actress wife, Carole Lombard, as well as gangster, Benny "Bugsy" Siegal, frequented the Lebec Hotel.[330] The dance bands of Tommy Dorsey and Harry James had attracted large crowds to the hotel. The hotel was considered the play land of Hollywood's richest stars and executives during the 1920s and 1930s but by the 1970s, time and the effects of deferred maintenance caught the attention of the county health department. They

[329] Lenke, Ibid.

[330] Anderson, Gordon, "Mountain pass winds through history," The Bakersfield Californian, 12-26-1983 p. B2.

revoked the hotel's license to operate on November 13, 1968, declaring it a dangerous building, listing eight misdemeanor violations involving mechanical, structural, plumbing, sewage and maintenance failures. Owner of the property at the time was Simons Corp. of Beverly Hills and the firm's president was Saul M. Meadows. William A. & Etta White held the mortgage on the property and filed foreclosure papers against Simons-Beverly Corporation. They took possession of the property and put it up for sale. The Tejon Ranch Company purchased the buildings and land. One week after escrow closed the Tejon Ranch Company destroyed the hotel. On April 27, 1971, they set it on fire while the Kern County Fire Department stood by to control the blaze. Remains of the once glamorous cement structure were hauled off and buried on ranch property.[331] [332] [333] Two tall Cypress trees are all that remain today.

Lebec Hotel in flames
Courtesy Bonny Ketterl-Kane

[331] "Old Lebec Hotel Goes Up in Flames," The Bakersfield Californian, April 27, 1971.

[332] "Lebec Hotel License Lifted," The Bakersfield Californian, November 13, 1968.

[333] "Lebec Lodge Group Faces Heavy Fine," The Bakersfield Californian, March 18, 1969.

At one time the board of supervisors had plans to make Lebec a showcase entrance to Kern County. Various improvements were envisioned including a new golf course. The opulent hotel would certainly have added merit to their vision. Frank Butler donated property for the golf course and the county actually started construction to implement their grandiose project. Unfortunately an election changed the powers to be and the Lebec "gateway" plan was scuttled. The golf course property was returned to Mr. Butler.[334]

Pershing Schools

Pershing School Number One was a wood and stucco structure formerly located on Lebec Road (the old Ridge Route) south of the former Southern California Gas Company building. This location is at the I-5 Lebec exit as you head south and was a short distance north of the old Lebec Hotel. Pershing School Number Two was a brick building located at Grapevine. Some students that had attended school at Lebec could not recall if it was Pershing School Number One or Two until Louise Lenke produced her old reader that clearly identified the Lebec schoolhouse as Pershing Number One. Pershing number one accommodated grades one through eight. An article in the <u>Los Angeles Times</u> of September 8, 1952, also confirms Pershing School number one was at Lebec.

Pershing School # 1 Lebec

[334] Lenke, op. cit.

All eight grades of the 1937 Lebec Pershing
number one school. Mabel G. Smailes,
formerly Miss Gillespie (center) was the teacher.
Courtesy William L. "Bill" Carter shown on
far left front row kneeling with arms folded.

The long abandoned Pershing School Number Two at
Grapevine was severely damaged as a result of the July 21,
1952, magnitude 7.7 Tehachapi-Bakersfield Earthquake and
was subsequently razed.[335] When El Tejon School opened
in 1939 opposite Fort Tejon, it absorbed both Pershing
Schools.[336]

Shady Inn

At 2.6 miles northbound on Lebec Road, originally part of
the 1915 highway, we come to the former site of Shady Inn.
Do not confuse this site with Shady Camp that was in Newhall or Shady Acres Camp that was located approximately
five miles south of Bakersfield. Shady Inn was located on the

---

[335] Brown, Nadine, Truempler, personal interview, June 9, 2001.

[336] Lenke Interview, 1998.

east side of Lebec Road between "South Drive" and "LE2 No Name Road" where the Lebec Community Church now stands. The touring guide described the site as follows: "Located 40.1 miles south of Bakersfield, 25c water, comfort stations, lights, tables & benches, shade or shelter; 3 cabins $1-$1.25; noted for its good meals, 50c." [337]

The old Tejon Ranch dairy was just beyond the Shady Inn site. It was located on the east side of Lebec Road where Lebec Road intersects with "North Drive." It began in the early 1920s and operated until about 1944. Originally, the Tejon Ranch personnel removed the adobe bricks from the ruins at Fort Tejon to construct two adobe buildings for the dairy headquarters. As of this writing, a house, a couple of tin garages, a covered hay-storage structure and two metal water tanks mark the site.[338]

At 3.9 miles we come to Lebec Oaks Road. On the northwest corner of this intersection is the old Mobil Oil Company refinery property and pumping station. Originally there were four or five cottages and a cookhouse that were parallel to Lebec Road for the workers. The cookhouse was right at the northwest corner of the intersection. A few more cottages faced Lebec Oaks Road. Housing was provided for both the refinery workers as well as the pipeline crew. The pumping plant was behind the cottages farther back on the property to the west. Abe Fromberg was Mobil's wholesale distributor at this location. At a later date Milt Lenke took over from Fromberg.[339]

At this point we continue our journey north on Lebec Road. As you cross over the I-5 Bridge, to your left is a remaining segment of the old road. Up ahead in front of El Tejon School you can see another portion of the original Ridge Route. At the Tejon Ranch Headquarters beyond the school we join I-5. Ninety Nine percent of the original road north of the Tejon Ranch Headquarters was destroyed with the construction of the freeway. Prior to moving into new quarters at Lebec, the

[337] Mohawk-Hobbs, 1928, op. cit.

[338] Wiebe, Mildred, op. cit.

[339] Kaufman, op. cit.

California Highway Patrol had a sub station next to the Tejon Ranch Headquarters building. It was located on the right hand side of the Fort Tejon northbound I-5 on ramp. The sub station building was originally erected as a field office for Caltrans during the construction of the I-5 freeway.

Fort Tejon

If you elect to cross over I-5 to the Westside of the freeway you can explore historic Fort Tejon. In 1926 the <u>Mohawk-Hobbs Grade and Surface Guide</u> shows Fort Tejon as being a supply point having a garage and café located three-tenths of a mile south of the current entrance to the fort. Two years later cabins were available. The business was not listed in the 1930 guide.[340] The guide also stated the ruins of the old fort were one-quarter mile west of the highway.

Mr. Yates Garage, Café with Hotel
& Cabins, south of Fort Tejon
Courtesy Tejon Ranch Company

As you make the transition to the west side of I-5, immediately after crossing the overpass there is a metal high-tension electric tower on your left. This is the Digier Road intersection. Charlie Yates first business venture was located south of Digier Road and south of the present day Fort Tejon entrance. It was located at the south end of the Fort Tejon parking lot where the southbound I-5 Fort Tejon on-ramp is

---

[340] Mohawk-Hobbs, 1926, 1928 and 1930, op. cit.

located. He built a gas station at this location on property given to him by Harry Chandler of the Tejon Ranch. Mr. Yates was Mr. Chandler's personal chauffeur. Yates was a single man and lived behind the station. He did not have a very good reputation because he had a bad disposition. Yates had a German Shepard tethered to a 30-foot chain and every time a customer drove into his station the dog would race out lickety split to the end of his chain and be jerked so hard it was a wonder he didn't break his neck. Frank Kaufman worked for the Southern California Gas Company in 1930 and when the Ridge Alternate was in the planning stage the gas company had to relocate their lines before highway construction got underway. They dug a rather large hole, exposing the pipes in preparation for the move. The area being worked on was near Yates service station. After the gas company crew finished up that evening, Yates removed dykes, allowing the hole to fill with water from the nearby Grapevine Creek. He did this twice and they finally had to hire a sheriff to stand guard all night so he would not persist in his mean-spirited tricks. He was just one of those individuals that didn't have a redeeming bone in his body.[341] The early automobiles would labor climbing up Grapevine Grade and the hot engines would drop oil and grease deposits onto the pavement. During wet weather, the water would combine with the oily grime on the highway causing tires to momentarily lose traction whenever they hit one of these oily spots. The resulting sensation gave the driver a feeling that his clutch was about to fail before he reached the summit. Pulling into Yates station, he told them to get a room for the night and he would replace their clutch and have their car ready the following morning. Of course there was nothing wrong with the clutch, it was only the slipping motion of losing traction on the oily spots coming up the hill. Yates never replaced anything. He simply stored the car until the following morning then duped the owners into paying for a clutch he never installed.[342] Another ploy he perpetrated on motorists when they requested a quart of

[341] Kaufman, op. cit.

[342] Meeks, op. cit.

oil was to grab a can from the top row of his display shelf. All of the oil cans on the top shelf were empty and he simply placed a spout into the empty can and pretended to replenish the engines oil. The unsuspecting motorist paid for a quart of oil he never received. He operated his station until the three-lane highway was converted to a four-lane divided expressway. At that time he moved to the east side of the road. His new station was located next to the former highway patrol office near the Tejon Ranch Headquarters building. The station was lacking in appearance and did not have a roof over the gas pumps to shelter customers from inclement weather. The attendant did not fare much better as his only protection was a building not much larger than a telephone booth. He also had several small cabins behind his station. About 1934 or 1935 he opened a restaurant north of the service station in a Spanish adobe structure. The restaurant served chicken dinners. The kitchen was on the south end of the building. Elizabeth Yaeck was the restaurant's cook while her husband Martin Yaeck ran Mr. Yates' service station. The restaurant seemed to be frequented more by locals than the traveling public. After five years of low patronage the restaurant closed. [343]

Fort Tejon Inn

Mr. Yates' defunct Spanish adobe restaurant building was converted into the Fort Tejon Inn. The back of the Inn faced the new three-lane Ridge Alternate highway. Eight rooms, each with a bath, were constructed inside the former restaurant. There was a large fireplace and swimming pool inside the lobby. All of the rooms were north of the lobby and common area. The interior was quite beautiful and had an open beam ceiling. When the Inn closed Martin and Elizabeth Yaeck made it their home. The 40 by 60 foot lobby became their living room. Mr. Yaeck filled the indoor swimming pool with dirt, turning it into a large planter so it would not be a hazard to his children.[344] The adobe was located on the east

[343] Kaufman, op. cit.

[344] Yaeck, Mike, Interview, December 8, 2000.

side of the freeway directly across from the Fort Tejon south-bound I-5 on-ramp.

Fort Tejon Inn looking south
Courtesy Tejon Ranch Company

Fort Tejon Inn looking north
Caltrans photo, Courtesy Tejon Ranch Company

Mr. Yates' Adobe Inn as well as the supply point buildings were all originally located on the west side of the original 1915 Ridge Route highway. Yates eventually closed his gas station and moved to Lebec where he built a motel at the north end of the old gas company property on Lebec Road. The complex had a swimming pool and 10 or 12 cabins, some of which he had moved from where his second operation had been. Each cabin was painted a different color.[345]

Crystal Springs Trout Farm

Around 1944 Mr. Yaeck opened Crystal Springs Trout Farm directly south of Fort Tejon on the west side of the highway where Leonard McLarty had operated his angling club in 1930, (see Tejon Angling Club under Grapevine).[346] Directly across from the trout farm and south of Yates station was Lenke's new Mobil station. Milt Lenke operated this station along with his station north of the Lebec Hotel Coffee Shop. During this time he was the Mobil bulk distributor in Lebec. Eventually Milt sold the Lebec station lease. The new owners closed the station shortly after acquiring it. Terry Lenke, Milt Lenke's son, opened a Chevron station immediately east of the trout farm on property leased from the Tejon Ranch. It was located at the southbound I-5 Fort Tejon on-ramp and was located on the same spot where Yates had built his station. Because the location did not produce the anticipated volume, Chevron did not renew his lease and the station was removed around 1988. Prior to this, Terry owned the Chevron station formerly located on the east side of I-5 next to the county fire station at the Lebec overpass. Terry said he had purchased the property from Chuck Hartley. This station operated five or six years and was removed around 1973.

Deadman's Curve

The most notorious curve on the road was Deadman's

---

[345] Kaufmanop. cit.

[346] Yaeck, Mike, Interview, op. cit.

Curve.[347] This curve was also known as "Death Curve."[348] The canyon below became known as the "junkyard" because of all of the vehicles that missed the curve and went over the side.

Uphill view heading south of Deadman's Curve
Courtesy Tejon Ranch Company

Downhill view heading north of Deadman's Curve.
This is the curve many teamsters failed to negotiate
if their heavily loaded rigs were not in low gear.
Courtesy Tejon Ranch Company

[347] Leadabrand, Russ, Exploring California Byways II, Ward Ritchie Press, Los Angeles, Jan. 31, 1969, p. 28.

[348] Wallace, op. cit., p. 24.

This view looking north illustrates the construction
of the Ridge Alternate and the soon to be by-passed
notorious Deadman's Curve. The Southern California Edison Station can be seen in the background.
Courtesy Tejon Ranch Company

Deadman's Curve Today

Charlie Dodge of Bakersfield told me that trucks hauled heavy loads of pipe from Los Angeles to the oil fields in Bakersfield. One of the more dependable trucks was the four-cylinder chain-driven Mack "Bull Dog." It had a stub nose and a large radiator that minimized boil-over. Unfortunately, the radiator was in close proximity to the cab and the heat produced on the steep climb would encourage drivers to navigate their trucks from the running board.

Motoring behind the slow pace of a fully loaded truck would test the patience of drivers. Some would attempt to pass, and the canyons below the road lay testament to their fate. For the truck drivers going down-hill, it was vitally important to shift into the proper gear to control the descent, as the mechanical rear-wheel brakes would not stop a fully loaded truck.

When I first began my research on the Ridge Route I spoke with an elderly gentleman who related the following story. At 17-years old my brother decided to sign on as a "Swamper" (truck drivers helper). On his first trip out of Los Angeles they were hauling a load of pipe casing for the Taft oil fields. Going down the Grapevine the brakes failed and the teamster ruined the gearbox trying to get the truck into a lower gear. Truck drivers were terrified of the grade. Losing your brakes almost guaranteed that you had an appointment with eternity. The truck raced down-hill out of control. Somehow they managed to stay on the highway and eventually rolled to a stop at the bottom of the grade. The old teamster, visibly shaken by the experience, got out of the truck. With one foot on the running board he lit a cigar without saying a word. After a few puffs he looked at my brother and said: "Son, if you want to get to Bakersfield it's that way!" The experience was enough to convince my brother to find another type of employment.

If you would like to get a commanding view of Deadman's Curve, head north from Fort Tejon and turn left onto Digier Road. Deadman's Curve is only 0.9 tenths of a mile from this intersection. On your way to the vantage point at 0.5 tenths of a mile, you will pass the old Richfield Oil pumping station now owned by Pacific Pipeline. Richfield had their picnic and camp-ground two tenths of a mile north of this facility near a small culvert that crosses beneath the road. It was located northwest of the culvert in a grove of Oak Trees. Although Richfield owned the property, Mobil also used the facility. Continuing north, the road begins to climb. When you reach the cattle guard, park your vehicle. It is private property beyond this point. Look down toward I-5 and you will see the infamous curve that countless motorists failed to navigate due to excessive speed, poor judgment and the frailty of early mechanical breaks. It was just above Digier road at this location in 1991 where one of the large yellow umbrellas erected by the Christo & Jeanne-Claude outdoor art exhibition toppled, crushing an unsuspecting tourist.

Southern California Edison Station

Directly north of Deadman's Curve on the west side of I-5 was the Southern California Edison substation. Mrs. Anita Stratton of Auburn, California, told me her great grandfather, Fred Yant Hixon, a native of Thomas Pennsylvania, managed the station in the 1920s. He was also in charge of the Eagle Rock station near Pasadena where the transmission line terminated. Fred and his wife had three boys and when the oldest boy, Grover Celeveland Hixon, was 12-years old, Fred's wife passed away. Fred raised all three of his sons by himself. Fred's oldest boy, Grover, married Sabina Ransom, and they had a daughter, Margaret. Margaret Hixon-Downing was Anita's mother. Anita's mother recalled spending a Christmas at the Edison station with her father-in-law. She said Fred would cut down a tree from the mountain, and they would decorate it. She also remembered Fred having some type of cold storage facility behind the house to keep food cold, as they did not have refrigeration. Anita was only 6-years old when her great grandfather passed away, however, recalls that he was a very nice man. There were three frame homes at the site including a corrugated metal storage shed. The reinforced concrete substation had been abandoned by 1934.[349]

---

[349] Department of Public Works, Division of Highways, Plan and Profile of State Highway, Route 4, District 6, Kern County, Section A, June 11, 1934.

Fred Yant Hixon & Granddaughter Margaret Hixon
at his Edison Station Home circa 1918
Courtesy Anita L. Stratton

At a later date Marie and Herman Carter lived in one of the old Edison homes at the abandoned substation site. Herman was the school bus driver for both Pershing Schools. Coming out the front door of their home and descending the porch steps a short walkway led to their front gate. Directly beyond the gate was the old Ridge Route. In 1936 when the three-lane Ridge Alternate was constructed at a much higher level, a mountain of fill dirt was dumped right up to their gate covering the old 1915 alignment and rendering their gate useless. The Carter's moved from the old Edison home in 1945.

Young William "Bill" Carter with his grandfather. The 1915 Ridge Route can be seen as the horizontal dark streak above Bill's head. Note the old road is directly in front of their gate.
Courtesy William L. "Bill" Carter

Young William with his older brother Quinton L. "Bud" Carter. Note the old road is covered over beyond their gate and the Ridge Alternate is at a much higher elevation.
Courtesy William L. "Bill" Carter

Camp Tejon / Christies' Camp

The camp was located on the original highway in Tejon Pass on the Grapevine approximately six tenths of a mile north of Deadman's Curve, down in between what today is the north and south bound lanes of the I-5 freeway. Heading south on I-5, Camp Tejon was located east of the second, emergency water stop. It was described in the 1926 <u>Mohawk-Hobbs Grade and Surface Guide</u> as being 35.5 miles south of Bakersfield, 50 cents, water, comfort stations, lights, tables & benches, kitchen or cook house, fine shade, 6 cabins $1.50. In later years it was known as Christies' Camp when Thomas W. Christie purchased the property. At this location the original highway was on the east side of the canyon. The camp was located on the west side of the road and west of Grapevine Creek. You had to cross a small wooden bridge approximately 20 feet wide and 10 to 12 feet long. The camp had a grocery store and tent cabins, café and gas pump. Most of the people parked and cooled their cars going south and carried water in tin cans from the creek for their cars. According to the <u>Mohawk-Hobbs Grade and Surface Guide</u> in 1928 they had 14 cabins and, by 1930, they had water faucets at the front door of each cabin. When the new three-lane alternate was under construction, the Griffith Company, contractors for the road, established a tent village at Christies' along with a large cookhouse to feed the men building the highway. Tom Christie put in a beer bar and slot machines for the highway workers and Saturday nights were said to be pretty lively![350] When the three-lane alternate opened, Tom operated a Shell gas station on the new road west of his old camp, located south of Oak Glen at the approximate location of the second emergency water stop.[351]

[350] Kaufman, op. cit.

[351] Meeks, op. cit.

Camp Tejon

Combs Service Station

In 1926 Edgar Combs had a Shell station and repair shop four-tenths of a mile north of Camp Tejon.[352] Mileage wise, Mr. Combs station was very close to the second emergency water stop which is two-tenths of a mile south of Oak Glen. This is the same location where Tom Christie operated his Shell station when the Ridge Alternate took out Christies' Camp and, at a later date, Kenny Yates, (brother of Charlie Yates) had his station selling some independent brand of gasoline. According to "the locals," Kenny Yates did not enjoy any better of a reputation than his brother up at Fort Tejon.

Oak Glen (Grapevine area)

Oak Glen was located on the west side of the Ridge Alternate, four-tenths of a mile north of Camp Tejon. It was between the first and second emergency water location on today's southbound I-5 Grapevine incline. An additional aid in locating the site is that it was 1.3 miles south of the first emergency water stop heading south on the current I-5 highway. The second emergency water stop is two-tenths of a mile south of Oak Glen.

---

[352] Mohawk-Hobbs, 1926 op. cit.

Oak Glen did not exist until around 1930, just three years before the 3-lane alternate opened. [353] Ray William Meeks and his wife, Velma Meeks, owned a home here prior to the construction of the Ridge Alternate. Their home was approximately one third of a mile west of the two-lane 1915 highway. Ray worked at the Mobil Refinery at Lebec. When the three-lane Ridge Alternate was built, it cut through a hill and was directly in front of their home. At this time, Meeks extended a roof from the front of his house and installed five gas pumps under its protection and opened his Mobil gas Station. He also had one Texaco gas pump.[354]

Meeks' Station, Ray with hat,
Robert Eugene Meeks on bike.
Sturm's Café in left background
Courtesy Jerold Ray Meeks

[353] Mohawk-Hobbs, 1930, op. cit.

[354] Meeks, Robert, telephone interview, June 8, 2001.

Sturm's Café with their house in background
Courtesy George Sturm

Sturm's Café inside view. Left to right, Odessa Sturm, her
brother Albert and George J. Sturm. Unidentified gentleman on right worked at Mr. Meek's gas station next door.
Courtesy Jerold Ray Meeks

Sturm's Home
Courtesy George Sturm

Just prior to December 7, 1941, Ray sold the place to Mel "Tex" Hogue and his wife, Lida. With the sale, Meeks relocated his family into company housing at the Lebec Refinery. Mel, a mechanic from Taft, converted the front half of the house/gas station into a small lunchroom.[355] Mileage wise, it was located at about the same spot as the old Combs station mentioned earlier. The Oak Glen State Highway Maintenance Camp was Mel's neighbor to the north. George John Sturm owned the property south of Mel's station. Sturm had built a café, an apartment unit and a large two-story house on land he purchased from the Barnett Farm & Cattle Company. His wife Odessa managed the café down on the highway that was popular with the men that worked at the Grapevine Mobil pumping station where Sturm was employed. The Worden family rented the apartment unit located behind the café. Sturm's large two-story house stood at the rear of the property. Constructing the house, Sturm incorporated a large bolder into one of the walls that in effect kept the house quite cool during the summer months. George (no middle name) Sturm, son of George J. Sturm, recalls helping his dad dig their well. They dug a well shaft 30-feet before finding water. His dad

[355] Hogue, Lida, telephone interview, June 8, 2001.

220

located two corrugated water tanks on the south side of the hill above the complex and used an electric pump to fill them. When Mel purchased the Mobil station from Mr. Meeks, Sturm had closed his café and the building had been converted into a garage. Mel was interested in utilizing Sturm's garage as part of his gas station operation. The two men came to an agreement with Mel leasing the building from Sturm. In 1942 after Pearl Harbor, Mr. Sturm decided to join the Air force and sold the garage to Mel. Included in the sale was Sturm's large two-story home.[356] Mel was on the school board at El Tejon School. He went out of business when the three-lane highway was converted to a four-lane divided expressway.[357]

These sites were located in section 5 directly north of the section 5 / section 8 boundary line in township 9 north and range 19 west. The small sub division of approximately 20 lots was previously part of the Barnett Farm & Cattle Company.[358] Sturm's two old, rusted water tanks on the side of the hill are all that mark the location today.

Grapevine/Grapevine Station

Grapevine was the small community located below Camp Tejon at the bottom of the grade, also known as Grapevine Station. J. B. Woodson was the engineer in charge of building the highway south from Bakersfield in Kern County. An existing wagon road did connect Bakersfield with Grapevine Station, however, there was a five-mile stretch of adobe, and in wet weather it became a gluey mess. It was not unusual to see cattle mired belly-deep, waiting for their owners to come and pull them out. Not even a strong horse could pull a light buggy along the adobe road when it was raining. The adobe and alkali condition presented a formidable problem for Mr. Woodson as it extended far to the east and west making a detour impractical. Material had to be hauled in for the Ridge

[356] Hogue, Interview, op. cit.

[357] Kaufman, op. cit.

[358] State of California Dept. of Public Works, Plan & Profile Maps, June 8, 1942 & June 11, 1934.

Route roadbed in order to build a proper embankment high enough to avoid the soupy mud. A special railroad was built to haul the large amount of ballast needed for the right of way. Occasionally they lost a section or two of track due to the unstable soil.[359] This entirely new right of way was provided by Kern County, the first section of which was known as the 17-mile tangent and by 1926 formed the longest perfectly straight stretch of road in the entire state. The new raised alignment was built west of the old mud impaired road.[360]

Seventeen-Mile Tangent approaching Grapevine)
Courtesy Seaver Center for Western History Research, Los Angeles County Museum of Natural History

Woodson, having conquered the task of building a stable road in such an unforgiving area now turned his attention to the Grapevine. Woodson had his young men stake out a road alignment on the side of the hill to avoid any problems Grapevine Creek could offer during wet weather. The new road up the canyon was progressing well until March 1914 when Grapevine Creek set a new flood stage and wiped out the entire highway Woodson had meticulously carved from the side of the mountain.

[359] Blow, Ben, "The Romance of the Ridge," National Motorist, 1933, p. 9.

[360] Hill, op. cit., p. 56.

Grapevine Canyon, note Grapevine Creek on the
left side of the road. This view looking south.
Courtesy Seaver Center for Western History Research,
Los Angeles County Museum of Natural History

He had no choice but to regroup and construct the road
at a higher elevation. He did this by using a series of loops
and switchbacks to gain elevation.[361]

Grapevine Loops with new three-lane
Ridge Alternate in left background

[361] Blow, op. cit., p. 10.

223

The small community of Grapevine was formerly located between the north and southbound lanes of the I-5 freeway. It was a small community of oil pumping station workers founded by Leonard Lawrence McLarty. Three small derelict 1920 cabins that McLarty built stood sentinel at the old town site until they were destroyed in late 1998 or early 1999 while Pacific Pipeline was attempting to locate a leak in one of their lines.

Exiting at Grapevine you can still access a portion of the original highway off to the left of the service road that goes under the freeway to the west side of Grapevine. Turn left from the service road onto Grapevine Road and you will be on the original alignment. Continue south approximately one mile. This is where the original community once stood. The Midway Gas Company had their pipe yard and patrol station cottage in Grapevine. The cottage was located to your left (east) about fifty feet south of where Grapevine Creek passes beneath the small bridge on Grapevine Road. A garage was located behind the house. Luther Smart and his wife lived at the site some time after the Southern California Gas Company absorbed the Midway Gas operation. Luther was responsible for patrolling the natural gas lines from Taft to Lebec. A stonewall that once surrounded the facility is the only vestige of the patrol station. The remains of the wall are hidden in the brush. Farther south on the same side of the road is a large cement slab foundation that once supported McLarty's garage. The small cabins mentioned above were also on the east side of the road and south of the foundation. West of the cabin's former site is a small wooden bridge obscured by trees. If you cross over the bridge and Grapevine Creek, you access the old Truempler home and the inactive Richfield pumping station building. The Truempler home is the last remaining Richfield Company house. Originally there were five homes. It is located directly to your right after crossing the bridge. Larry and Dot Truempler occupied the house during his tenure as a pipeline welder for Richfield. Larry retired in 1976. In 1977 he purchased the house from Richfield and moved it off of company property approximately 200 feet to the north, securing it to the former foundation of Pershing School Number Two that was destroyed in the 1952 Tehachapi earthquake. The house is quite nice inside having a large kitchen with two sinks and a large living room with beautiful old woodwork. The living room once served as the cafeteria for the pipeline and refinery workers. High ceilings keep the home cool in the summer heat. The front of the old home has a large, inviting front porch. The house is still occupied by Dot Truempler and her daughter, Nadine Brown. The family moved to Grapevine in 1941. Nadine told me they originally had gaslights as well as electric lights. The pumping plant generated electricity for the station and the company housing. They would shut the generator down at midnight.[362]

In addition to the gas company, Richfield had their pumping station at this location (See pipelines, Electric lines). Just beyond the small settlement the road veers to the left and begins to climb the mountain. This was the beginning of the famous Grapevine Grade that engineer Woodson built. Be aware that if you venture the grade the road ends abruptly, being severed by the northbound lanes of the I-5 freeway and there is little room to turn about. A barbwire fence prevents you from falling onto the freeway. At this point the road originally veered out onto what today is the northbound lanes of the I-5 freeway then veered back to the west side. The road finally crossed to the east where today a large overhanging (35 MPH) truck speed limit sign stands.

The following portion of Ridge Route history is dedicated to the memory of Lawrence Leonard McLarty for the impact he and his parents made in the development of both Grapevine establishments and especially for the formative influence that pioneering on the Ridge Route had upon the entire McLarty family. The inheritance of rich character, qualities of dedication, innovation, service to others and craftsmanship was the invaluable legacy this family derived from the Ridge Route experience. This memorial to Lawrence L. McLarty also commemorates the victims who succumbed to the severity of the early Ridge Route and celebrates the infinite worth of every soul who contributed to the heritage and convenience of Ridge

[362] Brown, Nadine-Truempler, telephone interview, June 16, 2001.

Route travelers today. Jan C. McLarty.

When Leonard Lawrence McLarty was a young man he was intrigued with the developing automotive industry. He worked at an automotive parts house in Los Angeles where he met and fell in love with Laura Martmer, the lovely young bookkeeper from Detroit. It was not long before they were married.

Laura & Leonard McLarty
Courtesy Jan McLarty

With Leonard's interest in automobiles he became acquainted with Barney Oldfield, the famous racecar driver. They did not have pit stops in those days, therefore each driver had his mechanic on board during a race. Leonard signed on as Oldfield's on-board mechanic and co-driver. During one of their races, Leonard sustained a crushed chest and broken collarbone. Leonard's wife was pregnant at the time and was so distraught she had a miscarriage. Gilmore Oil had sponsored their car and provided a settlement for his injuries. He would ultimately use this money to finance his start at Grapevine.

Barney Oldfield & Leonard McLarty

Leonard – Oldfield Crash
Courtesy Jan McLarty

Following the accident Leonard gave up racing and left Los Angeles to homestead property at Frazier Park in Kern County. At Lebec, Leonard found employment working as a mechanic for Tom O'Brien. On August 5, 1918, their first child, Lawrence Leonard McLarty, was born. With an expanding family he decided to press forward with plans to open a gas station, garage and café at the bottom of Grapevine Grade. Leonard negotiated a 99-year lease with Harry Chandler, publisher of the <u>Los Angeles Times</u> and member of a consortium of men that controlled the Tejon Ranch property. With the lease in place he began building at Grapevine. It was not long before his operation was up and running.

McLarty's Original Grapevine Station.
View looking northeast.
Courtesy Jan McLarty

Lawrence McLarty "in car" Grapevine Station.
View looking northwest.
Courtesy Jan McLarty

He quit his job at Lebec and moved his family into a small house at the new location. As the business grew, he acquired a Pierce Arrow wrecker and opened a motel, grocery store and post office. Laura baked and served pies and coffee at the café. At home she cared for their son, Lawrence, called Bud (and as an adult, Lawrie by his wife and Mac by his friends). A 1926 Mohawk-Hobbs Grade & Surface Guide reflected 12 "good modern rooms" in cottages, dbl. $3, lunchroom and soda fountain, one garage, open camp space.

McLarty's Garage, Café and Motel "under construction."
Note the Ridge Route climbing the
treacherous grade in the background.
Courtesy Jan McLarty

McLarty's Grapevine Restaurant
Courtesy Jan McLarty

230

Grapevine Restaurant, interior view
Courtesy Jan McLarty

McLarty's Grapevine Garage after being improved
Courtesy Jan McLarty

McLarty's Motel. Two derelict cabins, the
last remnant of the original town remained
until early 1999. Pacific Pipeline destroyed the
structures to facilitate the repair of a pipeline.
Courtesy Jan McLarty

When the Ridge Alternate was under construction west of
the old highway, Leonard once again approached Mr. Chandler and successfully renegotiated his lease for a site on the
new road. The new location was on the east side of the new
highway a short distance up the grade from his original place.
The new operation would host a grocery store, post office, motel, café and bar, garage, three wreckers, a six pump 24-hour
Union Oil 76 service station and an ambulance. A Union Oil
bulk distributing plant with two trucks were also located on
the property. Several employees were on the payroll to run
the operation, including a storekeeper, bookkeeper, chef,
bartender, two waiters, two waitresses, three attendants, two
mechanics and a cleaning person. Like all locations along the
Ridge Route it was difficult to get and keep good employees due
to the remote location. Because of this, room and board was
part of the wage compensation for enduring the isolation.

The Second Grapevine, looking southeast
Wayne Paper Box & Prtg. Corp.

The Second Grapevine Looking northeast
Courtesy Merle Porter photos, 1907 – 1989 Published by
Royal Pictures, www.merleporter.com
merleporter@merleporter.com

A nicer home had replaced the original small house down at the old Grapevine site so the family opted to continue living there. At the new Grapevine establishment, and perhaps because the family home was not in such close proximity to trigger Leonard's conscience, one of the waitresses, Lillian, captured his attention and an intimate relationship developed. Sadly, this relationship resulted in Laura divorcing Leonard. Leonard's co-habitation with Lillian resulted in a common-law marriage. Even with this, Laura remained committed to Leonard, even after divorcing him and later, when Leonard died, managed his burial at Forest Lawn Memorial Park where she is buried beside him. After the divorce, Laura and Lawrence moved in with Laura's sister in Highland Park. As part of the divorce agreement, Leonard provided a house for Laura and his son in Hollywood. Bud (Lawrence) attended Van Ness Elementary School. Later, they moved to an apartment in Glendale where Bud attended Roosevelt Junior High. While at this residence, Laura had a house built on Arden Drive in Glendale. They lived here throughout Bud's Hoover High School years and graduation. Bud would often visit his father in Grapevine. When his father came to Glendale to pick Bud up or bring him home in his Lincoln touring car he always took Bud to dinner at a fine restaurant. When Bud was old enough to get his driver's license at age sixteen, Leonard bought him a new 1935, 2-door Ford coupe.

Tejon Angling Club, a.k.a. The Fish Hatchery

One of Bud's fond memories during the decade of the new Grapevine was of his father's Tejon Angling Club a.k.a. The Fish Hatchery built in 1930, a short distance south of the main entrance to Fort Tejon. The small facility included a nice restaurant with Indian décor and red-checkered tablecloths.

Sign Advertising Fort Tejon and McLarty's Fish Hatchery

Hatchery Building
Courtesy Jan McLarty

Fish Hatchery Ponds
View looking Northeast
Courtesy Jan McLarty

A small building housed tanks for breeding trout.   Outside there were large concrete hatchery ponds. Nearby in the wooded area, Leonard created trout ponds at various points along Grapevine Creek.   Local fisherman enjoyed the Fort Tejon Angling Club only a short time. A fire destroyed the restaurant in 1932, and the club was never rebuilt.

Leonard was a social drinker and became habitually dependant on alcohol to the point that he started his day with a shot of gin. The eventual result was cirrhosis of the liver. During his decline, Hugh L. Spears, one of his employees began to assume most of the managerial duties. On Leonard's deathbed, Spears convinced Leonard that he owed him a great deal for keeping the operation running during the preceding months, and he succeeded in talking Leonard into signing half the business and property over to him and his wife, Gussie. The other half was willed to Laura McLarty. It was

1935 and young Lawrence was going on 17, and for the next four years Laura entrusted management of the business to Hugh Spears.

In 1936 Bud was graduated from Hoover High School and went on to Glendale Junior College. He met Jane Holbrook on a blind date and two years later on June 6, 1939, they were married. He was 21 and Jane was 19. After their honeymoon they moved up to Grapevine and took an active role in the business as co-managers along with Hugh Spears. Bud managed the gas station and garage and after taking the prescribed examination became the Postmaster for the second-class post office located in a corner of the grocery store. Jane assisted at the store and restaurant. She also counted money taken in by the restaurant, bar and slot machines (Kern County was lenient on gambling) and took the money to the bank. They became friends with Jimmy and Zoe Lanier. Jimmy worked for Richfield and his wife, Zoe, worked as a fill-in housekeeper at the Grapevine Motel when the regular maid was off duty. Their friendship with this couple lasted close to 20 years.

Jane & Lawrence
McLarty
Courtesy Jan McLarty

Besides managing the commercial aspects of the business, Bud and Jane would respond to accidents with their Buick ambulance. It was soon realized that the Buick was not suited for the treacherous Ridge Route terrain. They invited a representative from Sayers and Scovell's ambulance factory in Cincinnati Ohio to come to Grapevine and determine specifications for a new ambulance. When the custom ambulance was ready, Jane and Bud were given train passage to Cincinnati by Sayer and Scovell to pick up the new vehicle. The special extended chassis had a Cadillac engine. It had a siren and overhead red lights. It was the first emergency vehicle of its kind in the nation.

Run-a-way trucks were a common hazard that caused brutal accidents. An attempt was made to minimize truck-related accidents by establishing a weighing station near Lebec. If a truck was too heavy, they had to remove part of their load and leave it in the meadow near the grammar school. During hot summers, the smell of braking vehicles hung in the valley. Another cause of accidents during the springtime was the sea of wildflowers in the San Joaquin Valley. Motorists would be descending the Grapevine and become distracted as they looked at the flowers in the valley below instead of the highway.

When an ambulance was needed, the injured would be raced 32 miles into Bakersfield and taken to Mercy Catholic Hospital, San Joaquin Hospital or if they were poor, to the Bakersfield County Hospital. Fatalities were delivered to the Flickinger & Digier Mortuary. A $25 ambulance fee for the 32 mile trip was reimbursed to the Grapevine business by the hospital or mortuary.

One particular attraction that brought travelers from Los Angeles was Harry Chandler's Hunting Club in the valley near Arvin. The faces of these particular tourists were usually recognizable "big shots" and actors who stopped at the Grapevine restaurant and bar on their way to hunt quail at the club. The faces included notables such as Spencer Tracy and Melvyn Douglas. Jane particularly remembers Jackie Coogan arriving for dinner in a convertible accompanied by a luscious babe and another couple.

After Leonard died, Hugh Spears moved into the old McLarty home at Grapevine. Leonard's books, gun collection and business papers were stored in that house. Included in the business papers were legal documents regarding the disposition of his personal belongings. During the four years between Leonard's death and the arrival of Jane and Bud at Grapevine in 1939, Mr. Spears made strong political inroads with, among others, the Governor of California. He was also a member of the Prison Board. During the three years that Jane and Bud worked with Hugh, he showed them a gas station he had built (between 1939 or 1940) on property he had acquired in Tehachapi. He also developed a liquid gas company on the outskirts of Bakersfield. It was during those years that the house at old Grapevine burned, consuming virtually all of Leonard's personal possessions.

In December of 1941, Hugh Spears attended a political affair in Richmond, California. While traveling by limousine one rainy night in connection with that conference, he was critically injured in an automobile accident. Another passenger was killed instantly. His wife, Gussie Spears, left immediately by train to be with him. When he died two or three days after the accident, Jane and Bud drove up to bring her home. As funeral preparations commenced, Jane assisted with the children, eight-year old George Spears and 11-year old Patsy Spears. She took Patsy to purchase a dress for the funeral. The funeral, held in Bakersfield, was a publicized event attended by many political notables.

In the weeks that followed, Jane and Bud ran the business. In the meantime, Laura McLarty, residing at her Arden Drive address in Glendale contracted Dean Campbell, C. P. A. and professor at USC to audit the business. He arrived at Grapevine in early 1942 and meticulously examined financial records and business documents. His astonishing discovery was heartbreaking for Jane and Bud. Dean Campbell revealed to them clear evidence that Mr. Spears had been siphoning money from the Grapevine business. He used the money for at least two personal business ventures in addition to establishing a trust fund for his family. The partnership papers Leonard signed in his declining days giving one half of the business to Spears were missing which led to the supposition that they were consumed in the fire at the old Grapevine home. The situation was devastating. Dean Campbell's investigation revealed Spears had strong political ties. This weighed heavily against the fact that Jane and Bud were very young at the time and not politically connected. They wanted very much to fight for their inheritance and hired the law firm of Lloyd Massey & Howard J. Edgerton in Los Angeles to represent them. After reviewing the documentation Massey & Edgerton corroborated Campbell's findings and audit of the Grapevine business. After a complete evaluation, Mr. Massey recommended that the young couple negotiate a cash settlement and sell their interest in the business to Gussie Spears. This recommendation was most likely suggested due to the fact that all of the paperwork that would have enhanced Bud and Jane's legal position in court had been destroyed in the fire. After audit expenses and attorney's fees, Jane and Bud only realized about two thousand dollars of what should have been a substantial inheritance.

In May 1942 shortly after the legal proceedings were settled, Bud received a draft notice. Another surprise was in store for the couple. In June, Jane discovered she was pregnant with their first child. Bud liked the Air Force and decided he would try that branch of the service. With letters of recommendation from his many friends in Bakersfield and Kern County, Bud was accepted into the Army Air Corp.

He commenced his induction at Fresno California in 1943 just prior to the birth of his first-born son, Gerald Elliot McLarty, on February 18, 1943. After Basic Training in Santa Ana, California, and initial flight training at Hemet, California, he was sent for Detachment Training to Washington State University in Pullman. When Jane traveled to be with him in Pullman, he saw his son for the first time. From Washington he and his family went to Gardner Field in Bakersfield where he trained in small aircraft. He was then shipped to Fort Sumner, New Mexico, where he learned to fly Bombardiers and graduated with the rank of 2nd Lieutenant. After that he lived with his family in Mesa, Arizona, and served as a flight trainer at nearby Williams Airfield while receiving training in various aircraft. Next, while stationed in Lincoln, Nebraska, he received his rating in B29s and his squadron was assembled. They were transferred to El Paso, Texas, for training runs. They received their orders to enter the World War II Pacific arena. Ultimately, as he prepared to fly out from Mills Airfield near San Francisco, on the very threshold of entering military action, the war ended.

After the war, Jane and Bud settled in La Crescenta, California, where they had two more children, Jan Claire McLarty, in 1947 and Brent Alan McLarty in 1949. Lawrence Leonard McLarty was dedicated to supporting his family and being a committed father. He had a 35-year career as Warranty Administrator with Hydro-Aire Division of Crane Company (producer of anti-skid breaks for aircraft and space craft). He moved his family to La Canada, California, and eventually retired to Deland, Florida, in 1987. With his wife and daughter at his bedside, Lawrence passed away peacefully on January 5, 2000, at age 81.[363]

The metal tower that once held the large Union Oil 76 sign at McLarty's second Grapevine was destroyed in 2005. Without the tower it is now difficult to identify the location as you climb Grapevine grade heading south on Interstate 5 (formerly the Ridge Route Alternate, a.k.a. U.S. Highway 99). See picture on page 233. The second Grapevine was a target for out-of-control trucks descending Grapevine Grade. The small town was demolished no less than four different times by run away trucks. The worse accident occurred in September 1949. A twenty-ton truck loaded with motor blocks slammed into six parked cars killing two people and setting the gas station ablaze.[364] Today, in the current settlement of Grapevine located north of the original community, you can still continually smell the odor of hot brake lining as trucks descend the dangerous grade. In 1915 truckers heading to Los Angeles would hold up in Greenfield, south of Bakersfield. The highway would be lined with hay trucks, livestock rigs, tankers and fruit tractors. The drivers would drink coffee at

[363] McLarty, Jan C., Contributed courtesy of.

[364] Anderson, Gordon, "Steep, tortuous curves marked early travel," The Bakersfield Californian, Dec. 27, 1983.

the Tropics Café waiting for the sun to go down in order to reduce the possibility of overheating on the arduous Grapevine accent.[365] Other teamsters would wait at the base of the grade in McLarty's small community of Grapevine.

TEJON TROUT LAKES — 38 MILES SOUTH OF BAKERSFIELD — LEBEC, CALIF.

Trout Lake

Before closing the chapter on Grapevine, it should be stated that descendants of Hugh Spears categorically deny he ever established a trust fund or misappropriated money from the Grapevine business for personal benefit.

[365] Bezzerides, op. cit., p. 8.

CHAPTER 21

Accidents and Robberies

On one hand the Ridge Route was declared one of the most remarkable feats of highway engineering on the continent, and on the other it was said to potentially be the most dangerous road in the world bar none![366] Both statements were absolutely true. The road was constructed at a high elevation along the spine of the San Gabriel Mountains with canyons on both sides of the highway. This being the case, the motoring public experienced a panoramic view of stupendous proportions. The road was soon referred to as the "Scenic Ridge Route." Unfortunately, the beautiful landscape often diverted attention away from the highway. You can imagine the disastrous consequences. Slow moving trucks were another concern. Far too often a driver would become impatient and pull out to pass on one of the many blind curves. This forced the choice of a head-on collision or a sharp turn of the wheel that would propel the vehicle over the side of the highway into the canyons below. Most drivers caught in this circumstance jerked the wheel by instinct and went over the side. Either choice generally had the same conclusion, a meeting with your maker.

Speed was another factor. Most rural roads in 1915 were nothing more than wagon trails. The Ridge Route, being a well-graded and engineered highway enticed many drivers to use a heavy foot when it came to speed.

By 1920 the Los Angeles County Board of Supervisors instituted a novel regulation in an attempt to coral the speeding motorist. An officer was stationed at each end of the Ridge Route. Each motorist coming through in either direction was given a card with the time noted. If he made more than 15

---

[366] "All Aboard For Ridge Route...." op. cit. p. 9.

miles an hour on the road he would arrive at the far end ahead of time and was arrested for violating the speed limit.[367]

Even with all of my research on the Ridge Route and the many interviews and stories I have collected from old timers, I really did not comprehend what an early motorist was in for when they tackled the ridge. That is until I had the opportunity to accompany Daniel Holthaus on a ride over the old Ridge Route in his 1917 Model - T Ford. This experience brought it all into focus. His old Model - T Ford has less horsepower than my John Deere riding lawn mower! It was a challenge climbing up some of the hills. Of course the motor would get hot and the radiator would boil over like a teakettle and lose water. Daniel said old cars did not have pressure caps for the radiators. We had extra water with us to replenish the loss. On level stretches along the ridge we were able to maintain a fair speed. On the downhill grades my degree of concern increased commensurate with the speed because we were at the mercy of the crude braking system of the old "Tin Lizzy." I must admit I am being a little melodramatic here but reflect back in time and remember how remote this area was, and still is, should you develop car trouble. When we reached State Highway 138 on the north, we headed west toward Gorman Post Road (formerly the Ridge Route). We were fighting a strong head wind and with "both ears down" could only get about 15 miles per hour. Both ears down referred to the throttle and spark advance levers, both located on the steering column. With both levers all the way down in their maximum position, you would extract as much power as possible from the 20-horsepower motor. All of this said, the Model - T Ford did indeed get us over the Ridge Route, but more importantly, I now understand the feelings early drivers had when they saw such a formidable mountain in their path.

Daniel's 1917 Model - T Ford Touring car is rather unique. Oscar Peterson, a farmer in Center City, Minnesota, purchased the car during the summer of 1917. Mr. Peterson, an eccentric bachelor who didn't drive, bought the car to keep from

---

[367] "Cards To Curb Speed On Ridge," The Newhall Signal & Saugus Enterprise, January 23, 1920.

being pestered by car salesmen. That way he could tell them he already owned a car.

The car was driven 5.6 miles from Loren's Garage, the local Ford dealership, to Peterson's farm. The car was stored on wooden blocks inside his garage. Although he never drove the car, he licensed it for the next 20 years and kept the license plates under the rear seat.

After Mr. Peterson's death in 1937, his estate was auctioned off and the Model - T Ford, with 5.6 miles on it, still sitting on the wooden blocks Peterson had carved from tree stumps, was sold to E. R. Princeton, a Ford dealer from St. Croix Falls, Wisconsin, for the high bid of $87! Mr. Princeton named the car the "Rip Van Winkle Ford" and displayed it in his dealership's showroom. News of the "new" Model - T Ford spread quickly, and Mr. Princeton became somewhat of a celebrity. His car was featured in newspapers throughout the country, and also appeared in "Ripley's Believe It or Not." Princeton received many offers for "Rip," including one for $3,000 however, was advised by the Ford Motor Co. to keep it for advertising purposes. In fact, Ford Motor Co. leased the car as part of their display in the 1939 New York World's Fair. The car's last display was at the 1940 Minnesota State Fair. At the conclusion of that event, Princeton garaged the vehicle where it remained until stolen for a joy ride. The "thieves" drove 22 miles at which point a rear tire separated from the rim and the car was abandoned by the side of the road. After the car was recovered, Princeton stored it at several locations for the next 40 years. Unfortunately, the final location was a leaky, semi-enclosed Minnesota barn where it sat exposed to mice, rain and the elements.

By 1981, Mr. Princeton had retired to a nursing home and the car had been brought out to Maricopa, California, where his son, Eugene Princeton Jr. (Russ,) displayed it in his antique shop, still with 26 miles on it. Russ confided to Daniel Holthaus that as teenagers it was he and his cousin who had taken the car from his father's barn for the joy ride. In 1985 with the passing of his father, Russ Princeton took the car to an auction where it was purchased by Don Whipple of Fresno, California. Whipple mainly collected cars of the 1950s and 1960s and promptly stored the car in his garage resting on the same wooden blocks that Oscar Peterson had carved 75 years before.

In 1994, the "Rip Van Winkle Ford" was featured in Bruce McCalley's book, "Model - T Ford, The Car that Changed the World" but stated that its whereabouts was unknown. Daniel proceeded to trace down the car and purchased it from Don Whipple, still with 26 original miles on it! So there you have it. I had the distinct pleasure of motoring the Ridge Route in Daniel's brand new 1917 Model - T Ford. Now let us examine some of the terrible accidents that occurred on the Ridge Route.

September 17, 1925, The Newhall Signal & Saugus Enterprise: "FATAL ACCIDENT ON RIDGE ROUTE. Frances, the eleven year old daughter of Mr. and Mrs. C. W. Short of Stockton was almost instantly killed, and a son, and Mrs. Short were badly injured, when their car ran down a hill and turned over Monday afternoon, on the Ridge Route about 19 miles north of Newhall. The car was driven by Bert Miles, an employee of Short, who is a horseman. His race horses were in a trailer behind the car, and when the car upset the trailer and horses were thrown on top of the car. The little girl met death under the horses' feet. Mrs. Short and the little boy were cut and bruised, but Mr. Short escaped with comparatively few injuries, as did Miles. It seems the brakes were poor and Miles put the car in second gear, when it got too swift, he tried to go into low, but the car got away and ran down unrestrained. The family was hurried to the Newhall hospital where they were attended by Dr. Tuomy, and the body of the little girl was taken to Noble's undertaking parlor at San Fernando. The homicide squad came up from the Sheriff's office and investigated the accident. Short and his family were on their way to the Ventura fair, with three racers."

June 20, 1929, The Newhall Signal & Saugus Enterprise: "Two Meet Death When Gear Fails. Ellen Watkins, aged 13, and Fay Watkins, aged 12, daughters of Mr. and Mrs. W. R. Watkins, were killed, and the father, mother, and two sons,

246

Franklin Watkins and Harrison Watkins, cut and bruised when a truck driven by Mr. Watkins, went over an embankment on the Ridge Route, about a mile south of the National Forest Inn, Tuesday at 10:45 a.m. Two other children, aged two and three, were unhurt. The family, consisting of the father, mother and six children, as enumerated above, are residents of Bakersfield, and were on their way south. The Ford truck had another make of transmission and went out of gear on a steep grade. The brakes did not work. A trailer piled on top of the wreck after it went down the bank, pinning the two girls under it. Ellen Watkins was instantly killed, and Fay died while being brought to the Newhall Emergency hospital. On receiving the report, Captain Stewart and Deputy Sheriff MacVine went to the scene, also sending Dr. Redner and Nurse Eells. The ambulance was also dispatched, but it broke down and W. G. Noble, of San Fernando, came up and got the bodies of the two girls, while passing motorists brought the injured ones in. While the hurts of the parents and the two boys were painful, they were not serious."

August 8, 1929, The Newhall Signal & Saugus Enterprise: "Six Die In Crash Mother Only Survivor. Daniel Vargas, aged 60, and his son Frank Vargas, and four grandchildren, Panfilo, Jose, Francis and Inez, aged from 10 years to 18 months, were instantly killed, and Simona Varges, the mother of the four children, severely if not fatally hurt, when the car driven by Daniel Vargas got out of control on a curve of the Ridge Route a mile or more north of the National Forest Inn, and breaking through the railing, plunged several hundred feet down the mountain side, Thursday afternoon. The accident took place about four o'clock in the afternoon, and so far as the injured woman could remember, none of the rest were alive when she managed to crawl to them, after she fell. Mrs. Vargas then spent a night of torture trying to reach the road where she could give the alarm. Finally she attracted the attention of a passing motorist, who picked her up and brought her to the Newhall Emergency Hospital, after notifying Wm. Dailey of the nearest service, who relayed the notice of the accident to Pierre Daries, who notified the officers of sub-station 6. Deputy Stewart, Deputy Long and Deputy Pember went to the scene of the accident, and had the bodies of the dead removed to the Noble Undertaking parlor at San Fernando. The Vargas family lived near Bakersfield, and the husband of the injured woman is working on a ranch in that vicinity. The car was old and the brakes failed to hold it on the steep curve, Mrs. Vargas stated."

January 1, 1931, <u>The Newhall Signal & Saugus Enterprise</u>: "Roll Down Mountain. Mr. and Mrs. W. D. Shaw and O. L. Nelson, three travelers coming south over the Ridge Route on Christmas day were fortunate victims of an accident that ordinarily means death. Just south of Summit Reservoir station their car got out of control and rolled down a bank, some 150 feet, and turned over three times. Mrs. Shaw suffered a few minor cuts and bruises as did Mr. Nelson, but Shaw escaped unhurt, beyond the shaking up. The car was considerably worse for the tumble."

August 25, 1932, <u>The Newhall Signal & Saugus Enterprise</u>: "Car Carries Three To Death. Samuel Rabinowitch, Bernard Budnitsky and Kate Budnitsky were instantly killed Tuesday morning, when the car in which they were riding, went off the road near the Owl Garage a few miles north of Castaic, and rolled a thousand feet down the mountainside. Passing motorists saw the marks of the car where it left the road and notified Sub-Station 6, and Deputy Story and Deputy Pember went to the scene of the accident. The two men were dead, and the woman, who was huddled with her face in the dirt, breathed her last after the officers straightened her out. The car, a large sedan, was totally demolished, and from the marks made, the witnesses were of the opinion that it had literally sailed through the air for almost a hundred feet after leaving the paving, before striking the ground. The party had a large amount of stocks and legal papers with them, including deeds for some valuable property. Investigation showed that Kate Budnitsky was the mother of Bernard. The car evidently belonged to a brother of Rabinowitch, as it was registered to Joseph Rabinowitch. Relatives in Los Angeles were located by documents found in the car, and ordered the bodies taken to Los Angeles. There was no indication of what caused the accident, or who was driving. The spot where the accident occurred is a rather short, but not particularly dangerous curve, as the road has been made very wide. But if a driver takes it at high speed, and the car leaves the road, it is more than a quarter of a mile down to the bottom with no brush or trees to stop a plunging car."

The new three-lane Ridge Alternate (the second Ridge Route) through Violin Canyon opened October 29, 1933. Ten days later there was a spectacular truck accident on the new road. The new road with fewer curves was thought to be a much safer commute, history proved otherwise. Here is the account of the accident which occurred on the famous "Five-Mile Grade" just out of Castaic, now the north-bound lanes of the I-5 Interstate.

November 9, 1933, The Newhall Signal & Saugus Enterprise: "Three Die As Trucks Crash. Three truck drivers were killed, and two others seriously injured and four trucks destroyed and another wrecked, in a spectacular accident on the new Violin Canyon road, about six miles north of Castaic, which took place Wednesday about 5 o'clock a.m. Traffic on the road was suspended for some hours, as the burning trucks obstructed the road. The County Forestry Fire Truck was taken to the scene, and two or three wrecking crews got into action, and cleared the road for traffic about ten a.m. As near as can be ascertained, a Mack Truck and trailer, loaded with empty welding tanks got out of control some distance above the scene of the accident and ran into the big cut at a speed estimated at fifty or sixty miles an hour. The drivers, Wm. Jones and John McAvoy were both instantly killed. The run-a-way truck struck the rear of a truck load of sweet potatoes, the next in line was a load of grapes, these two being going south, as was the run-a-way. The three were piled up in a mass on the east side of the road, the Mack apparently running over the potato truck, and rolling on out of the mass for about 150 feet. All of these took fire and burned fiercely. A moment later another truck rushed down the hill and crashed into the mass. A fifth truck, going north, was struck and badly wrecked, but was apparently so far below as to escape the burning. The Ford truck was driven by John Pullio, who was accompanied by his brother, Nat Pullio. The latter was pinned under the mass of wreckage and burned to death in the resulting fire, his screams for help being heard as flames enveloped the mass. John Pullio was thrown clear, and only slightly injuried, except as to burns received as he frantically tried to rescue his brother. The driver of the northbound truck, Eddie Besyran escaped without injury, but a Negro, Paul Ernst, was injured by broken glass from the windshield. Leon Furra, driver of the last truck to crash, was accompanied by his father P. Furra. They escaped unhurt, or practically so, but the truck and its contents were burned. The place where the accident took place is ideal for such smashes. The road curves in the cut, and with the extreme grade that prevails cars and trucks from the north are practically helpless if they go at any more than slow speed. Besides, the grade is so long that brakes on heavily loaded vehicles are very apt to burn out, and it is possible that this is what took place. As a pertinent illustration, a hay truck, which came along while the wreck was being cleared, had smoking brakes which burst into flames just as it came into the danger, and only the near presence of the fire apparatus prevented a conflagration. One of the drivers of the original three trucks, C. McDowell, of Los Angeles, escaped injury, and hurried to Castaic and called officers. Deputy Constable Thompson responded and remained in charge of traffic till the road was clear. Ownership of two of the trucks was not ascertained, the registration slips and numbers being destroyed. The property loss was heavy, but no estimate was given. Summed up, of the eight drivers and others in charge of the trucks involved, five escaped with comparatively slight injuries, and three were killed, and four trucks were totally destroyed. Captain Stewart and the Signal man went up to the scene of the wreck on the new road, Wednesday morning. The conditions looked very favorable for the continuance of such happenings."

June 14, 1940, The Newhall Signal & Saugus Enterprise: "Ninety Sheep Victims Of Ridge Truck Wreck. A big Fageol trailer-truck loaded with 315 sheep was wrecked on the Ridge Route about 7:30 Tuesday morning with the result that practically the whole load was strewed over the highway and ninety of the animals either killed outright, or so badly hurt that they had to be destroyed. The truck, belonging to the Artozque Brothers of Stockton, was being driven south near the Ridge Tavern when a front tire blew out and the truck got out of control of the driver, John Goni, also of Stockton. The big outfit traveled 380 feet down grade and the truck broke loose from the trailer traveling ahead of it. The truck then turned over on its left side and the trailer crashed into it, breaking the front gate and spilling out sheep in every direction. Deputy Lockey, Deputy Keller and Deputy Young, arrived on the scene, and found that the driver and an insurance company were taking care of the mess, and after putting the wounded animals out of their misery returned without a leg of mutton. The driver was slightly injured."

Tanker truck on fire, Tejon Summit on the Ridge Alternate
Courtesy Harriet (Holland) Filoteo

December 27, 1983, The Bakersfield Californian, (excerpt) from Staff Writer Gordon Andersons' Grapevine, The historic link series: "In September 1949 a run-a-way 20-ton truck smashed into six parked cars, demolished and set afire most of Grapevine's buildings, killed two people and swept six more cars 150 down into a canyon."

1949 Grapevine Accident
<u>Los Angeles Times</u> Photographic Archive Department of Special Collections Charles E. Young Research Library, UCLA

This accident occurred at the second, relocated town of Grapevine on the three lane Ridge Alternate that was about a mile south of the original town. The Union Oil 76 gas station there became the unfortunate target for more than one out of control brakeless truck careening down Grapevine Grade.

December 28, 1983, <u>The Bakersfield Californian</u>, (excerpt) from Staff Writer Gordon Andersons' Grapevine, The historic link series: "The stretch of Interstate 5 from the Kern County line (Lebec) to the San Joaquin Valley (Grapevine) is infamous among truck drivers throughout the West. The CHP limits trucks to 35 mph – not only so drivers won't lose control of their big rigs – but because the low speed keeps the engines revving high and the air brakes pressurized. Truckers have argued for years for an escape ramp – someplace to steer their rigs should the brakes fail. The grading for a ramp was finally started in the fall." Of course today this ramp is in service on the east side of the northbound lanes of Grapevine Grade. Additionally, a second escape ramp was added in 2000 on the west side of the northbound lanes opposite the original escape ramp of 1983.

Los Angeles Times, (excerpts) from Staff Writer Eric Malnic's article Old Ridge Route: Long, Long Trail A-Winding, February 1, 1987: "Truck driver Oliver Bliss, 29, survives a 100-m.p.h. ride down Five-Mile Grade, just north of Castaic, when his brakes fail. A tanker truck breaks free in the same spot when the drive shaft breaks, cutting the brake lines, but again, the driver survives.

A run-a-way truck sends its load of wheel rims cascading down the Grapevine Grade below Fort Tejon, demolishing 12 cars and injuring as many as 20 people. A few weeks later, another truck on the same grade breaks loose and wipes out a service station.

In the first six months of 1956, a total of 16 trucks break loose on Five Mile Grade, claiming a total of five lives. One of the victims was Herbert Hayes, 29, of Huntington Park, who rode his brakeless truck to his death at 110 mph rather than endanger motorists below. Highway patrolmen said that during his wild, careening ride down the hill, Hayes ignored two chances to leap to safety as the truck slowed momentarily. Instead, they said, Hayes chose to stay with his truck, flashing his lights and blowing his horn as a warning to stay out of his path. At the bottom of the hill, they said, Hayes steered the rig over a 30-foot embankment and into a ditch below. He was crushed to death by the 20-ton load of cable behind him. Hayes was honored posthumously by the Los Angeles County Board of Supervisors and newspapers took up the cry for escape ramps and other safety improvements for the road-which had been branded by a National Safety Council representative in 1948 as 'one of the world's most dangerous highways.'

Floyd Winchell, a former resident CHP officer in Gorman during the Great Depression, recalls helping an Oklahoma man with his wife and little boy trying to get over the Ridge to the San Joaquin Valley so they could locate work picking cotton. They had no money, no gas, no spare tire and one wheel had been riding on the rim before they ran out of gas. Winchell went to Gorman and got them a can of hot soup and some bread for them. He siphoned some gas out of his own car to get them over the hill. From then on it was down-hill to Bakersfield. He wondered whatever happened to them."

Random Accident on the Ridge Alternate

December 26, 1983, <u>The Bakersfield Californian</u>, (excerpt) from Staff Writer Gordon Andersons' Grapevine, The historic link series: "Retired CHP officer, Jack Rummel, says that in 1955 he ticketed actor James Dean for speeding on the hill two hours before Dean was killed on State Highway 46 in a car crash."

When the last segment of (the third Ridge Route's) eight-lane Interstate 5 freeway opened on August 24, 1970,[368] the new interstate was still plagued with accidents. The average daily traffic count on the Ridge Route as of December 1999 is 53,000 vehicles, i. e. roughly 26,500 cars and trucks going north and the same amount going south. The road is engineered for a total of 30,000 cars per lane per day or for a total capacity of 240,000 cars per day for the entire eight-lane freeway.[369]

December 29, 1983, The Bakersfield Californian (excerpt) from Staff Writer Jim Mayer's article: CHP attacks Grapevine machoism. "Ever since he lost his brakes on the Grapevine and a California Highway Patrol officer had to clear the way for his speeding 18-wheeler, truck driver Jim Jappert pulls into the brake inspection area at the top of the grade. Once they've got a head of steam you're not going to stop 80,000 pounds, he said. The trucker from Springfield, Oregon said there are two reasons why the six mile long Grapevine is the most dangerous part of his 600-mile trip between an Oregon furniture maker and its southern California markets. The first is gravity. The hill is long and steep, and has no escape ramps like other mountain passes, he said. The second factor, he said, is a lack of respect. Motorists don't respect the momentum of the large rigs, and not all truckers respect the 6-percent grade. For every truck driver who pulls in for the voluntary safety check, at least one other driver doesn't take the time."

December 29, 1983, The Bakersfield Californian (excerpt) from Staff Writer Gordon Andersons' Grapevine, The historic link series: "Jerry Hall, a former California Highway Patrol officer was a victim of the Grapevine. He is a casualty of the truck accidents that have marred the mountain pass for decades, and a living reminder of the toxic chemical threat that grows every day. It was June 12, 1978, shortly after his graveyard shift began at the old Fort Tejon CHP office. He was on the southbound lanes when he saw a truck heading down

[368] Gustafson, Charles, Assistant Information Officer District 7, "Final Stretch of Ridge Route," State Public Works Bulletin, May – June 1971, p. 10.

[369] Jones, Nick, Associate Transportation Engineer, Caltrans, Los Angeles.

the grade at a high rate of speed. It crashed into a sign that warned trucks to go slowly, and blew up. We got there within a minute. There was a tremendous explosion. The southern San Joaquin Valley was lit up like daylight, Hall recalled. We found the freeway in flames. We found out later it was a toxic pesticide of some kind. I guess everyone has a little bit of John Wayne in them at one time or another. I tried to find the driver and was exposed to the fumes. That's when we found out it was bad stuff and I stayed. I didn't want anyone else to be exposed he said. The body of the truck driver was found under the wreckage. It took Kern County firefighters an hour to control the flames fueled by the 500 five-gallon cans of chemical. It took Hall, his doctors and the CHP the better part of a year to agree his mental and physical problems were a result of the exposure to toxic fumes. More than a week passed after the 1978 wreck before the Department of Transportation thought it had cleaned up the residue of the chemical. As a final inspection was being made, crews saw a grasshopper jump onto the roadway and die. Part of the freeway had to be replaced before officials were satisfied that motorists would be safe."

In addition to the possibility of having an accident, another menace confronting motorists along the remote Ridge Route was that of the highwayman. I suppose they were a hold over from the Wild West days when the stagecoach was held up. This modern day (1915) scourge of society would lay wait at a lonely section of road where one would slow down to navigate one of the many curves, then jump out and stop the unsuspecting motorist. What follows are a few newspaper accounts of such incidences.

The <u>Newhall Signal & Saugus Enterprise</u>, December 21, 1923: "Five cars have been held up and robbed by highway bandits near Lebec on the Ridge in the last few days. On one occasion a Ford car was taken away from its owner, a Bakersfield man. Recently a man in a big Marmon was coming down the Ridge when two bandits attempted to stop him. But instead of stopping he gave the machine more gas and ran over one of the highwaymen. And he did not stop to see how badly the bandit was injured."

The Newhall Signal & Saugus Enterprise, January 8, 1925: "Held Up On Ridge Road. Frank Lantam, traveling salesman from Oakland, reported in Santa Barbara recently that he encountered armed highway bandits on the Ridge Route eluding them only because his car responded quickly. He says while driving to Los Angeles in the night he had slowed down for a curve, when a young man leaped onto the running board and, leveling a revolver, commanded 'We'll stop here, bud and see what you've got in the car.' The robber also declared that he would shoot if Lantam put his hands on the wheel. Another bandit came running up, and Lantam says he stopped by shoving out the clutch, but left the car in second gear. Just then another car rounded the curve and, taking advantage of the interest of the robbers in that car, Lantam accelerated his car, and shot ahead, throwing the bandit from the running board, and the motorist made his escape. Other motorists, it is said have reported bandits operating almost fearlessly on the Ridge."

The next report although dated March 30, 1933, still took place along the 1915 highway.

The Newhall Signal & Saugus Enterprise, March 30, 1933: "Hold Up On Ridge Route. A report to the Sub-Station 6 officers states that David Hoffman a truck driver, was held up on the Ridge Route, about 4 o'clock p.m. Monday while traveling north. A man stood in the middle of the road and waved him down. 'Detour' he shouted, and Hoffman brought the truck to a stop. Then the man showed a big revolver and told Hoffman to 'stick'em up' which Dave promptly did. Then a second man got out of a coupe parked near by and came over and robbed him of $55 in money and a gold watch. In the car into which the two men got after the robbery was a woman. They drove off toward Los Angeles. The alarm was given, but so far no trace of the robbers has been discovered. They are described as about 5 feet 5 inches to 5 feet 8 inches tall, but the description of their dress was rather hazy."

The most heinous crime to occur on the old Ridge Route took place in October of 1953, 20 years after the road was bypassed in favor of the Ridge Alternate, (U. S. Highway 99). The following account has been edited. "John Richard Jensen, a 28 year old homicidal psychopath on leave from Camarillo State Mental Hospital used his liberty for the purpose of gratifying his lusts for degeneracy and murder. His very release raised serious question about the parole procedure that allowed his release." Jensen had picked up a 21-year old Marine Corp sergeant in San Fernando Valley on his way to Bakersfield from the Marine Corp Depot at San Diego. Jensen told the Marine he would gladly take him to Bakersfield, however, had to make a side trip on the way. "Jensen was driving a black 1937 Pontiac sedan that had been 'booby-trapped.'" Jensen had rigged cords to a stockless 22-caliber rifle that was located behind the passenger seat where the young Marine was sitting. On their way north, Jensen turned east from U. S. Highway 99 onto State Highway 138 then south onto the old deserted Ridge Route toward Sandberg's. Approximately a mile or so south of the once famous Sandberg Hotel, Jensen pulled the cord that fired the rifle into the Marine's back. Fortunately, the bullet hit a steel spring in the seat deflecting the deadly projectile. "The bullet missed its mark but caused the seat cushion spring to recoil and deliver a strong stunning blow to the Marine's lower back. Realizing that his murderous attempt failed, Jensen picked up a hammer and struck the Marine on the head. Jensen pulled him out of the car.

The Marine, dazed from the blow managed to kick Jensen knocking him to the ground. Jensen then grabbed a shotgun and shot the Marine in the chest. After pulling him to the side of the road Jensen dumped him in a shallow ditch and covered him with dirt. Jensen continued south toward Castaic. Miraculously the young man, covered in blood and dirt survived and managed to reach the old Sandberg Hotel nearly two miles away. "Lucky" Stevens, lease holder of the closed facility, stuffed a towel in the young man's chest to control bleeding then used his old crank wall phone to notify the sheriff, giving a description of Jensen's car from information the Marine provided. Jensen was apprehended at the south end of the Ridge Route near Castaic. "Lucky" Stevens told me they found the 12 gauge shot gun and 22 rifle that was triggered with the drawstring. The Marine's stolen watch and other personal items were also found in the car. "Lucky" told me that Jensen was eventually put to death for his premeditated murderous plot on the unsuspecting service man. It was fortunate for the marine that Lucky was living at the closed hotel, the last remaining building still standing on the remote and forgotten road.[370][371] Lucky's swift action indeed saved the Marine's life and helped the police apprehend Jensen.

Sandberg's
Courtesy Temblor Masonic Lodge Fellows Cal.

[370] "Psychopath Murderer declines to break down," The Newhall Signal and Saugus Enterprise, October 8, 1953.

[371] Stevens, op. cit.

1922 Snow Storm
Courtesy Pete Gianopulos

CHAPTER 22

The January 1922 Snow Storm

On Sunday, January 29,1922, Kern County was hit with the most ferocious snowstorm ever recorded in the region. Twenty five cars were stranded in a blinding snow storm on the Ridge Route between Sandberg's Summit Hotel and Bailey's Ranch at the west end of Quail Lake, (formerly Crane Lake). Motorists, including women and children, were in extreme danger due to the freezing weather and the lack of any food. A Pacific Telephone & Telegraph Company lineman was patrolling the Long Distance Toll Lines on snowshoes in an attempt to locate wires that had broken from the weight of ice when he spotted the stranded and desperate motorists. His attempt to reach them proved futile so he turned about and made haste to reach the local ranger station. The ranger, after hearing the lineman's report telephoned Bakersfield for help. In the interim, a group of brave men set out from Sandberg's with a team of horses to bring blankets and food to the stranded vehicles but after a mile were forced to return when the horses were unable to penetrate the impassable snowdrifts. When the highway commission in Bakersfield heard the news, a cooperative effort was established between the commission, the county board of supervisors and the sheriff's office to form a rescue party. Their plan was to use heavy caterpillar tractors and road drags. All available equipment would be pressed into service and sent to the Ridge Route.

Pacific Telephone snowplow helping the
state maintenance crew clear the highway

State Maintenance
Crew Plowing the
Road
Courtesy Caltrans

Section 7 L. A. 4 – D,
Sta. 400 places this
view north of Cas-
well's, Feb. 4, 1922
Courtesy Caltrans

On the southern end of the road, two touring cars and a truck loaded with food and various other items left Los Angeles hoping to get through and help anyone mired in the heavy snowdrifts. Mr. Hansen, the district plant manager of Pacific Telephone & Telegraph Company, dispatched a gang of his men from the line crew stating that they would make a determined effort to reach anyone stranded along the road. They headed north to tackle the Ridge as the thermometer continued to drop. If they were successful in their mission, Mr. Hansen said his men would return to repairing the telephone wires destroyed by the storm. With the Ridge Route closed motorists heading south had to wait out the storm in Bakersfield. Two hundred automobiles were tied up in that city. Hotels were overflowing and accommodations were difficult to acquire if at all. The Automobile Club of Southern California was credited in getting the word out that the Ridge Route was impassable thus minimizing a situation that could have been much worse.[372] [373]

On Tuesday, January 31st. word began to trickle in regarding the various rescue attempts. The Automobile Club of Southern California indicated in their most recent report that 100 people had been rescued from the peril of the storm. Club information revealed others were stranded between Sandbergs and National Forest Inn. A road gang was attempting to battle their way through to reach that stretch of the road. Earlier in the morning the rescue team from Bakersfield successfully reached 48 people that had taken refuge at the Tejon Ranger Station. After being given food, forty-two of the survivors that included five women and two children opted to endure the arduous hike to Lebec where they would find haven at the Durant Hotel. Management at the hotel made preparations for their arrival. Four women and two men refused to leave the ranger's cabin until communication was restored along the highway. The Automobile Club of Southern California also reported that several vehicles under their direction successfully pushed their way through to National Forest Inn rescuing more

[372] "Storm Traps Scores on Ridge Route," The Bakersfield Californian, January 30, 1922.

[373] "Wide Areas In Kern Buffeted By Storm," The Bakersfield Californian, January 30, 1922.

than thirty motorists on their way. The rescue party said they encountered snowdrifts from four to seven feet in depth but would press on if at all possible.[374]

On Wednesday February 1st The Bakersfield Californian reported that 200 people had been rescued. One hundred and fifty people were still stranded at Sandberg's Summit Hotel. [375]

By Thursday February 2nd the Automobile Club rescue team had managed to advance north from National Forest Inn reaching Kelly's where they found 38 people in acute distress. A 6-month-old baby at that location was said to be near death having existed on nothing but sugar water for two days. The rescue parties managed to press on and negotiate the entire highway. Miraculously those stranded on the Ridge in transit were all accounted for and there was no loss of life along the highway due to the storm. Road crews projected that the Ridge Route might be opened Saturday depending upon their progress in clearing the snowdrifts.[376]

North of Sandberg's in the 1922 snowstorm. Robert Lester "Bob" Chambers owned his own trucking company operating out of Taft. Bob is driving the truck coming down the grade. He would place newspapers in his shirt to insulate himself against the penetrating cold temperature.
Courtesy Gail Chambers

---

[374] "Three Have Feet Frozen; Many Are in Peril, Is Fear," The Bakersfield Californian, January 31, 1922.

[375] "Many Not Rescued From Snow Area," The Bakersfield Californian, February 1, 1922.

[376] "All Storm Victims Of Ridge Are Succored," The Bakersfield Californian, February 2, 1922.

CHAPTER 23

The Ridge Alternate (U. S. Highway 99)

By 1929 it became apparent that a new high-speed road was needed. An alignment was chosen through Piru Canyon. The new lower elevation "Ridge Alternate" highway would not only be 9.6 miles shorter it would be engineered to handle a much higher rate of speed. A three-lane concept was employed in building the road in hopes that it would minimize the passing maneuver that constantly plagued the old highway.[377] The greatest problem encountered during construction was the necessity to remove a small mountain. Avoiding the difficulty would compromise the high standards of alignment that were agreed upon at the beginning of the project. In a stretch of 400 feet, 230,000 cubic yards of rock were removed. This herculean effort created a huge pyramid that became a prominent landmark of the highway. [378] Pyramid Lake severs the Ridge Alternate and derives its name from the once prominent landmark. Work began on the new highway in 1930 and by late 1933 the 27-mile stretch between Castaic and Gorman opened for traffic. Like the original Ridge Route that opened in October of 1915, the Ridge Alternate officially opened on October 29, 1933, as U. S. Highway 99.[379] The new three-lane highway extended from Castaic to Gorman. From Gorman north, the 1915 Grapevine alignment was still in use. Years later when the Interstate number system was implemented, it became State Highway 99. By 1936 a new six and one half mile, three-lane alignment replaced the old tortuous Grapevine Grade of the original highway.[380]

---

[377] Fluter, op. cit. p. 10.

[378] Myers, op. cit., p. 16.

[379] "New Road Opened," The Newhall Signal & Saugus Enterprise, November 2, 1933.

[380] Gallagher, op. cit., p. 7.

Waiting for overheated engines to cool on the Ridge Alternate

From the beginning, economic studies indicated that within two and a half years the new road would justify itself. Speculation was that anyone using the highway would save time because you could safely maintain a higher rate of speed. You would also use less gasoline because the new road was shorter and the grades were less severe. In other words, in two and a half years these savings in time and gasoline would equal the cost of building the highway. The new road, thought to be safer, was plagued with accidents from the very beginning. Just 10 days after the road opened, three truck drivers died in a fiery crash on Five-Mile Grade, just above Castaic (see Accidents and Robberies). On the old road, head-on collisions were attributed to the numerous blind curves. On the new highway it was excessive speed. Far too often motorists would rear-end a slow moving truck. This perception problem with speed would be similar to freeway conditions today when in a split second you suddenly realize the traffic in front of you is at a stand still, and you frantically apply your brakes to avoid colliding with the cars in front of you.

In 1933 there were no freeways, however, the Ridge Alternate was similar to one if you considered speed. The third "middle passing-lane" was also a contributing factor

266

for accidents because it could be used by traffic traveling in either direction. It was soon referred to as the "suicide" lane. Impatient drivers would abuse the purpose of the lane and use it as an additional path for travel in their direction. The third lane soon became a major concern when it came to the matter of safety.

The Ridge Alternate was good for some time but increasing truck traffic began testing the limits of the highway. Studies were initiated in 1940 to address the capacity problems, however, the Second World War prevented any improvements. In 1947 construction crews began to upgrade and widen the highway. By 1952 the Ridge Alternate had been converted into a four-lane expressway.[381] Almost overnight it became the most heavily traveled long-distance roadway in the world.[382] A cement barrier separated the north and southbound lanes.

[381] Heckeroth, Heinz & Cohon, Barry, "The Ridge Route," California Highways and Public Works, p. 3, October 1965.

[382] Gustafson, Charles, op. cit., p. 11.

Ridge Alternate, U.S. 99

CHAPTER 24

Service Stops and Landmarks on the Ridge Alternate

Benny's Beanery

Benny's was a famous restaurant in Castaic that was located on the Ridge Alternate in the late 1940s. "Benny's Beanery" opened at the north end of Castaic. Benny and his wife "Babe" had a varied menu but it was his navy bean soup with ham that made him famous. People would come from miles away to have his soup. It was also a popular hang-out for the California Highway Patrol. The restaurant was located on the west side of the highway and south of the bridge on Castaic Road, formerly the Ridge Alternate. Today with the I-5 realignment the road simply dead-ends in a field not far from Benny's original location.[383]

Casa Baranca / The Ridge Tavern, a.k.a. El Rancho

An early landmark on the Ridge Alternate was Casa Baranca. The restaurant took its name from the large ravine (baranca in Spanish) on the west side of the highway. It was located about two miles north of Pyramid Lake on the east side of the road. This was the first restaurant you came to heading north from Castaic. The highway maintenance station was south of the restaurant. The restaurant closed in 1936. Charley Henderson re-opened it around 1938 changing the name to The Ridge Tavern. A Union Oil 76 gas station was also at this site. The Tavern looked like a big ranch house with four wagon wheels out front.[384] Bob Milander and his wife, Mildred, leased the restaurant in 1946 and 1947. Mr.

---

[383] Adkins, Tommy, Interview September, 2000.

[384] Lenke, op. cit.

Milander was killed in his private plane when it crashed into the mountains above Frenchman's Flat. The Restaurant closed upon his death.[385]

Caswell's

Caswell's was originally located on the 1915 highway. They relocated to the Ridge Alternate in 1934. They were located approximately one-half mile south of the Signal Cove Gas Station on the east side of the highway. Today, the Pyramid Lake Recreational Vehicle Resort at 45100 Copco Avenue, located 1.2 miles north of Smokey Bear Road on I-5, marks the site of the second Caswell operation. The former three-lane alternate pavement at this location has been covered over with the northbound lanes of the I-5 freeway.

Additional information can be found in Chapter 20 on "Service Stops and Landmarks on the Ridge".

Signal Cove Gas Station

Harriet (Holland) Filoteo, daughter of Harry Holland of Holland's Summit Café on the 1915 road, operated the Signal Cove Gas Station and towing service. Also on the property was "Mark's" Signal Cove Coffee Shop. The establishment was located on the east side of the three lane Ridge Alternate, 2.6 miles north of Smokey Bear Road.

The Signal Cove gas stations heavy-duty tow truck Courtesy Harriet (Holland) Filoteo

[385] Meeks, Jerold, telephone interview, June 11, 2001.

Gorman

Gorman remained a popular spot on the Ridge Alternate to grab a bite to eat, gas up and, if it was cold and raining, a place to seek refuge for the night.

Gorman on the Ridge Alternate. View looking southeast.
Courtesy Merle Porter photos, 1907 – 1989 Published by
Royal Pictures, www.merleporter.com
merleporter@merleporter.com

Gorman on the Ridge Alternate. View looking northeast.
Courtesy Merle Porter photos, 1907 – 1989 Published by
Royal Pictures, www.merleporter.com
merleporter@merleporter.com

The Giant Lemon

Caswell's and Holland's were the only businesses that migrated to the Ridge Alternate. Benny's Beanery, The Ridge Tavern, Young's Café and The Giant lemon were icons of the new highway. The Giant Lemon was a familiar landmark on the Ridge Alternate. Today a sweeping curve connects State Highway 138 to I-5 (north). The Giant Lemon was north of the curve on the east side of the highway. Verla Hoaglund managed the rather nice restaurant. The owner was Iner Hoaglund. Mr. Hoaglund's sister-in-law, Mrs. Osie Blood, was assistant manager. They originally started out selling drinks. Later they turned it into a fine restaurant, keeping the Giant Lemon appearance.[386] Anita Downing Stratton, whose great-grandfather, Fred Yant Hixon, ran the Southern California Edison Substation north of Deadman's Curve, recalls as a little girl of five, sitting in front of the large stone fireplace all night at The Giant Lemon sipping hot chocolate with her mother and father because a terrible snow storm had made travel all but impossible on the Ridge Alternate. It was 1941 and they were on their way from their home in Long Beach to Maricopa where they would spend Christmas with her grandparents, Grover and Sabina Hixon. Anita's father, George Downing, owned an oil field trucking business and was delivering a truckload of equipment to Bakersfield. The next morning when it was safe to proceed Anita and her two year old little brother, George Downing Jr., got into their new 1941 Chrysler with their mother, Margaret Hixon-Downing, behind the wheel. Margaret was following her husband's truck as they caravanned north. A short distance beyond the small community of Grapevine, after successfully descending the dangerous snow covered grade, Anita leaned against the rear door handle causing the suicide door (a door hinged to open into the wind) to open. She fell from the car onto the pavement receiving a head wound that required eight stitches at the Bakersfield hospital. It was a disappointing experience for her as she had received a pair of roller skates for Christmas that year and was not allowed

---

[386] Lenke, op. cit.

to use them until she had healed. Extremely lucky and none the worse from the experience, Anita's father told her mother "that was it" for having Christmas anywhere but home. From then on her grandparents came to their house in Long Beach every Christmas.[387]

Young's Café

Young's was a small café that was located four miles south of Gorman on the east side of the road north of the I-5, State Highway 138 transition and north of The Giant Lemon. Additional information regarding the site can be found under the history of "Kelly's" in Chapter 20 on "Service Stops and Landmarks on the Ridge".

Holland's Summit Café

Harry Holland's original operation was on the 1915 highway. When the Ridge Alternate opened he relocated to what today is the I-5 summit. His new gas station and larger restaurant was located on the east side of the highway. He also had several sleeping cabins. Additional information can be found under "Holland's Summit Café" in Chapter 20 on "Service Stops and Landmarks on the Ridge".

Holland's Summit Café on the Ridge Alternate. View looking south.
Courtesy Harriet Holland-Filoteo

[387] Stratton, Downing, Anita, Interview, December 9, 2000.

Holland's Summit Café on the Ridge Alternate.
View looking north.
Courtesy Harriet Holland-Filoteo

Holland's Summit Café on the Ridge Alternate
Courtesy Harriet Holland-Filoteo

Tejon Pass Summit on the Ridge Alternate
Courtesy Harriet Holland-Filoteo

Florafaunium

Another landmark on the Ridge Alternate highway in front of the Lebec Hotel was Emery Whilton's Florafaunium. Keep in mind the original highway at this location had been widened and became the Ridge Alternate. The Florafaunium was south of the hotel coffee shop and garage and sat behind the Don Pedro Fages historical marker.[388]

Emery Whilton's Florafaunium
Courtesy Pomona Public Library, Frasher Collection

[388] Hill, op. cit, p. 8.

A winter snow scene of Emery Whilton's Florafaunium.
The Lebec Hotel Coffee Shop is Whilton's next door
neighbor in this view looking north.
Courtesy Jerold Ray Meeks

The Florafaunium housed a collection of California birds, animals and wild flowers. Whilton, a resident of Taft, convinced the Kern County board of supervisors to move an old building from Bakersfield to Lebec for his museum. Kern County constructed the building for the 1939 World's Fair in San Francisco. When the fair closed the building was disassembled and moved to Bakersfield. His Florafaunium also served as the welcome center for motorists entering Kern County from the south. The Tehachapi, Bakersfield 7.7 earthquake of July 21, 1952, severely damaged the museum and it was torn down. The exhibits were relocated to Bakersfield.

Directly across from the historical Fages marker, Milton Lenke had a Mobil gas station. When the three-lane road went through it took out the station and Mobil relocated Lenke to the west side of the old road where two round cement foundations remain. They are about a foot in diameter and approximately one foot high. Mobil gave him the building for one dollar, but he leased the station property. This station was located north of the Lebec Hotel Coffee Shop near the southbound I-5 Lebec exit. Previously, Lenke had operated the Standard Station in

Gorman and after three years with Standard, purchased the Texaco Station that was once located where the south parking lot of Carl's Jr. is today. When Milt first arrived in California, he worked for Tom O'Brien at the Lebec Hotel's Coffee Shop down in front of the hotel.[389]

Lebec Hotel and Coffee Shop

The Ridge Alternate was almost on the same alignment as the 1915 Ridge Route road and was directly in front of the opulent hotel. With more dependable automobiles and the better highway, many motorists passed up the grand hotel and motored to Bakersfield where accommodations were cheaper. Although the hotel did not attract the number of overnight guests it once did, their coffee shop down on the highway remained a popular stopping point and produced more income than the hotel.

Lebec Hotel Coffee Shop
Courtesy Merle Porter photos, 1907 – 1989 Published by
Royal Pictures, www.merleporter.com
merleporter@merleporter.com

---

[389] Kaufman, op. cit.

Many people mistakenly believe the Ridge Alternate was the first highway over the mountains. All three highways, the first Ridge Route of 1915, the Ridge Alternate of 1933 and the current I-5 Ridge Route of 1970 (part of the National System of Interstate and Defense Highways)[390] take their name from the 1915 road that weaved its path over the (Ridge) of the mountains to form the (Route) that connected northern and southern California.

Poor's Shell Station

Francis and Ruth Poor operated the Meadow Creek Shell gas station and garage that was located on the Ridge Alternate, opposite the Lebec Mobil Refinery and pumping station. The pumping station is located at the intersection of Lebec Road and Lebec Oaks Road. Poor's station was on the west side of the Ridge Alternate directly east of this intersection. The Poor's leased the property from La Mar and Marie Jeppson who owned the small café and motel north of the gas station. Francis and Ruth Poor lived in Lebec and had a neighbor by the name of Rich, so here we had the Poor and Rich living by one another![391]

Meadow Creek Shell Station
Courtesy Barbara (Jeppson) Gleghorn

[390] Gustafson, op. cit., p. 12.

[391] Poor-Watson, Alberta, telephone interview, June 13, 2001.

Jeppson Café & Motel

La Mar and Marie Jeppson operated a small café on property they owned north of Poor's service station. Mr. Jeppson worked for the Lebec Mobil Refinery and pumping station, and he and his wife lived in company housing on the refinery property. Behind his café he built a four-unit motel. At a later date he built four more. The rear of the motel faced the old Ridge Route. The café, of course, faced the new Ridge Alternate. When the three-lane Ridge Alternate was widened to four-lanes, the motel was demolished and the café was moved back from the highway to the west. When I-5 was constructed Jeppson's Café was demolished along with Poor's gas station, however, the garage building was moved to Lebec. Both the café and gas station were built in 1946. The Jeppson's Motel featured "Simmon's mattresses, hot & cold showers and panel ray heat". Room rates started at $2.50. Their phone number was Lebec 2743.[392]

Jeppson's Café, view looking north. Courtesy Barbara Jeppson-Gleghorn

---

[392] Jeppson-Gleghorn, Barbara, telephone interview, June 13, 2001.

Jeppson's Café, view looking north, Dec. 1949
Courtesy Barbara Jeppson-Gleghorn

Jeppson's Café, inside view
Courtesy Barbara Jeppson-Gleghorn

Jeppson's Motel,
south end of Café in
background
Courtesy Barbara
Jeppson-Gleghorn

A short time after 1949 a trailer park opened directly south of the former location of Jeppson's Café and Motel and Poor's gas station, however, it did not last very long. It seems the area is low and the water table is high. Prior to 1949 water was being pumped from the site for use on a ranch down below the Grapevine. Due to environmental concerns the pumping operation was terminated, and the land reverted to a marsh thus forcing an end to the trailer-park operation. At one time, Velma Meeks was the cook at the Jeppson's café.[393]

Frank Butler

In 1942 Mr. Frank Butler, a screenwriter for Paramount Pictures, built a comfortable home 1.8 miles up behind the Lebec Mobil Oil Refinery and pumping station at 2140 Lebec Oaks Road. It was located on the south side of Lebec Oaks

---

[393] Kaufman, op. cit.

Road directly west of John's Road. The beautiful home had a large swimming pool in front and was built close to the mountain. Unfortunately, the house burnt to the ground in 2000 while it was being remodeled. Mr. Butler had an interest in the Lebec Hotel. If you recall, the hotel was the "watering hole" for the Hollywood elite. Mr. Butler, in addition to writing the "Road Show" pictures for Bob Hope and Bing Crosby, also wrote the screenplay for "Going My Way" and "The Greatest Show on Earth."[394] Another screenwriter living in the area was Dalton Trumbo. He was banned from Hollywood as a result of the McCarthy hearings that attempted to identify members of the Communist Party in the movie industry.

[394] Watson, Alberta, telephone interview, June 13, 2001.

CHAPTER 25

Interstate 5

In the 1950s growth in Los Angeles was expanding rapidly. Nearby in San Fernando Valley urban development was in full swing. The Ridge Alternate, being the direct north-south artery, would soon approach its designed capacity. By 1955 the California Division of Highways formulated plans to build a new six-lane freeway to replace the Ridge Alternate. Before they had secured funds for the project it was determined that eight lanes would be needed.[395] Plans for the new freeway were formalized between 1957 and 1958. Actual construction began in June 1963. At Castaic the steep Five-Mile Grade of the old Ridge Alternate was converted into the northbound uphill lanes of the new freeway. The newly built southbound lanes, a quarter-mile to the east, were engineered with a gentler grade and assigned to downhill traffic in order to minimize run-a-way truck problems. To incorporate Five-Mile Grade as a northbound route for the new Interstate, crossovers had to be provided that in effect reversed the alignments. Normally heading north on a north / south divided highway, you would have the northbound lanes on the right and the southbound lanes on the left. At Five-Mile Grade the layout was reversed. Doing so saved money and reduced the possibility of run-a-way trucks coming down off the grade. Before the present alignment was finalized one study suggested a 9,600-foot-long tunnel as part of a new route to connect the San Joaquin Valley to Los Angeles. Ultimately, the proposal was found to be financially impractical.[396]

The San Gabriel and Tehachapi Mountains, formed by earthquake activity are similar to a leaning layer cake. The

[395] Cronk, op. cit., p. 10.

[396] Heckeroth, op. cit., p. 10.

283

various layers of earth are separated not by frosting but slippery layers of clay. Constructing a highway across such terrain presents unusual engineering challenges, mainly in dealing with unstable soil. When the earth is disturbed or scraped away, rain can penetrate into the clay layers and initiate a serious landslide. This was the case in building the Interstate. The most serious slide occurred on the night of November 1, 1968. A newly-constructed embankment apparently sealed off an underground spring. Percolating upward, the water began to build up hydraulic pressure inside the mountain. The resulting landslide destroyed a quarter-mile section of graded freeway hurling it to the canyon below. To overcome the problem, three-inch pipes were driven into the mountain to siphon off the water. Two hundred thousand gallons of water poured out of the pipes each day for two solid weeks. After a great deal of work the soil was finally stabilized. In building the 45-mile Interstate 69 million cubic yards of dirt were moved, a job that would have been impossible without modern earthmoving equipment.[397] On Monday, August 24, 1970, the last section of the Interstate was opened to traffic.

Summation

The original 1915 Ridge Route was constructed, graded and paved at an approximate cost of $1,500,000.[398] As traffic increased in volume and speed, the sharpest curves of the road were "day-lighted" but by 1929 it became apparent that any further major improvement on the highway would not be justified in proportion to the resulting savings to traffic, thus marking the end of the road.[399] Construction of the road was financed with bonds and, although it was left to the elements, in 1933 when the Ridge Alternate opened, the bonds were not paid off until 1965.[400]

[397] Cronk, op. cit., p. 9.

[398] Dektar, op. cit., p. 9.

[399] Myers, op. cit., p. 16.

[400] Bezzerides, op. cit., p. 9.

The Ridge Alternate was constructed at a cost of $3,500,000.[401] Unlike the 1915 highway that was constructed with bond money, the Ridge Alternate was financed entirely with gas-tax funds and was paid for before it opened.[402] In 1947 after the Second World War, a $13,500,000-face lift was initiated to convert the road to a four-lane expressway.[403] Five years later in 1952, the four-lane conversion was completed.

In 1955 the California Division of Highways formulated plans for a six-lane freeway to replace the Ridge Alternate Expressway. Before any funding had been secured it was determined that eight-lines would be required. Construction began in June of 1963. The final segment of the project was completed on August 24, 1970. The original cost to construct the Interstate over the Ridge Route was projected to be approximately $90,000,000. After all was said and done the total cost of the project factored out to be $103,000,000.[404]

The minimum radius curve on the original 1915 Ridge Route was 70 feet. On the 1933 Ridge Alternate the minimum radius was 1,000 feet.[405] The 1970 Interstate 5 was engineered to have a minimum curve radius of 3,000 feet.[406]

The old Ridge Route has long silently awaited an unknown fate. It was left to the mercy of the elements in 1933 when the Ridge Alternate replaced it with a more direct path through Violin Canyon. My first encounter with the road occurred in 1955. I was 18-years old and had just started to work for Pacific Telephone. I needed transportation to go back and forth to work, and my parents helped me purchase my first car, a brand new 1955 Ford. I didn't need much of an excuse to get behind the wheel to enjoy my newly-found freedom. I stumbled upon the deserted, twisting Ridge Route winding

[401] Cronk, op. cit., p. 10.

[402] Bezzerides, op. cit., p. 9.

[403] Los Angeles Times, December 10, 1952.

[404] Gustafson, op. cit., p. 10.

[405] Gallagher, op. cit., p. 6.

[406] Heckeroth, op. cit., p. 3.

across the top of the mountains between Castaic and State Highway 138. I pretty much forgot about the road until 1991 when I was heading north over the new I-5 Ridge Route to visit my parents in Visalia with my son, Jim, as passenger. He commented that the first road over the mountains must have been a real challenge for the early cars, and I immediately recalled my 1955 adventure. Having some spare time, we left the freeway at Templin Highway and headed east in an attempt to locate the original road. In a mile or so we found it, and cautiously followed it north, ignoring the sign, which states that it is not a through road! Although in bad shape, it was passable, and we were able to drive all the way to State Highway 138. Here we came upon a county crew resurfacing the northern end of the road.

I interrupted their work momentarily to ask if this was still officially designated a county road. They didn't know, stating that they only maintained the pavement up to the national forest boundary. With this limited offering of information, I recall thinking that someone should look into the possibility of preserving this remaining stretch of the original Ridge Route. I wondered how you could go about saving a road when there is no agreement on where it begins or ends. I later found that it is generally defined as that section of highway, which winds over the San Gabriel and Tehachapi Mountains between Castaic Junction on the south and extending to the bottom of Grapevine Grade on the north.

The more I looked at the Ridge Route, the more I realized how this single highway affected the development of California. I began gleaning information from old newspapers and magazines, going to universities, libraries, contacting historians and searching through endless reels of microfilm. As I collected documents and pictures, I became more excited about the history of the road. Before I realized it, I became a "someone", who, with others, would help to preserve this remaining, virtually undisturbed, example of early highway construction.

The time came to find out what the requirements are for submitting a preservation nomination. I contacted the California State Office of Historical Preservation and, to my surprise, learned that I could not submit nomination papers. There was a technicality. My project area was for the major part on U. S. national forest land. In addition, I was told that it is much more difficult to qualify a road, as opposed to a stationary site. After so much effort, this setback rendered my hopes a devastating blow. For the first time I had doubts that I could accomplish my goal.

I contacted the Angeles National Forest headquarters and ultimately presented my intentions to Michael McIntyre, Forest Archaeology Supervisor. He told me that the Ridge Route had always been a candidate for historic recognition; however, no one had pushed to bring it about. Mike referred me to Doug Milburn, his colleague and fellow archaeologist. Perhaps we could work jointly toward nominating the Ridge Route for the recognition it deserved.

Douglas Milburn, foreground and Michael McIntyre, background, Angeles National Forest archaeologists. Picture taken at Kelly's Ranch.

Since I could not singularly submit the paperwork, I jumped at this opportunity. Doug and I worked together diligently for five years, I continuing to collect information and Doug inputting the information onto the various nomination forms. It was not an easy task, considering his limited time as the constraints of the recently tightened budget hit the national forests. Originally, Doug Milburn and I had planned to nominate that portion of the Ridge Route beginning at Castaic and ending at State Highway 138 to the north. Our paperwork also listed each historic site along the old highway such as Sandberg's, the Tumble Inn etc. The California State Historical Resources Commission held a public meeting on February 2, 1996, with an agenda of nominations (the Ridge Route being one of them) to be considered for approval. (State Historic Preservation Offices, or "SHPOs," have to approve National Register nominations before they can be forwarded to the United States Department of The Interior for Federal evaluation and acceptance). When our Ridge Route nomination came before the commission, a petition was submitted that opposed the nomination. Various property owners on the southern end of the road and outside of the forest boundary had signed the petition fearful that historic status would negatively impact the property they owned fronting the Ridge Route. I tried to reassure those present that we were only nominating the highway, which in no way should affect their property values. After hearing the petitioners, the late David G. Cameron, chairperson of the commission, removed our nomination for consideration suggesting we meet with the owners in an attempt to resolve their concerns. This was an unexpected setback after all of our hard work. Additionally, the commission informed us that we could not include Sandberg's, the Tumble Inn and other historic sites along the road on the same form. We were told that each historic site would have to be submitted on a separate form.

Due to the constraints related to the tightened forest service budget and the protracted negotiations that would be necessary to resolve the property owners concerns, we decided to expedite the process by truncating our nomination to include only the 17.6 miles of road entirely within the forest boundary. The historic sites along the route would have to be dealt with later.

Our reward came on September 25, 1997, when the National Park Service notified us that they had reviewed our nomination and placed the road onto the National Register. Mr. Paul R. Lusignan, the gentleman that reviewed our paperwork at the Department of The Interior, commented that our nomination forms were one of the most well documented submissions that he had reviewed in some time. So much so that with the information provided he also included each historic location along the highway, i. e. Sandberg's, the Tumble Inn, Kelly's etc. His decision to incorporate each historic site with the road's nomination negated the necessity to submit separate nomination forms for each venue, a process that would have extracted a great deal of time and effort. Our hard work had finally paid off.

Regretfully we had to forgo including that segment of the old road from the forest boundary south to the community of Castaic. The North Lake housing development in Castaic destroyed a portion of the original highway that formerly passed in front of Castaic Brick. Future developments in Castaic will most likely destroy additional sections of the road. Major developments are also being considered at the northern end of the road near State Highway 138. The listed portion of the old highway on Angeles National Forest property will at least be immune from the march of unrelenting development and afford future generations the ability to travel back in time on California's historic icon highway, the 1915 Ridge Route.

It was never my intention to write regarding the Ridge Route. My objective from the beginning was to get the road on the National Register so it would be preserved and protected. I saw this as a very unique opportunity because most of the road is intact and in its original state. Most of it is on National Forest property which has prevented it from being compromised over the years.

The road is historically famous in many aspects. It was one of the first highways built by the State, and the first mountain highway ever engineered over such unforgiving terrain. Politically this road prevented State division. Economically, this road provided the conduit to expand commerce benefiting both the north and the south. Today the Ridge Route is considered a major military highway. Although this Interstate Highway costs more to maintain than other similar routes, it will never be closed for any extended period. This was demonstrated by the record time the road was restored to service after the Northridge earthquake severed it in 1994.

Liebre Summit 1926
Courtesy Bernice Wilson
L-R: john Cederlind, Myrtle Cederlind, Bernice Wilson, nee Cinderlind and Jennie Holmquist

ACKNOWLEDGEMENTS

I want to thank Lois McDonald, former Editor of the California Historian, for encouraging me to document my research in this book. My personal appreciation is extended to Bonnie Ketterl-Kane, historian, author and founder of the "Ridge Route Communities Museum & Historical Society." Bonnie graciously shared information from her research and provided the picture of Holland's Summit Café. I thank my good friend, George Sigler for assistance with surface reconnaissance and documentation. The Sacramento Staff of Caltrans, operating under the constraints of a budget reduction, generously assisted in locating historic photos of the Ridge Route. I want to thank John M. Swisher, author and Regional Vice President of the San Bernardino / High Desert Region of the Conference of California Historical Societies, for his help with some of the political aspects of my project. I thank John W. Robinson, prominent author and leading authority on the San Gabriel Mountains, for his encouragement and support. David L. Cole, Editor of the Lincoln Zephyr Owners Club magazine provided valuable help with touring maps, gas stations, and information regarding the history of the Richfield Oil Company. His contribution was most significant and greatly appreciated. A special recognition goes to Douglas Milburn and Michael J. McIntyre, Angeles National Forest archaeologists, whose support and cooperation was vital in successfully placing the Ridge Route onto the National Register. These two gentlemen had to fill out reams of documentation so the Ridge Route nomination could be forwarded to Washington D. C. I am most indebted to my wife Marie for her help and support. Finally, I extend my appreciation and gratitude to all of the following people for their kind help and contributions.

Patti Ehret	Assistant Caltrans Administrator
Laurel Clark	Supervising Caltrans Librarian
Carol Gilbert	Caltrans History Librarian (Posthumously)
Fay Meek	Assistant Caltrans Administrator
Shirleigh Brannon	Caltrans History Librarian
Caltrans	Headquarters Photography Unit
Harlan H. Hill	Educator – Historian
Dace Taube	Curator, Regional History Center, USC
John Cahoon	Collections Manager, The Seaver Center for Western History Research
Mildred Wiebe	Tejon Ranch Co. Historian (Retired)
Charlotte Brown	Archivist, UCLA
Otto A. Sandberg	Sandberg Family History
Jack Rimmer	Fire Captain (Retired) Los Angeles County
Marvin and Bill Barns	General Petroleum History
Burton A. Burton	Sandberg Photos
Anna Pickner	Half Way Inn History
Frank Young	Young's Café History
Martha Forth	State Maintenance Camp History
Jack Farmer	State Maintenance Camp History
Glen Ralphs	Gorman History
Frank Kaufman	Kern County History
James E. & May Jean Graves	Martin's History
Tommy Adkins	Castaic Brick History
Milton & Louise Lenke	Lebec Hotel History
Charles H. Dodge	Ridge Route History
Sam & Gloria Azhderian	Castaic History
Harriet Holland-Filoteo	Holland Summit History
Edna Brodine	Ridge Route Trucking History
Gail Chambers	Ridge Route Trucking History
Dr. William A. Myers (Retired)	Southern California Edison Co. Historian
John W. Robinson	Author-Historian
Donald Arnot	President, Kern County Historical Society
Jan McLarty	Grapevine History
Nadine Truempler-Brown	Grapevine History
Sandra O'Brien	O'Brien Family History
Patrick O'Brien	O'Brien Family History
Walter Knapp	Kelly-Knapp Ranch History
Emmett Cooper	California State Fire Marshall, Petroleum Line History
Daniel Holthaus	1917 Model – T Ford
George A. Sedivy	Royal Pictures
Jack & Sidney Kelley	Directors, Ridge Route Preservation Organization (RRPO)
Bonnie Ketterl-Kane	RRPO Director, Author-Historian
Leon Warden	RRPO Director, Business Editor, The Newhall Signal

Index

ARCO: 34, 93
Arden Drive: 234, 239
Arizona: 63, 178, 240
Arkansas, Little Rock: 16
Army: 3, 10, 176, 240
Army Air Corp: 221, 240
Arrowhead Ginger Ale: 128
Artozque Brothers: 251
Arvin: 238
Ashland Kentucky: 178
Atlantic: 192
Atlantic Richfield: 34
Atmore, Minnie Mable: 126
Atmore, Richard: 66-78, 126-128
Auburn: 213
Auto Blue Book: 106, 176
Autocar: 56
Automobile Club of Southern California: 51, 73-75, 84, 85 87, 166, 263, 264
Avis, I. L.: 121, 122, 130
Azhderian, Sam & Gloria: 107, 108, 292

B
Bailey Ranch: 163-166, 172, 174, 261
Bailey, Marcos: 164
Bailey, William: 164
Baker, Leonard: 152
Baker, T. E.: 56
Bakersfield: iii, 2, 5, 12, 45, 50, 64, 71-73, 79, 84, 85, 94, 109, 126, 128, 129, 132, 141, 148, 161, 178, 179, 185, 192, 195, 196, 198, 203, 204, 212, 216, 221, 238-241, 247, 248, 251, 254–256, 258, 261, 263, 264, 272, 276, 277
Bakersfield & Los Angeles Fast Freight: 129
Bakersfield County Hospital: 238
Bald Mountain: 37, 38, 142, 159, 160
Bandidos: 21
Bank of America: 133
Banning, Phineas: 23, 24, 172
Barnes, Bill: 160, 161, 167
Barnes, Carolyn: 161
Barnes, Charlie: 162
Barnes, Marvin: 43, 153, 160-162, 167, 171
Barnes, Pete: 162
Barnes, Roy: 153, 161
Barnes, Tom: 162
Barneson, Harriett E.: 164
Barneson, John: 31, 164

Barnett Farm & Cattle Company: 220, 221
Barnhill, Jean Anne: 137
Barton, George: 167, 168
Battle of San Pasqual: 14
Bay Meadows: 186
Beacon Inn: 93
Beacon Stations: 93, 142
Beacon, Airplane: 93, 118, 142, 160
Beale, Edward Fitzgerald: 7, 10, 12-14, 25-27, 56, 158, 188
Beale's Cut: 17, 23-26, 56, 57, 63, 64
Bear Canyon: 133, 134
Beckley, H. G.: 60
Bell System: 180
Bell, Rex: 191
Belridge: 31
Benjamin, Ray: 196
Benny's Beanery: 269, 272
Berkley: 151
Bernhardt, Albert: 128
Berry, Dolores: 159
Best, J. B.: 85
Besyran, Eddie: 250
Beverly Hills: 201
Big Creek: 41, 42
Big Cut: 71, 119, 120
Birdsell, H. S.: 107
Black Gold: 178
Bliss, Oliver· 253
Blood, Osie: 272
Bolton, Professor Herbert Eugene: 4
Borel Power House: 42
Bouquet Canyon: 50, 57, 64, 72, 81, 82, 112
Bouquet Canyon Reservoir: 112
Bow, Clara: 191
Bower, Coie Francis: 179
Bowerbank: 58
Briggs, Adrian: 133
Briggs, Annie Rose: 133, 134, 141
Brinley, Charles: 25
British Petroleum: 34
Brock, Larry: 151
Brodersen, Bruno: 151
Brodine, J. D. "Dave": 109-111
Brown, Nadine Truempler : 225
Bucyrus Steam Shovel: 70
Budd, James H.: 47
Budnitsky, Bernard: 248

Budnitsky, Kate: 248
Buena Vista: 3
Buena Vista Aquatic Recreational Area: 3
Buena Vista Lake: 3, 4
Buick: 238
Burbank: 132, 153
Bureau of Highways: 47
Burlington Northern-Santa Fe Railroad: 10, 196
Bustillos, Charlie: 185, 197, 198
Butler, Frank: 200, 202, 281, 282
Butterfield Overland Stage Line: 2, 15-18, 24-26, 29, 63
Butterfield Station: 17, 171
Butterfield, John: 15, 16

C

"C" Blocks: 49
Cadillac: 149, 238
Cahuenga Pass: 1, 16, 17
Cajon Pass: 4
California: iii, 1-4, 7, 10-18, 21, 29, 44, 47-49, 51, 56, 61, 63,
64, 74-77, 88, 93, 124, 132, 138, 145, 147, 158, 160, 163, 174,
176, 178, 186, 213, 239-241, 245, 255, 276-278, 286, 289
California Aqueduct: 166
California Conservation Corp: 113, 125
California Department of Transportation: 256
California Division of Highways: 75, 283, 285
California Highway and Public Works: 75
California Highway Commission: 44, 48, 76, 77, 80, 81, 86
California Highway Patrol: 205, 252, 254-256, 269
California Historical Society, Los Angeles: 74
California Historian: 43, 291
California Originals: 152
California Spanish: 12
California Stage Company: 24
California State Historical Resources Commission: 288
California State Militia: 14
California State Office of Historical Preservation: 286, 288
California State Water Project: 112, 163, 166
Callahan Line Change: 102
Callahan, Cornelia Martinez: 100-105
Caltrans: 50, 59, 68-70, 72, 79, 82, 86, 89, 102, 120, 136, 139,
160, 163, 165, 166, 173, 174, 180, 199, 205, 208, 262, 291
Camarillo State Mental Hospital: 258
Camel: 10
Camel Corp: 10
Cameron, David G.: 288
Camp Tejon: 216, 217, 221

Cooke, Charles A.: 191
Copco Avenue: 171, 270
Corot: 12
Cottonwood Creek: 5
Cottonwood Trees: 166, 171
Count Edger Stanislaus V. Piontkowski: 145
Courtemanche: 114, 115
Courtemanche, Alfred: 135
Courtemanche, Charles: 114
Courtemanche, Frank: 135
Courtemanche, Harry: 114
Courtemanche, Louise: 114
Courtemanche, Mary Louise Ella: 135
Courtemanche, Nelson: 114
Cow Springs: 2
Cox, J. H.: 151, 152
Crane Company: 241
Crane Lake: 2, 162, 163, 167, 261
Crane, Rony: 163
Crenshaw Boulevard: 33, 179, 181
Crosby, Bing: 200, 282
Crystal Springs Trout Farm: 209
Cuddy Valley: 2
Cuesta Viejo: 23
Culebra Excavation: 71, 119, 120
Cullimore, Clarence: 12
Culver City: 93
Cummings, C. O.: 127
Cunniff, Michael: 135
Curry, Foster: 193
Curry's Lebec Lodge: 193
Cypress Trees: 201

D

Daly City: 138
Dailey, Wm.: 247
Dallas: 63
Daries, Pierre: 95, 96, 103-104, 247
Darlington, N. D.: 50, 51, 64, 81, 83
Davis, General Manager, Pacific Light and Power Co.: 41
Davis, Jefferson: 10
Days Inn Travel Lodge: 95
Deadman Canyon: 64
Deadman's Curve: 209-213, 216, 272
Death Curve: 210
Dean, James: 254
Deceta, Ignacia: 111

El Camino Viejo: 1
El Encanto Hotel: 191
El Paso: 67, 241
El Rancho: 269
El Segundo: 35
El Tejon: 14, 21
El Tejon Rancho: 14
El Tejon School: 203, 204, 221
Elderberry Forebay: 113
Elizabeth Lake: 1, 16, 42, 114, 142, 159, 163
Elizabeth Lake and Gorman Station Road: 159
Elizabeth Lake Sub Station: 42
Ellsworth, C. W.: 133
Emidio / Emigdio: 2, 32, 34
Empire Theater: 178, 179
England: 47, 103
Equilon: 35
Ernst, Paul: 250
Erskine, Cowee A.: 179
Eternal Valley Memorial Park: 17, 87
Eucalyptus: 88, 115
Evelyn: 127
Ever Green Café: 98, 99
Examiner: 51
Exxon Mobil: 31, 163

F

Fageol: 108, 250
Fages, Don Pedro: 3, 4, 275, 276
Fairbanks-Morse: 37
Fairmont: 2, 68
Fairmont Hotel: 191
Falcon Way: 177
Fargo, W. G.: 15
Fargo, Wells: 15
Farmer, Jack: 138, 140
Farmer, Martha: 138
Farmer, Rex: 138
FBI: 153
Federal Highway Act: 48
Federal Land Bank: 151
Feedmill Road: 91
Fellows: 37, 178
Fernando Station: 32
Field, Mr.: 93
Filoteo, Harriet (Holland): 251, 270, 273-275
Fish Hatchery: 234-236

General Motors: 186, 191
General Petroleum Corporation: 31, 33, 34, 37, 38, 41, 42, 103, 128, 129, 160, 163, 164
General Petroleum's Quail Lake Pumping Station: 160
General Pipe Line Company: 31, 32, 164
Gerald Desmond Bridge: 38
German: 144, 152, 153, 171, 206
German Shepard: 206
German Station: 171
Gertie: 192
Gianopulos, Pete: 260
Giant Lemon, (see The Giant Lemon)
Gillespie: 203
Gillette Mine: 133
Gillette, King: 133, 134
Gilmore Oil: 227
Gilroy: 16
Gleghorn, Barbara (Jeppson): 278-281
Glendale: 37, 38, 234, 239
Glendale Junior College: 237
Global Power Corp.:41
Golden State: 2, 34, 76
Going My Way: 282
Goni, John: 251
Gorman: iii, 2, 3, 17, 32, 37, 42, 74, 75, 128, 129, 141, 142, 159, 161-163, 167, 171, 172, 175, 176, 254, 265, 271, 273, 277
Gorman Coffee Shop & Hotel: 174, 175
Gorman Post Road: 37, 38, 162, 163, 167, 172, 175, 244
Gorman Ranch: 172
Gorman School: 142, 174, 175
Gorman Sr., James: 172
Gorman Station: 24, 171-173
Gorman, Jim: 172
Granite Gate: 143
Grant: 150, 151
Grant, John: 146
Grant, Marion: 146
Grant, Ulysses S.: 14, 158
Grant, Ulysses S. Jr.: 158
Grapevine: iii, 18, 32, 34, 37, 38, 42, 57, 75, 84, 85, 87, 94, 109, 162, 202, 203, 209, 212, 216, 217, 220-225, 227, 228, 230, 231, 233, 234, 237-242, 251, 252, 254, 255, 265, 272, 281
Grapevine Canyon: 3, 4, 37, 223
Grapevine Creek: 206, 216, 222-224, 236

Grapevine Grade: iii, 50, 57, 84, 85, 206, 225, 228, 241, 252, 253, 265, 286
Grapevine Road: 224
Grapevine Station: 17, 32, 33, 221, 229
Grapevine, The: iii, 18, 33, 34, 37, 42, 57, 75, 85, 87, 94, 109, 212, 216, 220, 238, 255
Graves, James E.: 105, 111-113
Graves, May Jean: 105, 112
Great Depression: 108, 254
Greenfield: 241
Greyhound: 175, 199
Griffith Company: 216
Grojean, Lillian: 152, 153
Guard Station: 124, 125

H
Hagle, Barbara: 55
Half Way House: 126
Half Way Inn: 126-128, 130, 141
Hall, Jerry: 255, 256
Hall, Mr.: 24
Hamlin, Ralph: 56
Hancock Park: 29
Hansen: 263
Harold's Club: 198
Hartley, Chuck: 209
Hart's Station: 18
Hayes, Herbert: 253
Hemet: 240
Henderson, Charley: 269
Henry Ford Avenue: 35
Highland Park: 234
Hixon, Fred Yant: 213, 214, 272
Hixon, Grover Celeveland: 213, 272
Hixon, Sabina: 272
Hixon-Downing, Margaret: 213, 214, 272
Hoaglund, Iner: 272
Hoaglund, Verla: 272
Hoffman, David: 257
Hoffman, Fred: 80, 83
Hogue, Lida: 220
Hogue, Mel "Tex": 220, 221
Holbrook, Jane: 237
Holland, Emily, Harriet, Ruth and Dolly: 169, 251, 270, 273-275
Holland, Gladys: 169
Holland, Harry: 142, 169, 270, 273
Holland's Summit Café: 168, 270, 272-274, 291

Hollandsville Station: 17
Hollywood: 1, 153, 154, 164, 200, 234, 282
Holmquist, Jennie: 290
Holthaus, Daniel: v, 244-246
Homestead Act: 151
Hoover Dam: 197
Hoover High School: 234, 237
Hope, Bob: 200, 282
Horseshoe Bend: 143, 144
Hosmer's Station: 18
Hotel Durant: 189, 192, 263
Hotel Hollywood: 191
Hudson Sprayer: 140
Hughes Lake: 4, 67, 99
Hughes, F.: 56
Humphrey, Hubert H.: 174
Hungry Valley: 37, 38, 164, 165
Huntington Lake: 41
Huntington Park: 253
Huntington, Henry: 41, 42
Hutchings, Georgia: 105

I

Imperial: 88
Indiana: 146
Incz: 247
Indian: 7, 15, 25, 61, 133, 134, 234
Indian Territory: 18
Irvine, R. C.: 47
Italy: 132, 196
I-5/Interstate 5: 2, 17, 32-34, 42, 61, 89, 102-104, 106, 112, 119, 126, 128, 142, 167, 171, 174, 176, 177, 202, 204, 205, 208, 209, 213, 216, 217, 225, 249, 252, 255, 269, 270, 272, 273, 277-279, 283, 284, 286

J

James, Harry: 200
Jappert, Jim: 255
Jeffery: 68
Jenkins, William Wirt: 134
Jensen, John Richard: 257, 258, 259
Jeppson Café & Motel: 279-281
Jeppson, La Mar: 278, 279
Jeppson, Marie: 278, 279
Jimeson & Wiesmann: 107
John Deere: 244
John's Road: 282

Johnson, Charles: 171
Johnson, J. A.: 185
Jolson, Al: 179
Jones, Seaborn "Pete": 188
Jones, Wm.: 249
Jones' Service Station: 100
Jose: 247
Junk Yard: 210

K

Kamprath: 57
Kane, Bonnie Ketterl-: 168
Kansas City Missouri: 75
Karnes & Klotfellers Restaurant: 109
Kashower, M. Co.: 117
Kaufman, Frank: 45, 206
Kaweah: 145
Kay, Ben: 133
Kearney, General: 14
Keaton, Buster: 191
Keller, Deputy: 251
Kelly Ranch: 126, 131-133, 141, 287
Kelly Ranch House: 131, 133
Kelly's: 126-128, 130, 133, 141, 264, 273, 289
Kelly's Half Way House: 126
Kelly's Half Way Inn: 126, 128, 130, 141
Kentucky: 164, 178, 196
Kern City: 56
Kern County: 35, 67, 84, 138, 152, 175, 188, 198, 201, 202, 221, 222, 228, 237, 240, 252, 256, 261, 276
Kern County Fire Department: 201
Kern County High School: 185, 196
Kern County Sheriff: 198
Kern River: 3, 7, 17, 21, 23, 42
Kern River # 1 Powerhouse: 42
Kettleman: 31, 37, 38
Kettleman North Dome: 31
Killingsworth, Arthur Earl: 126, 127
Killingsworth, Lila: 127
Kingman Arizona: 178
Kinsey Mansion: 163, 164
Kinsey Ranch: 137, 161
Kinsey, George E.: 137, 164
Kittridge Street: 132
Klaxon: 76
Knapp Ranch Park: 132
Knapp, Edwin Frank: 132

Knapp, Frank: 131-134
Knapp, Joe: 132
Knapp, Roy A.: 141
Knapp, Walter: 132, 134
Kongsberg, Norway: 145
Kress, M. C.: 4

L

La Canada: iii, 241
La Crescenta: 241
La Laguna de Chico Lopez: 2
La Liebre: 14
La Liebre Canyon: 37, 38
La Liebre Pumping Station: 32
Lake Hughes Road: 67, 99
Lambert, Frank: 115
Lancaster: 45, 50, 67, 85, 141, 162, 167, 174-176
Lancaster School: 141
Lang Station: 64
Lanier, Jimmy and Zoe: 237
Lankershim Boulevard: 32
Lantam, Frank: 257
Las Vegas: 197-199
Lea Wood, England: 103
Lebec: 2, 4, 32, 33, 37, 38, 43, 84, 88, 169, 180, 181, 185, 192, 196, 199, 200, 202-204, 209, 218, 220, 238, 252, 256, 263, 276-279, 281, 282
Lebec Community Church: 204
Lebec Garage: 184, 194, 195
Lebec Grammar School: 185, 196
Lebec Hotel: 4, 108, 141, 152, 178, 180-182, 184, 185, 187, 188, 190-194, 200-202, 209, 218, 275-277, 282
Lebec Lodge, Curry's: 193
Lebec Oaks Road: 204, 209, 278, 281
Lebec Post Office: 180
Lebec Pumping Station: 33
Lebec Refinery: 32, 33, 160, 220, 279, 281
Lebec Road: 4, 177, 178, 202-204, 209, 278
Lee Moor Contracting Company: 67, 68
Lenke, Louise: 202
Lenke, Milt: 204, 209, 276
Lenke, Terry: 209
Leona Valley: 142
LeTourneau & Lindberg: 60
Levitt, Ed & Dorothy: 158
Lewis, Art: 108
Libby Canyon: 155

Liberty V-12: 140
Liebre Gulch / Canyon: 37, 43, 135, 137, 165
Liebre Mountain: 43 – 45, 67, 126
Liebre State Highway Maintenance Camp: 134, 138, 139
Liebre Station: 17, 137
Liebre Summit: 121, 144, 290
Lillian: 234
Lincoln: 13, 234
Lincoln Highway: 76
Lincoln Nebraska: 241
Lincoln Zephyr: 144, 291
Lindbergh Jr., Charles: 192
Lindbergh, Anne: 191, 192
Lindbergh, Charles: 191, 192
Lindbergh, Jon, Land, Scott, Reeve & Anne: 192
Little Rock Arkansas: 16
Lloyd Massey & Howard J. Edgerton: 240
Lockey, Deputy: 251
Locomobile: 185
Lombard, Carol: 141, 200
Long Beach: 38, 80, 272, 273
Long, Deputy: 247
Lopez Station: 1
Lopez, Chico: 2
Loren's Garage: 245
Los Alamos: 14
Los Angeles: iii, 1, 2, 12, 16-18, 21, 23-26, 29, 31, 32, 37, 41,
42, 47, 48, 50, 51, 53, 56, 57, 63, 64, 67, 71-76, 79-81, 84, 85,
87, 90, 96, 108, 109, 114, 117, 119, 120, 122, 126, 128, 132,
144-146, 148, 152, 158, 159, 161, 162, 164, 170, 172, 174, 179,
181, 184, 191, 198, 199, 212, 226, 228, 238, 240, 241, 248, 250,
257, 263, 283
Los Angeles Area Chamber of Commerce: 74
Los Angeles Aqueduct: 1, 29
Los Angeles County: 44, 45, 72, 73, 81, 97, 99, 108, 112, 144,
153, 159, 222
Los Angeles County Board of Supervisors: 24–27, 63, 243, 253
Los Angeles County fire patrol station # 77: 45, 153, 159
Los Angeles County fire warden: 159
Los Angeles County Hospital: 141, 222, 223
Los Angeles County Museum of Natural History: 222, 223
Los Angeles County Road Department: 57
Los Angeles Examiner: 51
Los Angeles Express: 51
Los Angeles Railways: 41
Los Angeles River: 53
Los Angeles Star: 11

Los Angeles Times: 51, 103, 137, 146, 158, 202, 228, 252, 253
Los Angeles Water Bureau: 1, 29
Los Padres Gold Mine: 133, 134
Los Padres National Forest: 131
Lost Hills: 31
Louvre Saloon: 178
Love, Captain Harry: 21
Lowden's Garage: 87
Lusignan, Paul R.: 289
Lyons Station: 17, 18
Lyons, Sanford and Cyrus: 17

M

Mack Truck: 108, 110, 212, 249
MacVine, Sheriff: 247
Magic Mountain: 89
Mahoney Brothers: 67
Mahoney, Mrs.: 195
Main Street: 1
Malibu Canyon: 133
Malnic, Eric: 253
Manson, Marsden: 47
Manzana School: 175
Maricopa: 37, 245, 272
Marine Corp: 258
Marion Steam Shovel: 70
Mark's Signal Cove Coffee Shop: 270
Markel, Nelly B.: 108
Markell, Porter B.: 107, 108
Markell, Ruth: 107, 108
Marmon: 256
Marple Canyon: 103, 108
Marple, Thomas: 103
Martin, Mr.: 118
Martin's: 109, 111, 113
Martina, Gemma: 196
Martinez, Carlos, "Charlie": 103
Martinez, Leovigilda Del Campo: 103
Martmer, Laura: 226
Massey, Lloyd: 240
Maude, L.: 47
Mayer, Jim: 255
Maynard, Rea E.: 31, 164
Mesa Arizona: 240
McAvoy, John: 249
McCalley, Bruce: 246
McCarthy: 282

McDonald, Lois: 291
McDowell, C.: 250
McIntyre, Mike: 121, 131, 287, 291
McKee: 197
McKenzie, Bob: 155
McKenzie, James A.: 172
McKenzie, Mary: 172, 174
McKenzie, Westley: 155
McKittrick: 37, 56
McLarty, Brent Alan: 241
McLarty, Gerald Elliot: 240
McLarty, Jan Claire: 7-9, 12, 226, 228-232, 235, 236, 241
McLarty, Jane: 237-241
McLarty, Laura: 230, 234, 236, 237, 239
McLarty, Lawrence Leonard: 224-232, 234-237, 239, 241, 242
McLarty, Leonard Lawrence: 209, 224, 226-230, 234, 237-241
Meadow Creek: 278
Meadows, Saul M.: 201
Meeks, Jerold Ray: 189, 218, 219, 276
Meeks, Ray William: 218, 220, 221
Meeks, Robert Eugene: 218
Meeks, Velma: 218, 281
Memphis Tennessee: 16
Mercy Catholic Hospital: 238
Merril, Mildred Rose: 142
Mesa: 240
Mexican: 14, 53
Mexican Border/Line: 75, 77
Mexican Laborers: 12
Mexican War: 14, 172
Mexico: 145, 146
Midway: 31, 32, 37
Midway Gas Company: 37, 119, 224
Midway Route: 47, 50, 51, 71, 77
Midway-Sunset Oil Field: 31
Milander, Bob: 269, 270
Milander, Mildred: 269
Milburn, Doug: 131, 287, 288, 291
Miles, Bert: 246
Miles, George: 140
Mill, Catherine: 137
Mill, Clayton J.: 137
Mill, Howard: 137, 138
Mill, Paul T.: 137, 138
Miller: 126
Miller's Service Station: 98
Mills Airfield: 241

Minnesota: 244, 245
Minnesota State Fair: 245
Mint Canyon: 50, 64, 72, 81, 82, 85
Mission Art Company: 54, 58
Missouri: 16, 18, 75
Mobil Oil: 31, 33, 34, 50, 129, 163, 168, 177, 204, 209, 213, 218, 220, 221, 276, 278, 279, 281
Mobile Oil Refinery, (also see Lebec Refinery): 218
Model - A Ford: 140
Model - T Ford: 2, 244, 246
Mohawk-Hobbs Grade and Surface Guide: 87, 88, 122, 135, 205, 216, 230
Mojave: 33, 37, 50, 71, 160
Mojave Desert: 4, 60, 71
Monument Valley Utah: 25
Moore Station: 17
Moore, Charlie: 17
Moreland: 73
Moreno, Chata: 1
Moss, Harry: 151
Motel Gorman: 142, 176
Mountain View Lodge: 136, 137
Mr. Martin (National Forest Inn): 118
Muddy Springs a.k.a. Mud Springs: 2, 17
Mulholland, William: 29
Murrieta, Joaquin: 21

N

National Express: 15
National Forest Inn: 43, 45, 50, 114-119, 127, 135, 138, 142, 247, 263, 264
National Old Trails Road: 75
National Park Service: 289
National Register: iii, 43, 288, 289, 291
National Safety Council: 253
Native Americans: 7
Navy: 141
Nebraska: 241
Needham Ranch: 87
Needles California: 178
Neenach: 2, 44, 68
Nelson, O. L.: 248
Nevada: 13, 56, 75
New Mexico: 10, 240
New York: 33, 191
New York Herald: 16
New York World's Fair: 245

O

269
Pyramid Lake Recreational Vehicle Resort: 171, 270

Reservoir Summit: iii, 32, 38, 43-45, 121, 123-126, 128, 130, 136, 138, 140, 141, 153, 248
Reservoir Summit Restaurant: 43, 121, 122, 130
Reservoir Summit Service Station: 43, 122
Reynold, Bert: 99
Reynolds, Jerry: 67, 96
Rice Station: 17
Rich: 278
Richfield Oil: 34, 88, 93, 107, 127, 130, 135, 142, 150, 176, 193, 197, 198, 212, 213, 224, 225, 237, 291
Richmond: 239
Riehter Scale: 11
Ridge Alternate: iii, 32, 42, 87, 94, 102, 104, 112, 119, 128, 129, 136, 140, 142, 151, 164, 169, 171, 174, 206, 207, 211, 215, 217, 218, 223, 232, 241, 249, 251, 252, 254, 257, 265-267, 269-275, 277-279, 283-285
Ridge Road Garage: 106-109, 111
Ridge Road House: 106, 107
Ridge Route: iii, v, 2, 3, 29, 31-33, 37-39, 42, 45, 47, 48, 53, 57, 60, 65, 66, 69, 71-77, 79-81, 83-85, 91, 93-99, 103-105, 109, 112-114, 122, 124, 126, 129, 130, 133, 144, 146, 153, 158-160, 162, 165, 167, 171, 172, 174, 177, 178, 180, 184, 193, 202, 204, 209, 212, 215, 221, 225, 226, 230, 232, 238, 243, 244, 246-250, 253, 255-258, 261, 263-265, 277-279, 283, 284-291
Ridge Route Annie (Also see Briggs, Annie Rose): 141
Ridge Route Communities Museum & Historical Society: 104, 291
Ridge Route Rambler: 151
Ridge Tavern, (see The Ridge Tavern)
Rimmer, Jack: 44, 124-126, 136, 153, 159
Rip Van Winkle: 245, 246
Ripley's Believe It or Not: 245
Riverside: 47
Robbers Roost: 21
Robbins, O. P.: 27
Roberts Lane: 109
Robinson, John W: 146, 291
Rogers, Eva: 100
Roosevelt Highway: 76
Roosevelt Junior High: 234
Rosamond: 85
Rose: 32
Rose family: 134
Rose Station: 84
Rose, Annie: 133, 134, 141
Rose, Billy: 134
Rose, William: 115

St. Croix Falls Wisconsin: 245
St. Louis: 16, 19, 175, 191
Stagecoach, (also see Butterfield Overland Stage Line): 25
Standard Oil Company: 33
Standard Station: 105, 111, 141, 168, 175, 176, 277
State Bureau of Highways: 43, 47
State Department of Highways: iii, 43
State Highway 14: 17, 61
State Highway 33: 2
State Highway 46: 254
State Highway 58: 50
State Highway 99 (also see U. S. Hwy. 99): 265
State Highway 126: iii, 32, 88, 89, 91, 93, 94, 142
State Highway 138: iii, 33, 37, 38, 50, 128, 156, 160, 162, 167, 244, 258, 272, 273, 286, 288, 289
State Highway 204: 5
State Historic Preservation Office: 288
State of California: 44, 76
Station 40: 37, 38
Sterlings: 108
Stevens, Walter "Lucky": 150-155, 258, 259
Stewart, Captain: 247, 250
Stewart, Deputy: 247
Stockton: 60, 246, 251
Stockton, Commodore: 14
Stockton, Robert F.: 5, 14
Story, Deputy: 248
Stratton, Anita L.: 213, 214, 272, 273
Studebaker: 149, 196
Sturm, George: 219, 220
Sturm, George John: 219-221
Sturm, Odessa: 219, 220
Sturm's Café: 218, 219
Sturm's Home: 220
Sun freeze: 104
Sunfreze: 104
Superintendent of Indian Affairs: 7
Surveyor General: 13, 14
Sunshine Inn: 55
Swall Hotel: 87
Swall, Albert: 87
Swamper: 212
Swanson, Clarence A. and Bertha M.: 108, 127
Swanson, Irving A.: 108
Swede's Cut: 38, 71, 86, 119-121
Swisher, John: 291
Swiss: 144

Switzerland: 132

T

Taft: iii, 3, 37, 60, 177, 178, 212, 220, 224, 264, 276
Taft Midway Oil Fields: 37
Talbot: 197
Taylor: 180, 181, 184-186
Tehachapi: 21, 48, 50, 57, 63, 71, 239
Tehachapi Canyon: 5
Tehachapi Mountains: iii, 2, 21, 63, 71, 184, 283, 286
Tehachapi Route: 50, 85
Tehachapi Womens Prison: 152
Tehachapi-Bakersfield Earthquake: 203, 224, 225, 276
Tejon: 4, 5
Tejon Canyon: 5
Tejon Angling Club: 209, 234, 236
Tejon Hotel & Garage: 176
Tejon Lake: 188
Tejon Pass: 3-5, 21, 50, 169, 216, 275
Tejon Ranch: 7, 14, 156-158, 172, 188, 201, 204-211, 228
Tejon Ranger Station: 263
Tejon Road: 24
Tejon Route: 21, 25, 50, 53, 57, 77
Tejon Summit: 2, 11, 32, 163, 169, 177, 251, 275
Telegraph Road: 93, 94
Temple Street: 1
Templin Highway: iii, 34, 43, 44, 112, 113, 126, 286
Tennessee: 16
Texaco: 218, 277
Texas: 10, 35, 67, 133, 176, 241
Texas Pacific Railway Company: 63, 64
The Bakersfield Californian: 85, 251, 252, 254, 255, 264
The Bank Line: 33
The Fish Hatchery: 234-236
The Giant Lemon: 272, 273
The Greatest Show on Earth: 282
The Narrows: 56
The Ridge Tavern: 164, 251, 269, 272
The Spirit of St. Louis: 191
The Way of The Zepher: 144
Theresa: 127
Thomas Pennsylvania: 213
Thompson, Deputy Constable: 250
Three Points: 159
Tin Lizzy: 244
Tip's Restaurant: 94, 142
Tipton Missouri: 16

Tolefree's: 88
Toll Station: 147, 148
Torrance: ii, 33
Tosco: 35
Touring Topics: 80, 81
Tourist Wayside League: 121
Town For Lucky Children: 154
Tracy, Spencer: 238
Traveler's Hotel: 87
Tropics Café: 242
Truempler, Dot: 224, 225
Truempler, Larry: 224
Trumbo, Dalton: 282
Trust for Public Lands: 133
Truxtun: 14
Tulare: 109, 145
Tumble Inn: 38, 43, 135-138, 140, 288, 289
Tuomy, Dr.: 246
Turner Pass: 50

U

U. S. Grant Hotel: 158
U. S. Highway 99 (also see State Hwy. 99): iii, 32, 42, 76, 164, 169, 171, 241, 257, 258, 265
UCLA: 137, 252
Ultramar Diamond Shamrock: 35
Union Cemetery: 196
Union Oil: 232
Union Oil 76: 232, 241, 252, 269
Union Pacific Railroad: 23, 35, 64
United States: 41, 46, 67, 145, 191
United States Department of The Interior: 288
United States Forest Service: 95, 118
United States Navy: 7
Universal City: 1
University of California at Berkeley: 4
University of Redlands: 142
University of Southern California: 74
USC: 142, 239
Utah: 25, 172

V

Valero Energy Corporation: 35
Valley Circle Boulevard: 132
Van Ness Elementary School: 234
Van Norman Reservoir: 1
Van Norman, Harvey A: 1

Vanowen: 133
Vargas, Daniel: 247, 248
Vargas, Frank: 247
Varges, Simona: 247
Vasquez Rocks: 21
Vasquez, Tiburcio: 21, 22
Ventura: iii, 1, 29, 88, 91, 94, 103, 126, 142, 196, 246
Verdugo: 1
Vernon: 32
View Service Station: 113
Vineyard, James: 25
Violin Canyon: 65, 87, 108, 249, 285
Virginia Street: 198
Visalia: iii, 75, 286
Von Piontkowski, Marie: 146
Von Schmidt, Anna: 146

W

Warm Springs Road: 113
War Department: 12
Warsaw Poland: 145
Washington: 93, 109, 240
Washington D. C.: 10, 12, 197, 291
Washington State University: 240
Washington, Spokane: 109
Watkins, Ellen: 246, 247
Watkins, Fay: 246, 247
Watkins, Franklin: 246
Watkins, Harrison: 246
Watkins, W. R.: 246, 247
Wayne, John: 25, 256
Wayne Paper Box & Prtg. Corp.: 233
Webb, G. L.: 88
Wedgewood Range: 152
Weldon Canyon: 60, 61
Weldon, Arthur: 61
West Kern Oil Museum: 177
West Pine Crest Place: 100
Western Avenue: 179
Western Publishing & Novelty Co.: 90, 120, 144, 162, 170
Western Union Telegraph Company: 18
Whilton, Emery: 275, 276
Whipple, Don: 245, 246
White Star Auto Camp: 99
White, William A. & Etta: 201
Williams Airfield: 240
Williamson, Lieutenant Robert Stockton: 5

Willow Springs Station: 33
Wilmington: 35
Wilson, Bernice: 290
Wilson's, Jack, Service Station: 97
Winchell, Floyd: 254
Wisconsin: 245
Wood, Martin & Richard: 88
Wood's Garage: 88, 89, 109
Woodard's Café: 88, 89
Woodson, J. B.: 221, 222, 225
Wooley, Jack: 178, 179
Worden: 220
World War I: 67, 81, 145
World War II, (also see Second World War): 129, 153, 241
Worlds Fair: 245, 276
WPA: 142, 175

Y

Yaeck, Elizabeth: 207
Yaeck, Martin: 207, 209
Yates, Charlie: 205-207, 209, 217
Yates, Kenny: 209, 217
Yellowstone: 75
Yosemite: 193
Young, Albert Bernhardt: 128
Young, Charles E.: 137, 252
Young, Deputy: 251
Young, Frank: 128, 129
Young's Café: 128, 142, 272, 273
Yuma: 16, 63, 64

Z

Zalvidea, Father Jose Maria: 4